# Land Expropriation in Ancient Rome and Contemporary Zimbabwe

Also available from Bloomsbury

*African Americans and the Classics* by Margaret Malamud
*The Classics and South African Identities* by Michael Lambert
*'Your Secret Language': Classics in the British Colonies of West Africa* by Barbara Goff
*Zimbabwe's Fast Track Land Reform* by Prosper B. Matondi

# Land Expropriation in Ancient Rome and Contemporary Zimbabwe:

## *Veterans, Masculinity and War*

Obert Bernard Mlambo

BLOOMSBURY ACADEMIC
LONDON • NEW YORK • OXFORD • NEW DELHI • SYDNEY

BLOOMSBURY ACADEMIC
Bloomsbury Publishing Plc
50 Bedford Square, London, WC1B 3DP, UK
1385 Broadway, New York, NY 10018, USA
29 Earlsfort Terrace, Dublin 2, Ireland

BLOOMSBURY, BLOOMSBURY ACADEMIC and the Diana logo
are trademarks of Bloomsbury Publishing Plc

First published in Great Britain 2022
Paperback edition published 2024



Cover images: (*above*) Heroes Acre, Harare, Zimbabwe. Gary Bembridge/Wikimedia,
(*below*) Ludovisi Battle sarcophagus, National Roman Museum, Palazzo Altemps,
Rome, Italy. B.O'Kane / Alamy Stock Photo



A catalogue record for this book is available from the British Library.

Library of Congress Cataloging-in-Publication Data
Names: Mlambo, Obert, author.
Title: Land expropriation in ancient Rome and contemporary Zimbabwe : veterans,
masculinity and war / Obert Bernard Mlambo.
Description: London, UK ; New York, NY : Bloomsbury Academic, 2022. |
Includes bibliographical references and index.
Identifiers: LCCN 2021058937 | ISBN 9781350291850 (hardback) |
ISBN 9781350291898 (paperback) | ISBN 9781350291867 (ebook) |
ISBN 9781350291874 (epub) | ISBN 9781350291881
Subjects: LCSH: Veterans–Legal status, laws, etc.–Rome. | Veterans–Legal status, laws,
etc.–Zimbabwe. | Land reform–Law and legislation–Rome. | Land reform–Law and
legislation–Zimbabwe. | Eminent domain–Law and legislation–Zimbabwe. |
Eminent domain (Roman law) | Zimbabwe–Politics and government–1980– |
Rome–Politics and government--265-30 B.C.
Classification: LCC K4780 .M53 2022 | DDC 343/.0252--dc23/eng/20220331
LC record available at https://lccn.loc.gov/2021058937

ISBN: HB: 978-1-3502-9185-0
PB: 978-1-3502-9189-8
ePDF: 978-1-3502-9186-7
eBook: 978-1-3502-9187-4

Typeset by RefineCatch Limited, Bungay, Suffolk

To find out more about our authors and books visit www.bloomsbury.com
and sign up for our newsletters.

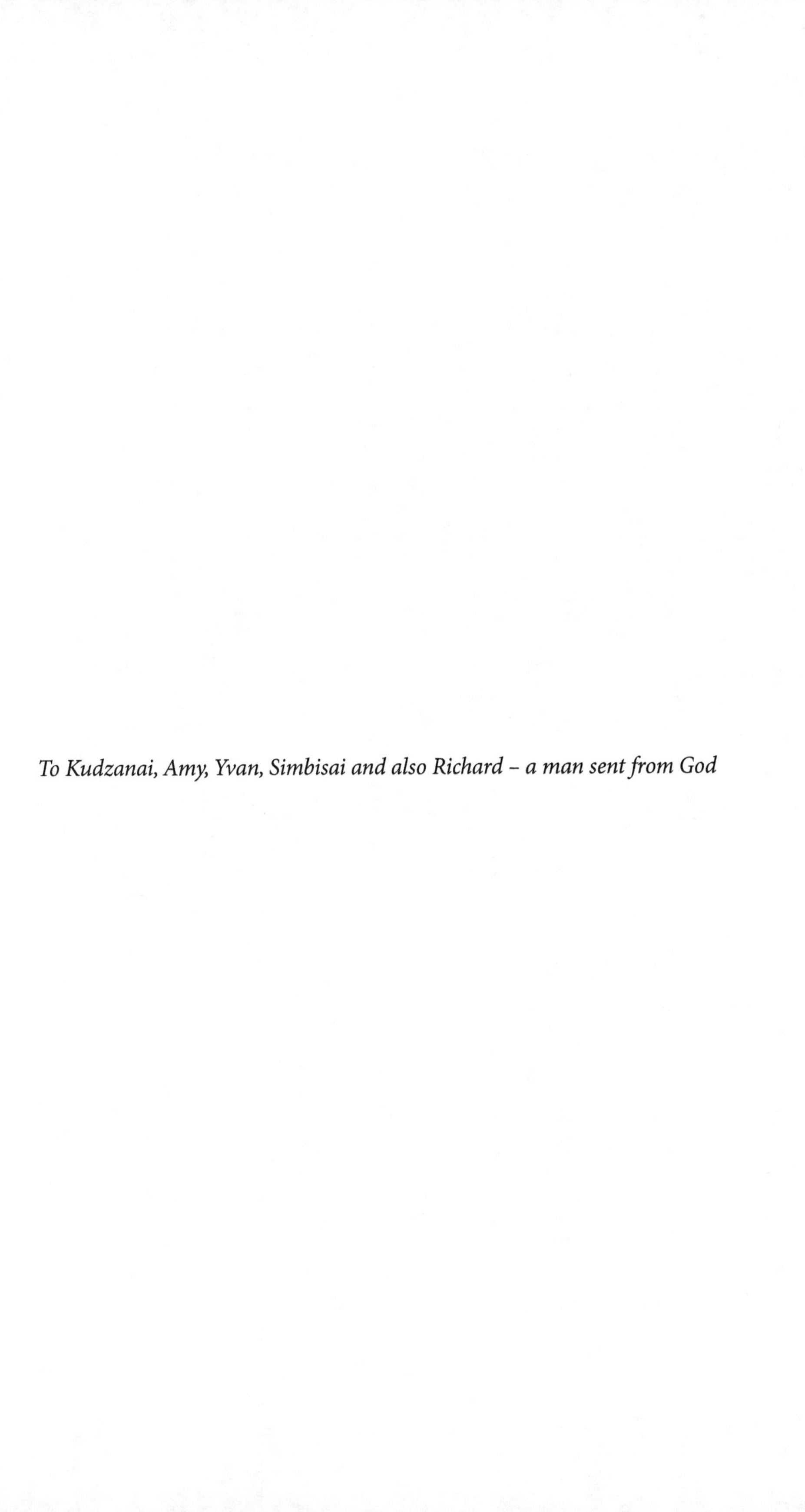

*To Kudzanai, Amy, Yvan, Simbisai and also Richard – a man sent from God*

# Contents

# Figures

# Foreword

David Konstan
*New York University, USA*

I went into a public-'ouse to get a pint o' beer,
The publican 'e up an' sez, 'We serve no red-coats here.'
The girls be'ind the bar they laughed an' giggled fit to die,
I outs into the street again an' to myself sez I:
O it's Tommy this, an' Tommy that, an' 'Tommy, go away';
But it's 'Thank you, Mister Atkins', when the band begins to play,
The band begins to play, my boys, the band begins to play,
O it's 'Thank you, Mister Atkins', when the band begins to play.

You talk o' better food for us, an' schools, an' fires, an' all:
We'll wait for extry rations if you treat us rational.
Don't mess about the cook-room slops, but prove it to our face
The Widow's Uniform is not the soldier-man's disgrace.
For it's Tommy this, an' Tommy that, an' 'Chuck him out, the brute!'
But it's 'Saviour of 'is country' when the guns begin to shoot;
An' it's Tommy this, an' Tommy that, an' anything you please;
An' Tommy ain't a bloomin' fool – you bet that Tommy sees!

Rudyard Kipling's famous poem, 'Tommy,' published in 1890, of which I have quoted the first and last stanzas, captures the predicament of the demobilized or veteran soldier, who is honored as a hero in wartime but despised and ridiculed when there is peace. It is told from the perspective of an ordinary soldier – Tommy Atkins was the generic name for the common trooper in Britain, a bit like John Doe in legal documents. Tommy is down and out, without a salary and apparently with little or no pension. As he says,

You talk o' better food for us, an' schools, an' fires, an' all:
We'll wait for extry rations if you treat us rational.

He is also isolated, alone. There are girls in the pub, and doubtless men, too; they are part of the generalized, plural 'you' to whom Tommy addresses his complaint. Of course, he is one among many such veterans. But they have, in this poem at least, no collective or corporate identity; Tommy seems to have no buddies with whom to socialize or who might back him up when he is mistreated in a civilian situation.

A similar malaise has afflicted former fighters in more recent wars, as they return, often psychologically wounded or traumatized, to a world that little understands them and in which they feel alienated and sometimes hostile. The movie *Coming Home* (1978) poignantly dramatized the condition of veterans returning to civilian life after the Vietnam War. Such former warriors, who might have exhibited extraordinary valour on the battlefield, may feel that their very masculinity is threatened, an anxiety symbolized, in the movie, by the confinement of the protagonist, Luke Martin (played by Jon Voight), to a wheelchair, and in Kipling's poem by the mockery of the girls. Yet soldiers, even after the fighting has ended, have an aura of the warrior about them, for their physical toughness and their experience and habits of combat. Where peace is fragile, especially in the context of internal conflict within the state, veterans may be summoned to support one or another side, not just in a military capacity – although their potential role in battle is not to be discounted – but also as icons of courage, self-sacrifice, and devotion to honour and the cause. In particular, they may project an image of ultra-masculinity, by which to shame or intimidate civilians, as they strut and posture and make a demonstration of their might.

But veterans are not just pawns in the plans of ambitious generals or politicians. They have needs, desires, and agency of their own. They may demand better food and schools, not just lament their absence. Or else, they may seek jobs, or, in societies that are largely agrarian, land, the bedrock of the economy. Land, however, is not an inexhaustible resource: granting land to a veteran may require expelling an established farmer from his property, and this, in turn, may well exacerbate social tensions. Just such a dynamic played out in the course of the civil wars in ancient Rome, where leaders like Julius Caesar won the loyalty of their troops by extravagant promises of acreage, always with the potential consequence that humble cultivators might be expropriated. Veterans might feel they earned their turn, having risked their lives and demonstrated their machismo on the battlefield and now again, at home, as they occupy public spaces and make a flourish of their virility with clanging arms and raised fists. Their support is crucial to a would-be leader, even as they depend on his promised largesse. And here there emerges that complex and treacherous dynamic of martial valour, economic deprivation, masculine posturing, and civil strife that may shake a society to its roots.

In this penetrating book, Obert Mlambo shows how all these factors were at play in two apparently very different contexts. The first of these is late Republican

Rome, as I have noted – a case that has been well studied from a strictly military and political angle, but where the veterans' own experience and above all the way their bodies were exploited in the construction of an ideologically charged masculinity have been largely neglected. The second context, far removed from Rome in time and space, is modern Zimbabwe, where the revolutionary fighters who drove out the British overlords who ruled what was then called Southern Rhodesia continued to play a critical role in the politics of the long time president of the decolonized state, Robert Mugabe (1980–2017). In both contexts, veterans sought compensation, and land was the crucial commodity; in both, leaders were prepared to mobilize the veterans' support, encouraging them to regard themselves as a privileged force in society. Of course, there were many differences. Ancient Rome was racked by rival generals, whose competition for power took the form of civil wars. Zimbabwe's ex-soldiers were veterans of a war of liberation, with its own ideological complexion. And yet, the similarities between the two are striking, and what is more, mutually illuminating. We have informative histories of ancient Rome from the pens of contemporaries or near contemporaries to the struggles, such as Livy and Dio Cassius. These help to orient the scholar to the issues as they were perceived at the time. Zimbabwe, in turn, is a living case study, where veterans continue to exercise a major role, and where it is possible to investigate their sentiments, beliefs, and self-image at first-hand. Just as studies of the economics of modern slavery, for example, have provided models for the understanding of ancient slave societies, so too a knowledge of the experience of modern Zimbabwean veterans offers clues to an appreciation of otherwise hidden aspects of ancient Roman soldiers in peacetime. Who would have thought to look, as Obert Mlambo has, to the possible schoolroom bullying of the young Horace by the sons of centurions as an example of veterans' machismo?

Mlambo combines an expert knowledge of both cases. He is by profession a Roman historian, and he has studied the sources closely, selecting revealing episodes with a keen eye to their ideological import. He has also immersed himself in the history of his own country, Zimbabwe, where he has explored the archives and conducted personal interviews with veterans and other players in the national drama. In addition, Obert Mlambo has mastered the modern literature on displays of masculinity and the construction of gender, as well as the sociological and anthropological theories that enable a deep understanding of the interplay of image and power. The result is a moving and compelling analysis of veterans' psychology, social conflict, political manipulation, and the need for land across two millennia.

# Prolegomenon

In life, we tend to have our horizons shaped or even limited by our contexts. What we know and believe about the world is often circumscribed by our environment. Roman history has afforded me a mental platform outside the contemporary world and its history, into which I was born. What I have learnt from Roman history, moreover, ultimately expresses itself in an inclination to inquire and research further, to press on to previously unasked questions, ones which exceed the usual frame of Roman historical inquiry, even change its very outlook – bringing up connections with other fields such as History, Religion, Anthropology, Sociology, Classical Reception, Black Classicism, Comparative Cultures, Postcolonial African History and Politics. Thus, the questions newly posed here involve ancient Roman parallels with an African context, and are linked to discussions of modern concepts – masculinity, gender, identity, embodied practice – and with this I am already outside the limits of an exclusively Roman history.

I take note therefore of the importance of culture, and I also note that, as cross-cultural studies confirm, it is possible to extend and merge cultural horizons by drawing insights from other historical and geographical settings. For example, German anthropologist, Thomas Widlok has done a comparative study of walking practices, involving bush walkers in Western and non-Western societies – reflecting on the evolution and history of bodily skills and the role of walking in anthropological enquiry itself (Widlok 2008). Joseph Alter's (1992) comparison of traditional Indian wrestlers with Western wrestlers shines a light on anthropological perspectives regarding the wrestler's way of life, ideology and identity more generally. The interaction of myself, as a Black Classicist, and of a Black African culture with the Classical tradition challenges and expands our views on the intersection of land, men and masculinity, gender, colonization, race, violence and war. In this book, I set out to move between an African context and that of ancient Rome, in order to examine three related phenomena, namely veterans, masculinity and land expropriation, and to challenge historical barriers and separations. The comparative analysis makes a contribution to broader discussions and advances theoretical thought on war, masculinity, violence and expropriation. Stathis Kalyvas (2006: 6) has observed that civil war violence often displays some critical recurring elements, in spite of its many different forms, and the various goals associated with it at different places and times. I hold that something similar applies to masculinity in military contexts, and intend to explore this.

I might be accused of comparing oranges and apples, but I maintain that it is not absurd even to compare apples and oranges. Both are fruits, both evolved on Planet Earth, both are suitable for vegetarians and among many other comparable stuffs, they both are made of matter. Cases at the extreme opposite ends on the spectrum of scale can be mutually informative by tapping into the richness of comparative material to shed more light on the role of masculinity and violence in land struggles than what a single case study might yield (cf. Widlok 2017). A selective approach to history may cause us to think of Caesar's war exploits as worthy of mention, whereas, for example, the war exploits of the pre-colonial African Zulu king, Shaka, may arouse no interest at all.[1]

Concerns might be raised that African and ancient Roman particularities could be lost in a comparison of Africa and Rome, as there exists the risk of merging of African masculinities[2] with those of ancient Rome. Yet what I have discovered, and will try to show you, is that there is something similar to ancient Roman masculinity in Africa. We may also remind ourselves of the more overt influence of Roman masculinity on the attitudes of colonial powers in the African continent. The actions of ancient societies may be studied with attention to noteworthy qualities like general norms, social and cultural practices, and contrast with our own society (Sharwood Smith, cited in McClymont 2007). The African and ancient Roman accounts of veteran-masculinities, land and expropriation explored in this book are not merely case material, but are viewed through a theoretical approach. My use of African and ancient Roman material follows the logic of what is called practice theory, and attempts to deal with both differences and convergences in the two societies. By convergence, I mean the independent occurrence of similar traits and patterns in the two distinct societies without a shared political or social environment or a common ancestry. Thus, the cross-cultural comparative analysis of the two cases serves to identify the cultural logic that connects masculinity, violence and expropriation beyond the particulars of each case.

I take practice as a key element of the human condition. Thomas Widlok (2017: xx) has argued that we never encounter humans in essence but always in their particular relational position of being powerful or weak, young or old, poor or rich, healthy or sick, as a member of this gendered group, that ethnic group, or a particular occupational group rather than another one. This does not imply, however, that accounts of the particular would make comparisons across different contexts impossible. Quite to the contrary, while humans are not reducible to essential attributes, any similarities found across diverse contexts are a strong indication of social patterns that follow an underlying cultural logic. We may also have recourse to Widlok's descriptive imagery, whereby ethnographic accounts can be imagined to be like the portraits of members of an extended family that are assembled on a wall: 'they are not "hung up" on principle of genealogy and lineage but they allow us to see convergences and differences along a whole range of possible connections.' (Widlok 2017: xix). The scattered fragments of information about expropriation in ancient Roman sources are interesting in their own right but do not fit together in a complete picture. For this reason, I have incorporated evidence of expropriation from an African setting into this book not as genealogy or history but as voices from another time speaking on similar themes. There is a way in which the African ethnographic material and Roman accounts are connected through such family resemblances. In using African ethnographic materials, I am seeking a recognition of patterns that emerge within the two societies. This underscores my reliance on anthropological approaches in the present task, which allow human beings to make sense of their actions.

Since I use my own social location, first and foremost as a Black African, and then as a Roman historian, the nature of the questions that I ask can be meaningfully addressed by a transcultural-comparative analysis of historical phenomena. Answers to the questions lie deeply embedded in the narrative accounts of land expropriation from the two societies contrasted in the present study. For example: Can a non-Western culture benefit from knowledge of Classics? Various important ideas have been handed down in Classical culture: the autonomy of knowledge, free speech, constitutional government, the value of private property (Decreus, cited in McClymont 2007: 147). These may be defensible in the abstract (e.g. by appealing to natural tendencies to knowledge, speech, orderly life, freedom and free control of the environment) but lodge more firmly in the mind when viewed in the context of a particular civilization (McClymont 2007). The *exemplar* value of Classics is also a part of their importance: their excellence gives us models and insights (Righi, cited in McClymont 2007: 147). This is by no means to claim that the ancients are paragons of our values as moderns.

Conversely, is it not a problem to study Classics from a narrow Western-background emphasis? Can Classics, in general, benefit from knowledge of non-Western cultures? Does Classics possess sufficient history needed to interpret its texts? The existing evidence naturally does not allow a psychological, to say nothing of a properly scientific, approach (MacMullen 1984: 440). Because of its deficiencies, Blakely (2013) for example, has considered the technological myths and rituals associated with the ancient Greek *daimones,* who made metal, as well as African rituals in which iron plays a central role. She has explored the associations of metallurgy with magic, birth, kingship, autochthony and territorial possession in both Greek and African cultures, and shed light on fragmentary references to the *daimones.* In this book, I consider African approaches to Roman history to be of benefit to its interpretation.

This could lead us to a debate regarding what Classics is and what it is not, which is outside the scope of the present task. In spite of the laudable interest of classicists in stuff outside the customary bounds of their specialty, some things must be excluded to give the term 'Classics' a definite content (McClymont 2007: 15).[3] Yet excluding some things from Classics should not entail discarding them completely. While I do not claim that African history and culture fall under the ambit of Classics, I defend the view that a non-Western culture can shed light on the discussion of related phenomena such as of war, land, masculinity, violence and gender in a Classical culture. With this in mind one may ask: What essential ideas, terms, meanings and images of masculinity and violence, distinct or alike, can be revealed when juxtaposing the ancient historian Dio Cassius' account of how the triumvirs' soldiers seized estates in Roman Italy, and an African account of how a group of guerrilla veterans in Zimbabwe seized a sugar-cane estate? The very variety of distinct narratives and incidents of expropriation found in the two societies, and the variety of situations, motives, causes, etc. they display, should encourage a careful examination of the concept of masculinity and the dynamics of violence between veterans and non-veterans in post-war environments. The narratives from the two societies do offer an entry point for analysing the modalities of martial violence and the complex terrain of veteran-masculinities, and how different forms, manifestations, constructions and ideas on masculinity enhance our ability to understand the phenomenon's multivalent nature.

I do not treat masculinity as if it stood alone, nor do I claim that it was manifested in the same way in the two societies. Masculinity functioned and was shaped in relationship to other factors (culture, militarism, violence, war, race, colonization, etc.).[4] The land expropriations in the two societies also took place in the context of war-ingrained masculinities, often articulated within the overarching framework of patriarchy. I explore this in detail in Chapter Three and Four. Examining the crisis of claims for rewards or compensation for veterans in the context of war, and its consequences – expropriations, confiscations, violence, etc. – the book fosters a deeper understanding of these social processes, relating the study of masculinity to the consideration of the veteran's body, and military violence.

In addition to masculinity, I give attention to land as a broad concept (cf. Shipton 1994: 348) – a means of establishing or challenging power relations, which includes not only estates and farms but also political space or political territory. The city of Rome, by way of illustration, was not only a site of politics, being the place where public power was both exercised and conferred, the terrain of politics and political communication (Ando 2019). It was also a city that ceased at some stage to be common property, becoming a city split and controlled by political rivals (see Luc. 1.87-9).

Thus, a more expansive and inclusive reading of expropriation is operational in this study. Whereas the dominant understanding of expropriation by veterans in the two contexts tends to restrict it to land, narrowly defined as physical space, I apply a wider frame. There is a strategic alliance between the veteran and the general, who sponsors and facilitates the land expropriations. The veteran is abetted by the general; in turn he expands the latter's sphere of influence ( see App. *BC*. 3.87, cf. Tac. *Hist*. 3.3). It is a marriage of convenience underwritten by a masculine code of loyalty and cooperation (see for example Dio Cass. 48.6). In this regard, the veteran does not simply 'colonize' the physical space of the farm, but takes over the political fields, more broadly understood. Applying a masculinity of conquest, he seeks to ensure that the very atmosphere where he has taken over is suffused with his being. He takes over physically, economically, materially and spiritually. As the sources portray the expropriations, client-armies especially of the *tresviri* expelled the expropriated from their lands, cities, houses, temples and tombs (see Verg. *Ecl.* 1.67-72, App. *BC*. 5.5). Expropriation by veterans in both contexts seeks to be complete. The idea is to transform and convert the conquered environment to subscribe to the ideology of the veteran and to assert the hegemony of the veteran.

By referring to 'ancient Rome' and 'Zimbabwe' in the title of this book, I indicate in broad terms the geographical location of the cultures under examination. Although I am cognizant of internal differences even within African countries, the label 'Zimbabwe' serves to situate the Southern African country (the description of which is detailed later on) within the broader socio-cultural milieu in which it exists. Postcolonial African politics, veteran-masculinities and violence can all be discerned in the Zimbabwean context. In that regard, I am by no means claiming that Zimbabwe stands for Africa in every sense, namely: history, language, size, economics, politics, religion, etc., but there exist broad, common issues in a postcolonial context at the intersection of war and the politics of the postcolony. Economic nationalism was not unique to Zimbabwe, but common in other African countries.

My particular focus on Zimbabwe involves the politics of space as a post-war resettlement political project, discussing the role of the martial prowess of veterans and its various enactment strategies in land expropriation contexts. I argue that the category 'Zimbabwean' history or even 'African' history is too limited to allow for broader and deeper discussion of the phenomena of 'veteran' and 'masculinity', and too narrow to shed light on the post-war dynamics of violence and expropriation in military contexts. This book goes beyond such categories and boundaries. Admittedly, Zimbabwean veterans tell a Zimbabwean story with not only particular contextual patterns, logics and practices, but also patterns and practices that are discernible not only in Africa (cf. Maquet 1972), but also in ancient Rome.

This book investigates two parallel cases of land expropriation and/or distribution, namely the client-army era of the first-century BC Roman Republic (from Gaius Marius to Octavian)[5] and contemporary Zimbabwe. More specifically, it investigates the expropriation and distribution of land by veterans of military campaigns or their military leaders or by representatives of the state, following domestic wars – whether of civil wars, as in the case of the late Roman Republic, or of the liberation war (1960s–1979), as in the case of Zimbabwe.

The book comprises eight chapters.

Chapter One is a methodological overview of the book – where I examine events and actions involving war veterans' violent dispositions in the light of the critical perspectives and methods associated with gender theories. The chapter is essentially an intellectual and philosophical justification for the present transcultural-comparative approach to study of two disparate societies. I approach definitional issues from a transcultural-comparative perspective, examining the methods and justification for the approach to the present task, as a way to challenge historical narratives of separateness.

Chapter Two examines the background to the two societies and gives a detailed exposition of the cultural and historical differences of ancient Rome and Africa. In this chapter, I define the concept of 'veteran' and clarify the concept as it occurs in both societies (and elsewhere), endeavouring, among other things, to examine its relationship with the expropriation of land and violent activities involving looting and destructive behaviour by military veterans.

The concept of 'veteran' did not function in a vacuum. There existed in both societies a patriarchal system of organization and honorific culture, which in each case governed the terms of gender, and which determined the distribution of land, property, rank and status. Discussing the role of culture in the investigation of the concepts of 'veteran' and 'masculinity', Chapter Three juxtaposes the two worlds of veterans to illustrate the relationship between land expropriation and notions of masculinity. Chapter Three is therefore devoted to a discussion of patriarchy and heroic honor in the two societies, examining how merit of war in the two societies determined behaviour of military veterans, the distribution of land, and prescribed appropriate behaviour for people in various classes. The chapter also explores how landlessness among ancient Roman and African men impacted their patriarchal masculinities, not only in the sense of fathering, the biological act in which a man's sperm results in birth of a child; but in the sense of fatherhood, the social role associated with the social care of children and rearing a family – an important convergence of the importance of land in two societies separated by two millennia.

Patriarchally organized societies in which men's masculine dispositions are steeped in honorific cultures have the effect of building the veteran up to larger-than-life proportions. This has implications for how military veterans conduct themselves in society. Therefore, Chapter Four explores the aggrandized image of the veteran and his disposition to warfare-madness and violence – examining the link between such behaviour has to expropriation, violence and notions of masculinity in ancient Rome and Zimbabwe. I specifically investigate whether warfare-madness is linked to behaviour driven by masculinity and the extent to which a madness of warfare complicates or clarifies our efforts to understand episodes of expropriation in military contexts.

Chapter Five explores how military veterans in both societies can be understood as having constituted hegemonies and how in turn such hegemonies enabled them to lay claim and control over land, territory and power. I deploy the concept of homosociality in my particular endeavour to understand client-army veterans as a society of men, whose existence and way of operation was dependent on dominating other men and women. The Zimbabwean comparanda (and examples from other modern military contexts) are contrasted with the Roman situation to show how the recent history of war veterans in more or less similar conditions may be useful in understanding how military men organize themselves, and how notions and ideals of power influence the creation of a society of men bound by distinctly martial masculinities and identities.

Marx theorized that there was a dialectical relationship between the body and the social and natural worlds, and insisted that the body acting upon the world is, in turn, acted upon by the world the body has helped to create (Cowan 1990: 22). Drawing on Marx's ideas, Chapter Six situates the practical and symbolic value of physical bodies of veterans in a broader socio-cultural and political framework. In Foucauldian terms, I examine the body of a Roman veteran in its mode as crafted, and in the service of a certain self-crafting. I highlight how discourses have a powerful effect upon how a soldier lives through their body. My use of ideas related to Marx's thought leads me to emphasize a dual concern with ideology and the material aspects of the body, while my use of ideas related to Foucauldian thought leads me to emphasize the discourses and the mastery relating to the bodily life of a soldier. Among other concerns, I explore how the Roman military veteran claimed and wielded certain types of authority, based on his particular body-type, and on bodily substances such as blood, sweat, bones, wounds and scars. The soldier's battle scars, according to Jonathan Walters, '. . . are . . . the signifier, permanently inscribed on his body, of his social status as a full man.' (Walters, cited in Gale and Scourfield 2018). In this way the interaction of the body and society can be brought into relief, and the way in which veterans as humans used and acted on and through their body can be illuminated.

Chapter Seven suggests a new attentiveness to the manner in which masculinities were constructed and performed in land expropriation contexts. I analyse instances of the performative display of valour in Roman literary texts and compare them with performative displays of valour by Zimbabwe's guerrilla fighters, as displayed on various platforms such as protests and marches, and on the media. The purpose of this endeavour is to explore how veterans of both societies, through performative masculinity, enacted, elaborated, and gave nuance and palpable form to ideals of power, including those that governed the attitude to gender. Likewise, they expressed, through performative masculinity, their emotional proclivities, fears and anxieties. In the case of Roman client-army veterans, political activity often expressed itself in the political agency of their bodies as they occupied space within the city walls, on the Capitol, in military camps, in the Assembly, in the Forum, etc. This consideration serves to shed light on the spatial and topographical dimension of violence and territorial claims and expropriation in general.

Chapter Eight sums up the main discussion of the present study, namely the exploring and analysing issues of expropriation within the context of the political economy of physical bodies of war veterans' representation of masculinity. The chapter observes that juxtaposing the two societies refracts veteran-masculinities in ways that deepen our understanding of societies from far-off times and how such remote societies speak to each other and to realities of ancient and present-day manifestations of phenomena that scholars tend to study in closed compartments. The chapter emphasizes how the meaning of the human body generally, and that of military veterans in particular, is linked with both physical nature and culture as manifest in history and society.

# Acknowledgements

This book project was made possible thanks to the Humboldt Foundation, a charitable institution on which I have many times relied for funding. The Institute of African Studies and Egyptology and the Global South Studies Center both of the University of Cologne hosted me during sustained periods of my postdoctoral research in Germany. I am grateful for the support I generously received from my host, Thomas Widlok, and from Clemens Greiner (Global South Studies Center). Without them, this book could not have been completed. It was a great pleasure to work with Bloomsbury Press. I am particularly compelled to mention Lily Mac Mahon for her exceptional kindness and professionalism. Gratitude is also due to Bloomsbury Press' astute reviewers, whose criticism and feedback was tremendously helpful.

The Fondation Hardt in Vandœuvres, Switzerland, an institute for the study of classics and antiquity, together with its staff facilitated access to critical documents for the writing of the book. The following staff members at the Fondation Hardt assisted me in one way or another and I acknowledge them here as follows: Director, Professor Pierre Ducrey, General Secretary, Dr Gary Vachicouras, Librarian, Dr Pascale Derron, Administrative Secretary, Ms Patricia Burdet, and Housekeeper/Chef, Ms Heidi Dal Lago. Being a non-French speaker, moreover, might have made my life miserable at meal-times at the Fondation, but I offer my thanks to Ms Heidi Dal Lago for speaking German with me, and for the excellent food! A travel grant from CA IV – Cultures and Societies in Transition of the University of Cologne, expedited research and writing in 2019 at the Fondation Hardt for which I am very thankful.

I am deeply indebted to David Konstan for reading, critiquing and improving the entire manuscript, and for writing the foreword to this book. Many thanks to my scholarly friends, Alexander Thein and John Douglas McClymont, who were available to discuss with me a vast amount of Roman texts during research for this book. Again, to John Douglas McClymont, I am grateful for his collegiality and remarkable editorial stewardship of this book ever since the time I conceived the idea of writing it. Ezra Chitando sacrificed his time to read the whole draft manuscript and made incisive contributions to this book. Special thanks to Joseph Farrell for his kindness and contribution to this book. Other scholars contributed towards this book in various ways: Jeffery Wills, Ilya Berkovich and Kathleen Coleman.

My thanks also go to the many war veterans of Zimbabwe's liberation war who were generous enough to sit with me for many hours and explain their experiences.

Last but not least, my eternal gratitude goes to the love of my life Kudzanai, daughter Amy, and son Yvan for their unwavering support and patience during a project which robbed them of precious time with me! Needless to say, I bear all the responsibility for the contents of this book in which all errors, omissions and mistakes remain my own.

# Abbreviations

| | |
|---|---|
| BACCOSSI | Basic Commodity Supply Side Intervention Scheme |
| BSAC | British South Africa Company |
| CFU | Commercial Farmers' Union |
| MDC | Movement for Democratic Change |
| RENAMO | Resistência Nacional Moçambicana |
| ZANLA | Zimbabwe African National Liberation Army |
| ZANU-PF | Zimbabwe African National Union-Patriotic Front |
| ZIPRA | Zimbabwe People's Revolutionary Army |
| ZNLWVA | Zimbabwe National Liberation War Veterans Association |

1

# General Introduction

## Introduction

*Even the men who have obtained their discharge still follow the standard under the name of veterans another word for protracted misery. A few, indeed, by their bodily vigor have surmounted all their labors; but what is their reward? They are sent to distant regions, and, under color of an allotment of lands, they are settled on a barren mountain, or a swampy fen. War of itself is a state of the vilest drudgery, without an adequate compensation. The life and limb of a soldier are valued at ten pence a day: out of what wretched pittance he must find his clothing, his tent-equipage, and his arms; with that fund, he must bribe . . . intense cold in winter, and the fatigue of summer campaigns; destructive war, in which everything is hazarded, and peace, by which nothing is gained, are all the soldier's portion.* (my emphasis).

Tac. *Ann.* 1.17; Arthur Murphy 1908: 20; cf. Dio Cass. 54.14.3

*During the liberation war, our nationalist leaders would promise to reward us for our* courageous sacrifice. *They promised us suburbs and farms of the white men. We all expected, soon after the war,* to go on a rampage to grab for ourselves nice houses and farms. *My wife, father, mother, three brothers and two sisters were all killed, our homestead burnt and all our cattle were shot by the Rhodesian soldiers . . . The farms we as veterans of the liberation war expropriated from white farmers have become our homes. I dislocated my right hip fighting for my country during the liberation war.* I can no longer walk properly. I now walk like a pregnant woman as I have lost my physicality! *This farm is not even enough compensation. The blood we shed, the limbs we lost, the scars we carry on our bodies are the ultimate fealty to our fatherland. The farms we have expropriated are a seal of our manliness.*[1] (my emphasis).

Interview with a Zimbabwe liberation war veteran

A problem of historical inquiry arises when narratives plucked from ancient Rome and contemporary Africa – disparate historical, temporal and geographical contexts – are juxtaposed as if the two societies were historically, geographically, temporally or sociologically connected. The antitheses of time and perpetual change, to borrow Marc Bloch's turn of phrase (Bloch 1953: 28), beg questions relating to the possibility of utilizing material from different time periods and geographical spaces. Such a challenge, in my view, was admirably addressed by Ika Willis' inauguration of a relationship between 'ancient Rome and now'. In the book *Now and Rome: Lucan and Vergil as Theorists of Politics and Space*, Willis argues for a transformation in how we should think about history.

Even if one were to think of two consecutive historical epochs taken out of the uninterrupted sequence of the ages (Bloch 1953: 28), there would still be compelling questions which, for want of clarity, may be posed thus, following the precedent of Bloch (ibid.): to what extent does the connection which the flow of time sets between the two periods predominate, or fail to predominate, over the differences born out of that same flow? Should our knowledge of the earlier period be considered indispensable or superfluous for the understanding of the latter? Or vice-versa? Must we believe that, because the past does not entirely account for the present (or vice-versa), it is utterly useless for its interpretation? (Bloch 1953: 517, 521). Does mere temporal and spatial proximity guarantee similarity?

Extracting comparative evidence from narratives of the ancient texts poses a difficulty in that being an African, I do not share the culture of the ancient authors, nor indeed their language – posing a danger of distortion and prejudice in understanding the ancients. Yet to bring nothing to one's reading of the text can also be a pitfall because our general sensitivities govern those aspects of the text which we notice the most (McClymont 2007: 77). Sharwood Smith (1977) argued that the reader must always bring something to the text. Would I have better understood Meliboeus' lamentation upon losing his farm to an 'uncouth veteran' (Verg. *Ecl.* 1.71), before, I myself, had seen and experienced the terrible reality of what it meant for a farmer to lose his farm to a group of marauding veterans to which my sister, who is a liberation war veteran, also belonged? Would I have appreciated what it meant to feel a sense of ownership of a home and a farm before I myself had walked the breath and length of a farm which my own veteran sister, who used to be homeless and landless, got by means of appropriation? In the words of Bloch: 'It is always by borrowing from our daily experiences and by shading with new tints that we derive the elements which help us to restore the past.' (Bloch 1953: 44). Taylor has argued that:

> the vocabulary of a given social dimension is grounded in the shape of social practice in this dimension; that is, the vocabulary would not make sense, could not be applied sensibly, where this range of practices did not prevail. And yet this range of practices could not exist without the prevalence of this or some related vocabulary.
>
> Taylor 1994: 194

By virtue of having witnessed my own sister in the company of a group of her fellow guerrilla fighters, expropriating farms from white farmers, I had a better appreciation of how the notion of masculinity was performed live – something that gave me a mental platform and the visual images to envision and approximate episodes of land expropriation in first-century BC Roman Italy.

Thus, in my approach to the present study, I endeavour to explore an African-Roman correspondence on issues involving ancient and contemporary perspectives on war veterans, masculinity and land expropriation, without simplistically equating the phenomena contrasted in all respects. In the different human contexts, the phenomena of masculinity, war veterans, land expropriation and violence are refracted. When contrasted, could these phenomena reflect explanatory meanings valid beyond a single historical epoch and place?

It is my contention, as argued by Bloch, that some societies which are very remote from one another can surely be more alike, at least in ways that are crucial for some explanatory problems, than neighbouring countries (Bloch 1953). As Marc Bloch has argued, a comparison of medieval French serfdom with bonded labour in Senegal in the twentieth century could shed some light on important new truths (Bloch 1953: 28).

The main question at the centre of this book concerns itself with land expropriation considered in relation to the ways in which the concepts of 'veteran' and 'masculinity' may be utilized to explore the nature of power and strategies adopted in land expropriation by client-armies in first-century BC Roman Italy. I revisit episodes of land expropriations, as depicted mainly by Appian and Dio Cassius, with a broader aim to examining the iconography of masculinity in relation to land expropriation. I argue that Appian's and Dio Cassius' narrative accounts, including other Roman historians, along with some literary poets such as Lucan, Horace and Vergil on land expropriations, are productive of gender images and meanings, involving a 'veteran-masculinity' – a masculinity linked to violence, fighting for land as remuneration and also as a reward of honour – a masculinity which violated and feminized its victims or opponents. Since any interpretation of episodes of expropriation depicted in the ancient sources is bound to contexts which existed more than two millennia ago, this book attempts a juxtaposition of ancient Roman war veterans with living war veterans from a modern situation, to understand more about what we can otherwise only access through texts. As such, my investigation of the Roman sources examines episodes in which 'masculinity' appears in land expropriation by veterans, in order to lay out a 'reading' which indicates how the concepts of masculinity may help explain the meaning of such passages.

The narratives and accounts relating to ancient Roman and Zimbabwean war veterans examined in this book are taken as descriptions of phenomena, and I interrogate and contextualize them for what they tell the reader. Roman historians did not necessarily provide accurate descriptions of what they recorded.[2] It is my task in this book to make sense of these narratives. In her book, *Speaking with Vampires: Rumor and History in Colonial Africa,* Louise White underscores the importance of narrative accounts in historical writing. The material basis of historical truth, she argues, is not eroded in narrative accounts, not even in anecdotes, and the mediation of language is no stronger than the events it describes (White 2000: 25). My analysis is therefore located firmly in disparate narratives and anecdotes which reveal common predicaments of military veterans and their plight as military men, something which in both worlds inevitably cultivated distinctively military forms of masculinity (cf. Berkovich 2017), marked by an indifference to law in a civil society.

What is more, some narratives from both contexts contain descriptions of physical bodies of war veterans. Bodily substances such as blood, scars and wounds, and also weapons of war, military fatigues, military standards and battle scenes, are also examined in this book as essential resources for constructing and performing masculinity (see Lendon 2005; McDonnell 2006: 14). They reveal images of masculinity and the nature of war veterans' masculinities, and they too ascribe terms in which meanings and details of notions of masculinity are contained. Although such narratives yield historical evidence which belongs in different historical contexts and different human histories and experiences, I argue that when juxtaposed *to* and/or *with* each other, they share generic qualities and detail along with epistemologies that can allow for insightful comparative descriptions and interpretations of the phenomena of veteran, masculinity, violence and land expropriation, in shaper relief. I use both prepositions *to* and *with* to describe the relationship between phenomena in ancient Rome and Zimbabwe because the putative relationship of the two, I argue, is both asymmetrical and in some respects symmetrical as the present study shows.

The narratives and accounts relating to ancient Roman and Zimbabwean[3] war veterans examined in this book serve to frame several issues within the context of masculinity, land expropriation and the political economy of the physical bodies of war veterans.

- Firstly, I explore the ways in which physical bodies of war veterans inform the representation of a veteran-masculinity with a view to linking the importance of the relation of cultural expressions of physicality – particularly the body of the war veteran – and the relation of masculinity concepts and land expropriation to observable features of the physical body – in what may be termed, if I may borrow an expression from Harold and Deluca (2005: 274), "a forceful rhetorical form that captures and expresses ideas in ways words cannot.".
- Secondly, I explore the roles played by images of a veteran-masculinity in bridging the symbolic gap between, on the one hand, various paraphernalia – such as military boots, military fatigues, weapons[4] (swords, shields, guns, axes), body-parts and bodily substances – such as blood, sweat, wounds, scars, etc. respectively – and, on the other hand, the struggles for ownership and control of land, money and influence in which masculine subjectivities[5] and masculine failures[6] of war veterans were determined. The inclusion of paraphernalia and weapons here takes cognizance of a definition of masculinity[7] that includes also certain inanimate objects that are connected with the male gender because of some essential quality, such as relative superiority or strength.[8] Regarding body-parts and bodily substances, practice theorists have argued that practices are the chief and immediate context within which the preponderance of bodily properties crucial to social life are formed, not just skills and activities but bodily experiences, surface presentations, and even physical structures as well (Schatzki 2006: 11). Thus, the practice theory's importance for the present task lies in its relationship to my materially focused approach, in highlighting how activities of war veterans interweave with ordered constellations of non-human entities (ibid., 12). Indeed, because human activity is dependent on the non-human environment within which it takes place, understanding the practices of war veterans in the two societies should involve apprehending material configurations.
- Thirdly, I examine the manifestation of similar energies of masculinity in different forms in the continuum of land expropriation activities by war veterans recorded in the narratives of the two worlds of veterans.
- Fourthly, through a cross-cultural comparison, I discuss the overlapping functions of discourses of masculinity – shared among war veterans and their leaders in both societies. I explore how such discourses could mobilize

fantasies of the possession of land, houses, etc., and mastery of expropriated possession. This is in respect of promises made to veterans by their generals during the wars in which they fought, which often never materialized. How did the promises work as part of discourses of masculinity in motivating war veterans? What role did the discourses play in creating a sense of entitlement among war veterans? How did such discourses of masculinity cause war veterans to self-identify as masters and champions of the worlds in which they existed? I, therefore, examine how a war veteran's masculinity[9] shored up and affirmed through speeches and promises of land and money by his general, and how discourses of masculinity served as a bulwark against tribulations, calamities, suffering, anxieties and fears faced in war.

- Lastly, I examine narratives and anecdotes bearing images of masculinity and other themes (distinct or related to masculinity) involving war veterans' engagements in expropriation, and in situations where they exhibited irrational impulses or a madness of warfare. My examination takes note of situations where a veteran-masculinity went mad (cf. Boucher 2004), especially when client-armies took over the Roman state – a phenomenon that characterized the last years of the Roman Republic. In the post-2000 Zimbabwean state under Robert Mugabe (1980–2017), the war veterans went berserk in the manner in which white farmers were killed and their farms ransacked (Sachikonye 2011; Meredith 2002). Without necessarily attempting to decouple masculinity from the behaviour of soldiers linked with a tradition of a berserk warrior and a berserk state, I explore the relationship of the two in my attempt to make sense of episodes of expropriation and the violence that accompanied the processes.

In conceptualizing veterans masculinities of the two societies, I develop my argument around the constant feature of how both were organized as patriarchal societies. Thus, I conceptualize patriarchy as denoting the prerogatives of male privilege and power, in which actions and language of claims for land, money and war booty by war veterans functioned as the loci and producers of cultural meanings that were themselves linked with ideologies of gender. I argue that veterans of the two societies existed at the intersection of patriarchal power and the challenged contexts of war, landlessness, social inequality and poverty. The two societies provide contexts in which both gender and masculinity were produced within the overarching framework of patriarchy. Therefore, patriarchy in the two societies connoted relations between men – relations which had land as a material base and which, though hierarchical, established interrelationships and concurrence among veterans and entitled them to dominion over other men and women.

There is scholarship on masculinity in the ancient world (Rosen and Sluiter 2003; McDonnell 2006; Rubarth 2014), but nothing explicit (to the best of my knowledge) as yet on masculinity and land expropriation in first-century BC Roman Italy. Despite abundant evidence that issues of Roman masculinity have received their due, the issue of veterans, masculinity and expropriation in first-century BC Roman Italy require specific analysis. This book does not aim to identify general truths about masculinities, but to map out some trends that characterized episodes of land expropriation in the late Roman Republic. These are entities to be investigated from different scholarly and theoretical perspectives to explore masculinity's latent as well as manifest meanings in land expropriation contexts.

As such, this book places more explicit emphasis and focus on the agency of first-century client-army veterans. Veteran settlements of the first-century BC are largely seen in the light of the strategic importance in the schemes of their generals, in which they feature more as instruments of power at the service of their leaders. According to Gabba, the 'veteran phenomenon' of the first-century BC, chiefly characterized by granting of land to soldiers, has to be seen in the context of the army's political importance and of the establishment by its leaders of extra-constitutional power (Gabba 1976: 43). Keaveney (2007, cited in Thein 2010: 81) is not of a dissimilar view in his reference to Sulla's complete mastery over his men, who made no demands for farms to which Sulla had to respond.[10] This view of emphasizing the role of veterans at the service of military leaders is upheld by Cicero (see Thein 2010: 79 n.3[11] and Appian (App. *BC*. 2.141). In this book, I stress the importance of the view that client-army veterans featured as actors rather than only as a group whose relationship was shaped by patronage and land in which the general called the shots. In their demands for land, as argued by Thein (2010: 81), Caesarian and triumviral veterans were highly assertive and even aggressive – an indication of a gradual decline in military discipline, compared to earlier periods when generals had taken the initiative. For my part, I explore this feature of client-army veterans within a well-specified foundation of masculinity theory. The concept of masculinity allows for a juxtaposition of more nuanced images which can demonstrate masculinity's multiple manifestations in the expropriations. Client-army veterans and their generals adopted and marshalled a wide range of masculine positions in their struggles and quest for acquisition of land.

While Gabba described the power exercised by client-army generals to give land to their veterans as 'extra-constitutional', Brunt analysed the land question in Republican Rome through the concept of 'political power', to describe similar processes (Brunt 1988: 69). Scullard touched somewhat on this power[12] of Roman generals, but only broadly by drawing a contrast between the use of military *auctoritas* in land distribution for veterans on the one hand, and tribunician *auctoritas* on the other.[13] While military *auctoritas* helps us to comprehend, for example, the Sullan and Caesarean veteran settlement schemes in which veterans marched into their allocated farms or colonies in military units under their standards (*sub vexillo*), the concept does not help us to understand how warfare, masculinity, land and gender images influence the meaning of the symbolic and cultural construction of client-army soldiers. The notion of *auctoritas* is not an explanatory label neither can it be a substitute for analysis. Although Eder argued, with specific reference to how *auctoritas* was exercised by Octavian, that it was both concrete and creative (Eder 2005: 16), it can only be stretched so far as a descriptor of the power exercised in land expropriation processes.

For my part, the word *auctoritas* (whether military or tribunician) must be used only as the starting point for thinking about power as appropriated by military generals to give land to their veterans, its constraints and how it was acquired and applied. At its most basic, *auctoritas* simply means authority or, in modern terms, political capital.[14] This category is far too narrow to account for first-century BC land expropriations in Roman Italy.

In respect of Sulla, for example, ancient writers (Appian, Cicero, Sallust and Plutarch) highlighted the materialism of the army which followed him on his march on Rome in 88, in his campaigns against Mithridates from 87–85 BC, and then in his invasion of Italy in 83 BC (Thein 2016: 450). Citing Harris (1971), Hinard (1985) and Fündling (2010), Thein (2016: 451 n.8) emphasized the acquisition of booty as the main fact of the Sullan civil war of 83–82 BC in which as he argued, the ravaging of the countryside provided soldiers with booty, while also served a coercive function, to terrorize the civilian population into submission.

My argument in the present study focuses on the action of the client-army veteran in his social and political struggle for his earned turn through expropriation of land and the Roman political fields. I apply the notion of intersectionality to argue that no action is ever simply 'one' thing; every action is simultaneously many things at once, hence my reading of expropriations through the notion of masculinity, along with martialism, war and violence, to analyse episodes of land expropriation in Roman Italy.

My point of departure places emphasis on the socio-political struggles and the value of land, in which the *status* and *gender* construction of the army veteran is paramount. Expropriation and the violence undertaken by client-army veterans, I argue, can be interpreted as a manifestation of social identity animated by an ideologically charged sense of masculinity. The first-century BC expropriations were occasions for performing specific forms of masculinity, centred on a discourse of the heroization of veterans.

My investigation and study of veterans and their representation in first-century BC Rome explores various versions of masculinities in the veterans' context. These include a masculinity based on the veterans' particular warrior body-type, and on bodily substances such as blood, sweat, bones, wounds and scars. We may also speak in the veterans' case, as Connolly (2007: 92) did in the context of elite Roman oratory, of an oratorical masculinity where veterans "exploited the 'natural' language of gender to describe and evaluate themselves, and through which the visible and verbal signs of masculinity become both evidence and a source of power." Through speech[16] and careful posturing and control of body, gestures and voice, the veterans were able to perform combat-related masculinities and to communicate the need for land and other material rewards in a forceful way. An 'oratorical masculinity' or 'controlled masculinity' and its application served to perform leadership by generals, and as a means for handling their veterans' hostile demands for rewards.[17]

There was also a masculinity wielded by weapons in the city of Rome.[18] The soldier had to be armed. Donning armour and bearing weapons completed the Roman soldier's *habitus* (Phang 2008: 105). After the triumvirs had marked out estates in Italy for their veterans, what proceeded was something like a ritualized parading of their forces, who in their numbers, gathered in Rome wielding arms of war and whose physical presence enforced the bill proposed by Publius Titius the tribune, to legalize the Second Triumvirate, effectively putting into effect the planned confiscations of lands, houses and estates belonging to the proscribed in Italy.[19] Thus, more nuanced, flexible meanings of masculinity are of greater descriptive utility in discussing episodes of expropriation or communication for the need for land and other rewards or demands by client-army veterans. This book contrasts such practices by Roman veterans and veterans from a modern society, including the practice of brandishing of arms, and practices of assembly. Since it has been argued that norms and concepts get their meaning, and their normative authority and force, from their embodiment in publicly accessible activity (Rouse 2007: 43), the Zimbabwean context enabled me to explore how such practices can be understood in similar ways as methods of summoning combat-related masculinities by Roman veterans.

I discuss below how the comparative methodology conducted in the present study works.

## The comparative methodology

My comparative analysis attends to land expropriation in the two societies as a complex system of meaning – the task at hand is a work of interpretation. In order to better understand Roman client-army expropriations, I temporarily take them out of their holistic context and look at them in conjunction with expropriations by guerrilla war veterans of Zimbabwe's independence war. Reification is a pitfall to be guarded against in any comparison (cf. Alter 1992: 8), and thus, rather than construing Zimbabwean episodes of expropriation as ontologically similar to those of ancient Rome, I opt to treat them as heuristically useful and analytically beneficial (cf. Alter 1992: 8) as the Zimbabwean case enables consideration of possible emotions to bring to life and better understand the Roman texts.

There are two methodological questions to consider: a) how may comparative history as a method work in this book? b) If the two sets of veterans belong to different cultures, is there no difference in their concept of masculinity and of the concept of the war hero? And can we then say that the military veterans of ancient Rome were war 'heroes' in the same sense that Zimbabwean veterans consider themselves as such, if 'masculinity', 'heroism' and 'veteran' are concepts conditioned by one's culture? These questions pose methodological difficulties, for which I seek to offer some solutions. I attempt to address this methodological difficulty by examining the applicability of the concept of masculinity as a unit of comparison of the two worlds of veterans.

## The concept of masculinity as a unit of comparison in the present study

In spite of the existence of cultural differences there are common features in the experiences of war veterans in the two societies, such as the predominance of man and associated masculine ideals, as integuments of veterans' self-presentation. Nevertheless, there is need here to briefly discuss the applicability of masculinity as a unit of comparison in the present task. There is also need to reflect whether the concept of 'masculinity' is a legitimate category of inquiry in a comparative enterprise involving the late Roman Republic (cf. Stewart 2014) and a modern society. Admittedly, I take cognizance of the fact that masculinities are situated in specific geographies, temporalities and ethnographies (Berg and Longhurst 2003). As has been demonstrated by Hearn (1987), Cornwall and Lindisfarne (1994), and

Butler (2011), what compounds the problems of the current enterprise is the manner in which masculinities draw and encroach on numerous elements, domains, identities, behaviours and objects. Also compounding this challenge are differences not only between Roman and Zimbabwean masculinities, but even within Roman and Zimbabwean masculinities themselves.

Being cognizant of these challenges, I argue that all humans being human, there exist natural resemblances between different human cultures which can serve as a background against which differences between cultures can be articulated. Trigg (1982: 5) notes that the classical disciplines presuppose that there is in fact a common human nature. By virtue of this common possession, the cultures of ancient times may be said to have points of contact with our condition and problems. The term 'culture' here is understood in the broad sense of the term used by Tylor, as the complex whole which includes knowledge, belief, art, morals, law, customs, and any other capabilities and habits acquired by a person as a member of society (cf. Fagin 1985: 84). Culture includes patterns, explicit and implicit, of and for behaviour, acquired and transmitted by symbols, and constituting the distinctive achievement of human groups. These patterns may be embodied in human bodies and artefacts. At the core of culture lie traditional ideas (historically derived and selected), and their attached values. Culture systems may, on the one hand, be considered as products of action, and on the other, as conditioning elements of further action (cf. Kroeber and Kluckhohn 1963).

This understanding of culture specifically mentions 'society', implying that what belongs to nature rather than society is pre-cultural or extra-cultural. Thus, nature and culture-society are two areas, providing the context in which human beings exist. This is not, however, to say that nature and culture are hermetically sealed areas that never interact; culture is related to nature, and nature's expression is influenced by culture. This is especially the case when discussing a social role like that of the 'soldier' or 'war veteran', and particularly when one is exploring the theme of masculinity.

While ideas of 'male dominance' and 'patriarchy' are considered to be neither sensitive nor appropriate tools for analysis (Cornwall and Lindisfarne 1994: 18), I argue that relations of power are an aspect of every society and every social interaction. Connell's theory of masculinities (1995, 2001) demands that masculinities and femininities be understood primarily as gender terms. Gender terms are naturally contestable because competing, contradictory discourses and conflicting systems of knowledge are deployed in their analysis. Moreover, if notions of masculinity and of gender itself are fluid and situational, we need to consider the various ways people understand masculinity in any particular setting (Cornwall and Lindisfarne 1994: 18). This takes us to some difficult questions confronting theorists in defining masculinities. I refer to the following questions following the precedent of Connell: a) Is everything that men do masculine? b) Is masculinity a coherent object of knowledge? c) Is there unity in men's lives? This question allows for the application of concepts of hegemonic masculinity and homosociality to explain Roman client-army soldiers' relations among themselves and with their leaders; something I attend to in greater detail in comparisons broached in Chapter Five. d) Do all men have the same masculinities? This particular question allows for investigation of the various forms through which masculinities were exhibited by client-army soldiers – an examination of hegemonic versus secondary masculinities.

The following section makes an attempt at a working definition of masculinity in the context of the present study.

## The concept of masculinity: A description

Masculinity is not necessarily equated with men; it is "…simultaneously a place in gender relations, the practices through which men and women engage that place in gender, and the effects of these practices in bodily experience, personality and culture." (Connell 1995: 71). Exploring such practices allows for the discussion of the ways in which patriarchal order can be challenged, questioned, creatively subverted even in patriarchally very rigid societies such as the Roman Republic. Comparisons of ancient Roman women and African women's struggles with patriarchy illuminate our knowledge of the cultural logic of female power in gender discourses and practice. An example of the interaction of male and female power is, in particular, Julius Caesar's recognition of the *virgo muliebris* (power of the Vestal virgins) who kept his will, and in general the role played by the Vestal virgins in the Roman state (see Greenfield 2011). This is particularly useful in my discussion of Roman women's struggles and negotiations with the Roman patriarchal system in Chapter Two. This in turn enlightens our understanding of how ancient Roman women attempted to negotiate and challenge men's privileged and dominant masculine position, even on issues of land and property ownership,[20] sometimes by transgressing culturally and patriarchally sanctioned boundaries.

In locating the examination of masculinities in ancient Rome in the broader context of gender, I draw on Connell's key arguments regarding the relational nature of masculinities. Connell argued that masculinities and femininities are 'inherently relational concepts'. (Connell 1995: 44.) Only in relation to each other can the two concepts have meaning. Engaging Connell's ideas on hegemonic masculinities, defined as cultural dynamics by which a group claims and sustains a leading position in social life (Connell 1995: 77), it is possible to understand more about lived realities of client-army veterans in terms of how ownership of land through expropriation and territorial claims and expropriation mediated their hegemonic masculine identities.

I also draw upon Solomon-Godeau's (1997) classification of masculinity into two polar types – a 'masculinized' and a 'feminized'[21] masculinity to shed a light on Rome's client-army veterans' relations.[22] It must be noted that there is consistency between 'masculinized/feminized masculinity' and 'hegemonic/subordinate masculinity'. The two pairs are not different concepts per se, but the former is more expressive of gender ideologies while the latter qualifies the nature of male power in relation to various versions of secondary masculinities. For example, in their public speeches, Zimbabwean war veterans used epithets (such as *mbwende*/cowards, *zvimbwasungata*[23] /sell-outs etc.) which ridiculed as effeminate those who did not fight to own land, while glorifying as manly those who expropriated land from white men. Effeminacy was therefore differentially and negatively defined in relation to the masculine norm in the veterans' discourses on prizes of war. For example, Octavian in his address to his veterans spoke thus: '. . . for it is worthwhile, in order to win the greatest prizes, to wage the greatest contests … to allow no woman to make herself equal to man …' (Dio Cass. 50.28). Veterans maintained, in rhetoric and behaviour, hegemonic norms of masculinity. This shall be my watchword in analysing and interpreting the actions of Roman veterans throughout this book.

Pursuant to how my comparative method works in the present study, the following section explores the nexus of masculinity, culture and biology to demonstrate how these three serve as our windows to see through different post-war societies and to gain some insights regarding the political economy of masculinity and social processes of expropriation and violence during first-century BC Rome.

## Masculinity, culture and biology

Research has shown that masculinity as socially constructed is not always related to biological sex. Gail Bederman (1995: 6) criticized the idea of manhood as a 'transhistorical essence, substantially unchanging over time, rooted in biology, and therefore not amenable to historical analysis – or to human efforts to change gender relations.' Neither is she satisfied with the attempt to treat masculinity as an immutable yet coherent set of 'ideals, traits or sex roles', given the presence of simultaneous contradictions in any age's concept of masculinity (ibid.). She opts instead to view manhood as a historical and ideological process (ibid., 7). On the other hand, Connell (1995) referred to challenges involving the complex interlocking sociological, personal and structural factors in the production of masculinity. There is, therefore, need to acknowledge that, in each of the two societies under investigation, there exist specific historical and cultural contexts that texture the creation of particular ways of enacting masculinity among military veterans.

The differences of the two societies are narrowed down if we look at them from the viewpoint of Connell's assertion that masculinities are produced in the process of social and *cultural* interaction in which social actors exploit the resources and strategies available to them in their specific social settings (Connell 1995, 2001). To this stance the objection might be made that it reduces masculinity to cultural processes. Such processes are indeed attested to by Dio Cassius when referring to Antony in a speech of Octavian. In the speech Octavian argued that (my italics):

> εἰ δ' οὖν ποτε καὶ ἐκ τῆς σὺν ἡμῖν στρατείας ἀρετήν τινα ἔσχεν, ἀλλ' εὖ ἴσθ' ὅτι νῦν πᾶσαν αὐτὴν ἐν τῇ τοῦ βίου μεταβολῇ διέφθαρκεν. ἀδύνατον γάρ ἐστι βασιλικῶς τέ τινα τρυφῶντα καὶ γυναικείως θρυπτόμενον ἀνδρῶδές τι φρονῆσαι καὶ πρᾶξαι, διὰ τὸ πᾶσαν ἀνάγκην εἶναι, οἵοις ἄν τις ἐπιτηδεύμασι συνῇ, τούτοις αὐτὸν ἐξομοιοῦσθαι.
>
> Dio Cass. 50.27.3–5

> 'even if Antony did . . . at one time attain to some *valor* through campaigning with us, be well assured that he has now spoiled it utterly by his changed manner of life . . . For it is impossible for one who leads a life of royal luxury, and coddles himself like a woman, to have a *manly thought or do a manly deed*, since it is an inevitable law that a *man assimilates himself to the practices of his daily life*.'
>
> Cary 1917

The Greek literally says 'because there is every necessity that whatever kind of practices (ἐπιτηδεύμασι) someone is engaged in (συνῇ) he is assimilated (ἐξομοιοῦσθαι) to these.' Επιτηδεύμασι is from ἐπιτήδευμα which means business or practice (Liddell and Scott 1889: 304). Συνῇ is from σύνειμι, to be with, or to be engaged in (ibid., 771), ἐξομοιοῦσθαι is from ἐξομοιόω (ibid., 275).

A cultural-reductionist view of masculinity does not advert to the more stable elements of biology and nature underlying it. Masculinity was associated with heroic actions, sacrifice and dedication to one's nation. Fighting for and defending Rome, for example, was regarded a service to its citizens, where an excellent and patriotic man would readily give up both *body* and life (see for example, Dio Cass. 36.27.6, Cary 1914: 45).[24] With that positioning as a 'manly man' inevitably came a host of other social meanings, expectations and identities, upon which veterans acted, adopted or adapted in the context of their physical bodies' involvement in land claims, contestations and expropriations.

Nevertheless, the problem of contradiction in concepts of masculinity is a real one. I try to address it through recognition that there may be different ideas of masculinity in a given culture, even if biological maleness is an attribute that might be thought of as common/natural to all biological males (cf. Dio Cass. 36.27.5, Cary 1914: 45). This assumption has also been challenged, as there seem to be ambiguous cases in nature, for example, the Roman fixation on the figure of the hermaphrodite (see Barrow 2018: 76ff). The apparent ambiguity of maleness may however be reduced if we distinguish maleness from manliness. Through Dio Cassius, in Pompey's speech, we learn that manliness does not come of its own accord to just anyone, but a man must be born with a natural bent for it, and must not only learn and practice the art of being manly, but must enjoy good *fortune* to achieve great exploits (Dio Cass. 36.27.5, Cary 1914: 45. Appian says the same in reference to Sulla's unbroken success against his enemies (see App. *BC.* 1.97).

This Roman client-army masculinity, like Zimbabwe's guerrilla veteran's masculinity, is related integrally to its narrative patterns. For the latter, narratives of war exploits by guerrilla fighters involve feats of adventurism and courage as I shall highlight in detail later. In Plutarch's *Life of Caesar* we are told that those soldiers of Caesar who had not notably distinguished themselves in previous campaigns became significantly more valorous when fighting under him. Plutarch gives examples of Acilius, who carried on fighting when his right hand was cut off, and Cassius Scaeva, who was wounded in his eye, his shoulder and his thigh (Plut. *Caes.* 16). The word for 'valour' here is ἀνδραγαθία, which means 'the goodness of a man': it is derived from ἀνήρ, meaning 'man' in the sense of male, and ἀγαθός, which not only means 'good' but when used of heroes in Homer may be translated as 'brave' or 'noble' (Liddell and Scott 1876: 2). This word is redolent of masculinity.

To return to the theme of culture vis-à-vis my comparative method: I centralize cultural production of images of masculinity in conjunction with the physical body of a veteran. I argue that Roman client-army veterans claimed, embodied and wielded authority based upon their warrior body-type in their claims for land rewards. Since the identity of being a war veteran involves physical factors such as violence, the body and its substances such as blood, sweat, bones, (Dio Cass. 44.51.1) wounds (Dio Cass. 42.53.3) and scars, – as detailed in Chapter Six – I examined how such factors shed a particular light on client-army veterans' construction of concepts of masculinity and the body in land expropriation.

## Practice theory

My comparative investigation makes use of the 'practice theory'. The Zimbabwean war veteran's cultural context is accessible live. This is not possible with the ancient Roman veteran. Geertz has argued that culture can be studied by observing closely those publicly accessible practices, either through micro observation of largely mute and unnoticed practices or through 'thick description' of the publicly observable symbolic and ritual practices that structure the possibilities of meaning in a given 'cultural system' (Geertz, cited in Swidler 2006: 85). Meanings of masculinity generated through descriptions of clearly observable Zimbabwean war veterans' rituals, practices, actions, are contrasted with rituals, practices and actions of veterans described in the ancient Roman texts under investigation. Thus, practice theory helps me to make sense of the cultural and social significance of human activity; the nature of subjectivity, embodiment, meaning and normativity; the character of language and power; and the organization, reproduction and transformation of social and political life, in my context, by military veterans (Schatzki 2006: 10). This approach, to borrow Schatzki's turn of phrase, helps mark the frontiers of my analysis of the 'body-activity-society complex' in ancient Rome.

The juxtaposition of the ancient Roman and the Zimbabwean contexts allows for an examination of the relationship between the construction of concepts of 'masculinity' and 'veteran' on one hand, and land ownership and expropriation on the other. In order to place the phenomena of the study – 'veteran', 'masculinity' and 'expropriation' in sharper relief – I examine parallels or contrasts relating to Roman veterans and veterans of Zimbabwe's guerrilla veterans insofar as they relate or do not relate to what is observed elsewhere. For example, I contrast the complex performances of acts of masculinity deployed as strategies to expropriate land by Zimbabwe's liberation war veterans with similar performative displays by Roman client-army veterans. The function of the element of performativity, which comes out clearly in the Zimbabwean context demonstrates the role of the masculine ideal in the broader matrix, dynamics and mechanics of land expropriations when contrasted to Roman client-army veterans.

I am also especially attentive to expressions in classical languages and Shona (my native language) respectively, that are linked to masculinity. In classical historical documents relating to politics and history, I took note of language (in the Greek and Latin) linked to manliness, valour and martial prowess, and language that attributes effeminacy in such a way as to imply inferiority. The best interpretation of Latin or Greek words whose meanings converge with Shona words denoting the same phenomena, in my view, does not reduce similarities to some level of universal truth, but allows for an understanding of the cultural logic behind a language redolent of masculinity and its deployment in the construction of images of power, status, rank and authority in the two societies.

## Roman historical and literary sources

This section details a discussion of the nature of the ancient Roman and some of the modern sources analysed in this book, their limitations and gaps, and how such gaps can be plugged by evidence from disparate historical contexts. The comparative methodology, I hope, can illuminate any critical reader, through the African context in general and the Zimbabwean situation of war veterans in particular, to be able to identify with what the ancient Romans have expressed in the literary, historical and other evidence that they have left behind.

Appian and Dio Cassius offer detailed narratives (Finley 1986: 12) of episodes of expropriation and struggles for land rewards between individual generals and their hordes of fighters. It is necessary to note that both historians were drawing on a series of previous accounts which went back to their respective contemporaries of the events which they describe. Appian (first to second-centuries AD) shows awareness of economic and social as well as political factors and provides a continuous narrative from the Gracchi to the battle of Actium. Dio Cassius' books 36-60 (68 BC to 46 AD) survive largely complete – the period which covers a large portion of the late Roman Republic, which this book is mainly focused on. However, the oddities of relying on Appian and Dio Cassius in envisioning the processes of land expropriation are far-reaching, especially when one takes into account their direct quotations from speeches of their characters (Finley 1986: 12). Referring in particular to Thucydides' speeches,

Finley stresses that there is no good reason for taking the speeches to be anything but inventions by historians, not only in their precise wording but also in their substance (Finley 1986: 13). However, there is a certain quality that I find important in the speeches created by Appian and Dio Cassius. Whilst one may regret that such speeches are unhistorical, in a literal sense, the psychological insight which they reflect is quite suited for envisioning images of masculinity and the dramatic nature of the struggles for land of Roman client-army soldiers (cf. Walsh 1961: 220).

My interrogation of meanings of masculinity within episodes of expropriation also takes account of the wider Roman historical field. Thus, the ancient sources cited throughout this book come from different periods in classical history – Polemo being in the second century AD (Gleason 1995: 22), Plutarch being in the first to second century AD. Dio Cassius, for example, imported third-century AD issues in his discussion of first-century BC issues concerning land struggles for veterans. This has been said to have displaced and diffracted authentic material (Reinhold and Swan 1990: 170). However, a common factor here would be the environment of the Roman empire, for example, issues experienced by Cassius Dio's Rome were very much similar to those of first-century BC Rome. The imperial government of Dio's time, like during the period of client-armies, enlarged armies corrupted by excessive pay and largesse and by slackening of military discipline (Reinhold and Swan (1990: 157). His description of soldiers as utterly mercenary was typical of first-century BC client-armies. It must be noted that 'empire' as I use the term refers not only to the empire contemporaneous with the principate of Augustus and later leaders, but also to the complex unity of Italian territory and annexed territory beyond Italy, the *imperium*, that existed even during the Republican period, and from which the empire of the principate took its rise. Like many cultures which rose to prominence primarily through military aggression, images of the soldier's life and the ideal man's life were often the same in Roman society (Stewart 2016: 11). Perusing literary and visual sources from any period of Roman history, as Stewart (ibid.) argued, draws attention to the importance of this connection to the idea of a common Roman military ethos through which all citizens could bask in their armies' glory.

It also seems reasonable to suppose that, as a consequence of subjection to the same leadership, there was, amid the cultural variety of the Roman-conquered territories, an underlying cultural relatedness in the colonized cultures incorporated under the developing Roman *imperium*, which would allow us to view their masculinity-ideas as related, hence my reference to material from different periods of Roman history. Thus, Roman veterans' masculinity culture was a result of social interaction and certain practices and habits that pervaded the cultural milieu within which the veterans existed; this informed the competitive face-to-face world of veterans – a society which influenced and shaped veterans behaviour – something like what was explored by MacMullen (1984) in his article, '*The Legion as a Society*'.

## A mosaicist approach

I also adopted a 'mosaicist approach', a method of juxtaposing for analysis, ancient sources drawn from a variety of literary genres – an approach adopted by Kelly Olson (2014: 183) in her article '*Masculinity, Appearance, and Sexuality: Dandies in Roman Antiquity*'. Envisioning the process of land expropriation in ancient Rome, something that happened more than 2,000 years ago, requires an assemblage of multiple sources. Because of the fragmentary character of the sources, I had to gather discrete and disparate traces of the period and assemble them in order to shed light on the circumstances and background of what we otherwise can only know by scrounging for whatever material that we can lay our hand onto. I emphasized the importance of treating the widest range of source material in envisioning the expropriations. For example, my use of some passages from selected Roman literary sources – Vergil's *Eclogues*, Horace's *Odes* and *Satires*, and Lucan's *De Bello Civili* – draws upon Westall's approach (2014), by concentrating on perspectives that can be demonstrated to flow from the texts, together with historical references to the authors' own time. These sources are for me interpretations of evidence recorded down in form of poetry.

I must at once state that poetry, for example, appeals to different levels of the human: ideas, feelings, imaginations, aural sensitivity (Rigault in McClymont 2007); and these qualities are universal. The texts of Vergil, Horace and Lucan analysed in this book appeal to the mind. They evoke feelings of pity, fear; fantasy; narrative fiction appeals to the imagination (not all that is imaginatively vivid must be believed by the hearer to be false). The relevance of the poetry of Vergil, Horace and Lucan and other literature is related to the human dimension which it touches. I value even the fabulous tales of poets such as Q. Ennius quoted by Pliny (Plin. *NH*. 7.38). I argue, the poems of these poets affect the various levels of the human in a more or less structured way. The intellect is given thoughts to consider; the emotions are aroused by poetic rhythms and narrative structures; the imagination is offered stories relatable to an African context. Thus, I treat Vergil, Lucan and Horace as sociohistorical texts and reflections of the reality they portrayed (see Kirstein 2017). When Lucan, for example, discusses a historical event poetically (Lintott 1971: 488) in his epic, *De Bello Civili*, in the words of Robert Kirstein (2017: 191), 'he depicts scenes of violence that include fictive objects set in a fictional, self-contained literary world'. Garrett Fagan as quoted by Serena Witzke (2016: 250) explains:

> Ancient anecdotes and fiction can act as mirrors that reflect social attitudes, assumptions, and realities, even if the immediate context is highly dubious or even fantastical. This is because in order to be effective, satires or novels have to present their audience with recognizable social paradigms.

From these texts, we can extract much evidence about the realities of civil war crises in Rome and its effects such as violence and expropriations. According to Robert Kirstein, the scenes of violence depicted in literary texts are possible reflections of actual violence in the context of historical testimonies for that epoch (Kirstein 2017: 191). Thus, my focus on Lucan's passages, for example, is mainly an endeavour to make an historical interpretation of the text. Like Kirstein (2017: 191, 195), I interpret the text in Lucan's *De Bello Civili* as part of a cultural discourse on violence, and I give the text a literary and metaphorical interpretation of gender. The conclusions that I make in this book are thus based on my analysis, not only of Appian and Dio Cassius and other ancient history texts, but on metapoetical – in the case of Lucan (see Paolo Asso 2010: 220), Vergil and Horace whose inclusion in my discussion of perspectives of the concept of masculinity should be seen in the light of narratives of ancient historians – and, of course, generic discussion linked to the texts. Although it has been argued that Lucan exhibited no illusion of heroism in the Homeric sense, no promise of glorious deeds alluded to in the Iliad's proem (Roche 1997: 95), I maintain that the theme of masculinity and heroism is evident. For example, Lucan represented Caesar and his men as Giant figures of Roman history, in the process, depicting the civil war with Pompey through the analogy of a Gigantomachy masculinity, in which the struggle of Hercules against Antaeus evokes the political forces that face each other in the civil war (Asso 2010: 221–2; Luc. 3.315-20). The two opposing factions are depicted as acting like gladiators in the arena, an image that evokes Hercules and Antaeus pitted against one another as wrestlers in the arena (Luc. 1.708-9, see also Roche 1997: 264). This image of gladiators clearly mirrors Roman masculinity in practice in the amphitheatre as opposed to the battlefield. The gladiators' duty was to fight valiantly and be ready to die at the will of the audience and the emperor. They fought on behalf of, and for, the Roman people and its empire. These men were objects demonstrating and displaying fighting skills and by extension, traditional Roman virtues in the amphitheatre (Takacs 2009).

I also analyse the representations of masculinity in the poetry of Vergil, Horace and Lucan as a way to complement the evidence of imperial historians. The imperial historians' narratives suggest an implied devotion of veterans to the masculine ideal, but they often offer a rigid view of land expropriations, which has the effect of blurring the performative element of the process, stripping the expropriations of the dramatic effect. It is in this regard that Lucan, Horace and Vergil provide possible perspectives on masculinity that can be demonstrated to flow from their poetry. From an epistemological principle, as Finley argued, poetry enhances the imagination as a means of discovering the truth 'as it really was' (Finley 1986: 53–4). For my part, I do not attempt to re-discover client-army veterans' expropriations as they really happened. The poetry of Horace, Vergil and Lucan is important insofar as they enhance how the episodes can be re-imagined. Thus, the history–poetry relationship is critical in my analysis of masculinity. Wilhelm von Humboldt argued that an event:

> is only partially visible in the world of the senses; the rest has to be added by intuition, inference, and guesswork ... The truth of any event is predicated on the addition ... of that invisible part of every fact, and it is that part, therefore, which the historian has to add ... Different from the poet, but in a way similar to him, he must work the collected fragments into a whole.[25]

I must also hasten to say that I am not pursuing Wilhelm von Humboldt's conception of history (which involved methods that control intuition and other kinds of subjectivism) in my treatment of ancient Rome, as my approach is not verificationist, but is aimed at generating hypotheses and questions on masculinity, veterans and expropriation, through examination of available data (Glaser and Strauss 1967: viii). This is because Roman sources are fragmentary and rudimentary, which make the theories we arrive at probabilities of lesser weight, which we assert tentatively in a spirit of openness to further evidence.

Our limited knowledge coupled with the poor state of evidence on first-century BC client-army veterans' involvement in land expropriation calls for an open-minded approach to the study of Roman history. My approach involves a critical search for illuminating insights in disparate historical settings and contexts, involving land expropriations by military veterans. I draw upon perspectives on comparisons of disparate cases from the work of Timothy Scarnecchia (Scarnecchia 2006), who explored a comparative model of fascism developed by Paxton (2004) to demonstrate a wider significance of fascist Italy's political tradition for understanding the current crisis of dictatorship in Zimbabwe (Scarnecchia 2006: 224–5). He explored the instrumentalization of war veterans by the ruling elite to maintain a grip on power through stifling democratic space. In Italy, for example, the ruling elites entered into a compromise with militias in return for recognition of veterans' demands for land and employment (ibid.). The militias violently intimidated and weakened the opposition parties in both rural and urban areas (Scarnecchia 2006: 224–5).

One reason why one might find the study of ancient Rome problematic is that in modern times we are quite remote from the original context of ancient authors, and thus there is a lot we do not know about ancient times in general and the context of fragmentary and rudimentary material in particular. So the problem of incompleteness does need to be acknowledged, and thus we need to ask how the problem of access to incomplete and rudimentary evidence might be alleviated. One prerequisite is the attitude that any and all sources of illumination that can be used should be used. With so unsatisfactory information about the Roman period in question at our disposal, we need to take appropriate account of every bit of information we can get. This means that an multidisciplinary approach is essential; we cannot afford to cut ourselves off from sources of knowledge because, 'Such-and-such is not my discipline.' Therefore, cognizant of this, in this book I seek to generate new perspectives on the interplay of war veterans, masculinity and land expropriation – perspectives that could be applied to our understanding of the ancient world.

A further implication of the need to work with every available scrap of information is that the researcher must not be afraid of comparing material with other material. We should not exaggerate in a nominalistic fashion the amount of similarity between material that is needed for comparison to be meaningful. It is part of the 'theoretical sensitivity' techniques of the grounded theory approach that contexts of comparison should be as broad or as narrow as is required for the generation of insight (Strauss and Corbin 1990: 90). The Romans were human beings of our species and from our planet. They were not Martians; they have human nature in common with us. So we should not be afraid of comparing ancient sources with us and with each other; we should not be afraid to draw parallels between personalities ancient and modern, and with the 'prime mover' theory of history referred to by Fagin (Fagin 1985: 515).

Finally, the concepts of masculinity can make visible for analysis what imperial historians' narratives of land expropriation, due to their lack of concepts (now at the disposal of modern historians) (e.g. Finley 1986: 26.) could not quite articulate. Renowned comparativist Marc Bloch argued that using modern concepts to describe ancient ideas would not be sufficient if we had not known living men and living examples (Bloch 1953: 44). In the same vein Gaetano De Sanctis compared First World War veterans' movements to those of ancient Rome, by conventionally discussing the political problem of the '*veterani*' after the Jugurthine War and defining it with the concept of '*combattentismo*', which was actually a neologism created in the 1920s to refer to the widespread belief that ex-combatants from the First World War deserved a special treatment in post-war society (De Sanctis 1932: 213).[26]

Ramsay MacMullen in his article *The Legion as a Society* plugged a gap in the ancient sources by using interviews from the Second World War to explain the organization of the Roman legion (MacMullen 1984). In reaching beyond Roman history to refer to interviews from Second World War veterans, the aim in MacMullen's words (1984: 447) would be:

> ... to bring to bear whatever wisdom and clarity the modern evidence may afford, and the unanimity to be discovered among them suggests that they may be used to shed light on quite other times and circumstances.

Similarly, contemporary Zimbabwe provides something 'real': primary evidence for the motives and actions of war veterans. Narrative accounts of Zimbabwean war veterans are products of lived experience, of thought and reflection. This places me at a good position to pose questions and to come to conclusions that ancient historians would not necessarily think of with their more limited concepts and evidence. Thus, by means of defensible ideas of human nature, society and culture, aided by textual and other data, one can reconstruct a picture of the ancient human world, and thus Classics can have a human object of study.

## Conclusion

In this chapter I marked the general theoretical terrain and approaches to the present study. I explained the challenges posed by the ancient Roman texts as sources of historical evidence for reconstructing episodes of land expropriation in the first-century BC. Ancient Roman sources, both literal and historical, are not sufficient for our understanding of client-army veterans' motivations in the context of the cultural matrix of gender, masculinity, violence, war and land. From these sources issue narratives on land expropriation from which emerge an opaque view of latent and manifest meanings of veteran-masculinities. A juxtaposition of ancient Roman client-army veterans with living war veterans from a modern situation, allows an understanding of what we can otherwise only access through texts. As such, I investigate the Roman sources to examine episodes in which 'masculinity' appears in land expropriation by veterans, in order to lay out a 'reading' which indicates how the concepts of masculinity may help explain the meaning of such passages.

# 2

# Ancient Rome and Africa: Background and Differences

*But a man may wear himself out just as fruitlessly in seeking to understand the past, if he is totally ignorant of the present . . . For here, in the present, is immediately perceptible that vibrance of human life which only a great effort of the imagination can restore to the old texts.*

Marc Bloch[1]

## Introduction

In the previous chapter, I outlined the aims, methodology and arguments involving the comparative approach deployed in the present study. My comparative approach is intended to suggest that images of expropriation discernible in the ancient Roman sources can heuristically be analysed in comparison with an African context, to explore the cultural meaning and logic embedded in the social processes of land acquisition, ownership, loss of land and property through expropriation in first-century BC Rome.

This chapter examines the historical backgrounds, in ancient Rome and Zimbabwe, against which veteran activity may be understood, and looks at the meaning of the term 'veteran'. It also examines fundamental differences in the two worlds of veterans which relate to notions of war, gender and masculinity. These involve, among other things, socio-cultural differences in the physical and spiritual constitution of a veteran in the ancient Roman world and an African context, and differences in the function of a 'female masculinity' in land struggles in the two societies.

## Ancient Rome: A background

Ancient Rome was originally under a regal government (based on kings accompanied by a senate) and shifted in 510/509 BC to a more republican government where two magistrates called consuls were in charge (Petrie 1963: 14). During the Republican period, the tribune Tiberius Gracchus, in 133 BC, introduced a scheme of land reform which provided for the distribution among the poorer citizens of any state land that did not have an authorized possessor. This led to a conflict between the senate, who sided with the rich and their prescriptive rights, and Tiberius, who resisted along with the popular assembly. There were a lot of poor Romans without land, it must be noted, but the struggle for land was not simply senate vs people; some senators favoured reviving land allotments, whose victims would be the Italian allies – so it was a complex issue.[2]

The agrarian law was passed, but Tiberius was murdered shortly thereafter, when attempting to be re-elected to the tribunate. His younger brother, Gaius, renewed the struggle between the senate and the people and attempted various political measures, including a law designed to prevent favouritism by the senate in allocating provinces. Tiberius' reform broadly aimed to tackle the plight of the soldiery in order to gain support from this section (Plut. *Ti. Gr.* 9.5, Dio Cass. 24.4-5). Citing Plutarch and Tibiletti, Scullard argues that Tiberius' land bill had veterans in mind (Scullard 1960: 63).[3] Gaius also acted in a manner that exhibited a quest for the affection of the soldiery when he made a provision of clothes and food for the same, at a time when the senate had turned its back on the army which was doing its duty in Sardinia (Plut. *C. Gr.* 2.1-20).

The main problem the senate faced with the Gracchan attempts at reform was the fear that patronage of settlers would lead them to gain excessive power. The sources generally suggest that the Gracchi's land redistribution programme was designed to attain personal *regnum* (dominion). Gaius Gracchus founded three additional colonies, two in Italy and one on the site of Carthage, which prompted the reactionary proposals by the tribune Livius Drusus (Coles 2020: 47 n.289). The agrarian reforms introduced by the Gracchi did not long survive them, but the struggle between the senate and the popular party did (Petrie 1963: 45–7). The Gracchan settlers and the veterans had two things in common: they were mostly rural in origin and their desire was to obtain a secure source of livelihood by having their own land (Brunt 1962).

During the Republican period, war veterans had no fixed claim to land, but could obtain such rewards through the influence of powerful generals (App. *BC.* 5.5) under whom they served – hence the willingness of war veterans to side with a few generals against the senate. Every army so raised consisted largely of men who were attracted by the reputation of the general and the sphere of war in the hope of winning no small booty in the fighting and a piece of land on its conclusion (Smith 1955: 128).

When the Republican period was entering its final stages, in the first-century BC, Roman armies were overwhelmingly rural in origin. According to Brunt (1962), levies throughout Italy in 87, 84–82, 52, 49, 43 and 4I BC, and on various occasions in Cisalpina, Etruria, Picenum, Umbria, the Sabine country, near Arpinum, in Campania, Samnium, Lucania, Apulia, Bruttium, among the Marsi, Paeligni and Marrucini were from the rural areas. This stresses the importance of land in the lives of fighters. Generals were able to carve out their careers using land to build their armies. Lucius Domitius, one of Pompey's lieutenants, had acquired vast amounts of land under the Sullan regime (Dio Cass. 41.11.2), which he used to mobilize a large number of soldiers, in preparation for the war against Caesar. Julius Caesar built his army on promises and on the parcelling out of acreage to his men. The foundation of the first triumvirate was based on expropriation of political fields and territorial partition between Julius Caesar, Pompey and Crassus. One key pillar of the agreement hinged on the support of Caesar in providing land to Pompey's Mithridatic veterans as I shall explore in detail later on.

Plutarch's account emphasizes the role of land in Caesar's victory at Pharsalus (a civil war that was fought between Julius Caesar and Pompey).[4] Caesar knew how to motivate his men and to inspire loyalty, bought or otherwise. He used this knowledge to engender fierce loyalty in valorous troops that won him Italy before Pompey had even galvanized his own levying efforts, using promises of acreage. This effectiveness, and the rewards system tapped into by Caesar from his time of governorship of the province of Hispania, following his praetorship, up to his preparations for the Parthian war, was instrumental in establishing for him a key advantage over Pompey.[5] The dedication of Caesar's land-motivated soldiers caused Pompey to reflect upon the uncertainty of his own troops, most of whom had joined up with him only recently, and were motivated only by the gains they might secure should Caesar fall to him.

Octavian and Antony offered a great deal of land and money to their forces after Philippi. Appian recorded that:

> After the victory of Philippi Octavian and Antony offered a magnificent sacrifice and awarded praise to their army. In order to provide the rewards of victory Octavian went to Italy to divide the land among the soldiers and to settle the colonies. He chose this himself on account of his illness. Antony went to the nations beyond the Aegean to collect the money that had been promised to the soldiers.
>
> App. *BC.* 5.3, White 1913: 381

Referring to the struggles for power between Octavian and Antony, Dio Cassius captures the role of land thus: 'Both sides placed the greatest hope of power in the allotment of land, and consequently the beginning of their quarrel was concerned with that.' (Dio Cass. 48.6, Carry 1917). Veterans were indeed responsible for the see-saw kind of situation which saw Antony and Octavian wrestle for supremacy in Roman politics. Antony's career in Roman politics, though short-lived, was made possible by the support he got from Caesar's veterans stationed at Campania. Antony's agrarian law of 44 BC, aimed to attract the support of veterans as the law was envisaged to benefit them. The entire legislative programme was pushed through with their help. When the senate finally declared Antony and his supporters enemies of the state, he marched towards Transalpine Gaul and fled to the Alps accompanied by three veteran legions recruited for him in Italy. Their readiness for recruitment in the hope of gaining land as payment placed them on a high political ground in Rome.

In order to deal with Antony, whom they had designated an enemy to the Republic, the senate had to lure veterans with land. The senate honoured the 5,000 denarii and farms which Octavian had promised them. Antony's veterans were also promised some money and farms for deserting Antony. In keeping with his vision of maintaining the support of veterans, Octavian absorbed Antony's defeated army which had surrendered at the naval battle of Actium, and assured to provide them with farms in Italy after their demobilization. Octavian had learnt of the dangers of restless veterans from the contemporary political situations, so he ensured their future loyalty, the case of Catiline being a good example.

Octavian later re-named himself Augustus, by which name posterity better know him. Augustus attempted to reward veterans of Rome with land: some veterans were settled in 41 to 40 BC and 36 BC and these settlements involved widespread confiscation of land. In 30 BC and 14 BC lands were bought for war veterans, and under Augustus legal arrangements were made for the rewarding of soldiers on discharge (Brunt and Moore 1967:41–2). Rewarding the veterans was not, however, an easy task; from 7–2 BC Augustus had to pay veterans from his own resources, public revenues being insufficient, and in AD 14, after Augustus' death, there were mutinies on the Rhine and Danube, and mutineers complained that they had to serve thirty or forty years and were then fobbed off with grants of mountainous or marshy land in distant territories (ibid., 42–3).

It can be observed from the foregoing that land ownership in Rome is historically linked with political and military struggle; and since the prime movers of these struggles were mostly males, especially soldiers, operating in a largely patriarchal social milieu, this book explores how masculinity was enacted and bound up with land ownership as well as physical appropriation of political fields. How was land acquired both as a reward for political struggle and military effort, and in what ways was the process an expression of masculinity?

## Zimbabwe: A background

Zimbabwe is a small, landlocked Southern African country with a population of approximately 13 million located between the Zambezi River and the Limpopo River where people have always contested for land, even before the arrival of the pioneer column in the 1890s (Masiiwa and Chipungu 2004). The Shona and the Ndebele were two major ethnic groups living in the territory now called Zimbabwe. The country has its origin in the former British colony of Southern Rhodesia and today shares borders with South Africa, Zambia, Mozambique, Botswana and Namibia (Mlambo 2018: 167).

The livelihood of the Shona was originally dependent on both agricultural and pastoral activities while the Ndebele were cattle keepers whose economy was based on highly organized military structures (Masiiwa and Chipungu 2004). Since the beginning of colonialism in the 1890s, land has been a major bone of contention. Blacks were confined to Tribal Trust Lands or native lands by the passing of the Land Apportionment Act in 1930 and the Land Tenure Act of 1970, except for those required for labour in the towns and cities. The 'native' land became overworked and overgrazed, so that peasant agriculture became subsistence agriculture, with the farming families often depending on assistance from their wage-earning relatives in the urban areas (Auret 2009: 101). These events led to the independence war (1960s–1980), as the indigenous people fought to reclaim their land. After independence in 1980, the colonial land imbalances persisted as the government of Zimbabwe had gone slack on the issue of land redistribution. This triggered violent scenes of expropriations of white-owned farms and even farms belonging to fellow Blacks, by veterans of the liberation war, led by their former guerrilla leader Robert Mugabe. In this movement they expropriated land in collaboration with other actors (landless rural peasants and some rural and urban working class). This historical legacy provides an essential explanation for the thinking and behaviour of appropriation among veterans and their wartime leaders.

The expropriations of land also worked as a form of accumulation by the Zimbabwe African National Union-Patriotic Front (ZANU-PF) elites of valuable power, influence and land. The terms 'expropriations' or 'farm invasions' refer to what is commonly known in the native Shona language as *hondo yeminda* (war for land), or *jambanja* (smash-and-grab) (Scarnecchia 2006: 234) or violent invasions (Worby 2001). Zimbabwe's liberation war veterans dubbed this movement *kutora ivhu* (taking [back] land), or the Third *Chimurenga*, as the expropriations became ideologically linked to a narrative of continuous struggle for decolonization since the 1890s (Mlambo 2018). The word *Chimurenga* refers to wars fought against colonial occupation, and its use connects the liberation struggle (1960s-1980) and the land occupations of the 2000s with the 1896/7 Shona–Ndebele uprising against the British South Africa Company (BSAC), known as the *Chimurenga*. The liberation war was thus an important historical event for the ex-liberation war fighters. The First *Chimurenga* (also known as the Shona–Ndebele rebellions) were fought to reclaim the land from the colonialists. The indigenous people lost these wars and the land remained in the hands of the colonizers.

At this point, having discussed the general historical background to war-veteran activity in ancient Rome and Zimbabwe, we may now look in more detail at the connotations of the term 'veteran'.

## The term 'veteran': Ancient Rome

The term 'veteran', in late Republican scholarship is used to refer to soldiers who had a special loyalty to their commander in the period of the 'client-army', for example, the time of Marius, Sulla, Pompey, and later Caesar and Octavian. My definition of veteran in first-century BC Rome is informed by Appian who recorded that veterans were those who fought on behalf of another, i.e. client-soldiers. The Greek word for 'fought on behalf of' is ὑπερηγωνίζοντο (App. *BC.* 1.96). The prefix ὑπερ- means 'on behalf of'. The term ὑπεραγωνίστης, related to ὑπερηγωνίζοντο, means 'one who fights on behalf of another', or a champion.

Citizen-soldiers returning from frontier warfare in the second-century BC who constitute part of the Gracchi problems do not fit in this category, although they form part of the historical process of the problem which became a factor in Roman politics in the first century.

The time-expired soldiers of the legions are also part of what I refer to as veterans. The term 'veteran' in the late Roman Republic does not necessarily imply advanced age or long service. In the second and first century BC, recruits were expected to serve not more than six continuous years, since six years of service were counted as the complete full service, and anyone who had completed the six years was entitled to share in any available *praemia* (Keppie 1983: 36).[6] According to Polybius, foot soldiers served for 16 legal years, and the cavalry served for 10 legal years in his time (Polyb. 6.19.2). Keppie (1983: 36) thought it safe to conclude that 16 years of service was the maximum that could be legally demanded of a citizen between the ages of 17 and 46, but in practice six years was the regular term. However, the client-army era disregarded these strict limits, as retired soldiers could be enlisted into private armies of individual generals inspired by rewards in the form of acreage, booty or money. The idea that the veterans, as mercenaries, were holding out for financial compensation is implied in Lucan (Luc. 5:244-248, Graves 1956), where he tries to explain the cause of the mutiny of Caesar's veterans as follows (my italics):

> . . . seu maesto classica paulum
> intermissa sono claususque et frigidus ensis
> expulerat belli furias: seu praemia miles
> dum maiora petit damnat causamque ducemque,
> et scelere imbutos etiam nunc *venditat* enses.
>
> Either the leaving off of the trumpets with their sorrowful sound or the confined and frigid sword had expelled the madness of war; or the soldier, while he *sought greater rewards*, condemned both the general and his cause, and offered his crime-stained sword even now for sale.

It is important to note that the term *venditat* suggests also that financial rewards and not just rewards of valour were sought by veterans. The meaning of the word for booty, *praeda,* has overtones of a martial ethic. Caesar spoke to his soldiers about the dangers of Pompeian victory in the civil war, which included the loss of the colonies meant for them as veterans to pirates, as a betrayal to both Rome and the soldiers that fought for her (Luc. 1.343-5). The word *praemium*, reward, is related to *praeda,* meaning 'booty', so that its derivation suggests the booty of war.[7] In Luc. 5.308, there is a reference to *praemia Martis,* the rewards of Mars, showing the connection of *praemium* with war. This shows how veterans are generally characterized in literal and historical texts.

## The Zimbabwean concept of 'veteran'

In talking of 'veterans' in the context of Zimbabwe, I focus on adult guerrilla soldiers who share a more or less similar ideology of the liberation war.[8] The identities of Zimbabwean liberation war veterans are grounded in the anti-colonial struggle which culminated in the country's independence in 1980, and was the work of men and women from various political organizations in the country (Mlambo and Gwekwerere 2019). These men and women are the archetypal embodiments of the liberation struggle.

It must be noted that on their part, the war veterans discarded the term 'ex-combatants' and insisted on being called war veterans (Muchemwa 2011: 128). This was a strategic move on their part. Accepting the label 'ex-combatant' had the effect of relegating their efforts to a period that had long since been passed. Furthermore, their bodies would only be associated with 'combat' which is only one aspect of war. However, by re-inscribing their bodies and demanding to be known as 'war veterans', they sought to do a number of things at once. First, the label would secure a place for them alongside other recognized war veterans from the First and Second World Wars, alongside the American war veterans. Second, the description would serve to remind both the citizens and the ruling elite of their heroism and expertise in the art of war. Third, such a reminder would facilitate access to resources such as land and pensions as it would have the effect of drawing attention to the war veterans' capacity to re-mobilize their bodies whenever the situation required them to do so.

The terminology of 'ex-combatants' would moreover imply a group of men who were no longer interested in fighting; and of course the liberation war veterans were by no means ready to stop their fighting, but wished to continue. Their efforts were described as a *Chimurenga* or war of liberation using nomenclature that called to mind the previous First and Second *Chimurengas* in the country's history.

The idea of 'war veterans' as people who are not 'ex-combatants' but still ready to fight is also seen in the Roman war veterans who, throughout the client-army era, were mobilized and re-mobilized at different times, by different generals.[9] Dio Cassius mentioned of Caesar's veterans whom Octavian recalled from

Capua to fight his wars against Antony.[10] The passage below typically demonstrates this point (my italics):

> Multi undique ex veteribus Pompei exercitibus spe praemiorum atque ordinum *evocantur*, multi ex duabus legionibus quae sunt traditae a Caesare arcessuntur. Completur urbs, clivus, comitium tribunis, centurionibus, *evocatis*.[11]

> Many men from the previous armies of Pompey were recalled from all parts by the expectation of rewards and high positions. Many were *recalled* from the two legions which had been handed over by Caesar. The city, the hillside, and the place of assembly were filled with tribunes, centurions, and *people who had been recalled*.[12]

Sallust describes Sullan veterans who joined Catiline in the 60s BC as spendthrift upstarts who had squandered their ill-gotten properties and hoped for new civil wars and confiscations, to escape their debts (Thein 2010: 84; Thein also cites, Sall. *Cat.* 16.4, 28.4). Even after the battle of Philippi, Octavian recruited an army, comprising both new recruits and Caesar's veterans re-mobilized (*RG*. 1).

## Difference in the significance of the 'veteran'

One main difference in connotation between the term 'veteran' when used in a Roman or Zimbabwean context respectively is that the economic and political crisis of Zimbabwe was manifested through the veteran phenomenon, in which land expropriations, though perceived as rewards of valour, were also seen as a means of economic emancipation from the British colonial legacy of bondage and landlessness. What is more, male and female war veterans' experiences and understanding of the land question in Zimbabwe was shaped by issues of race and belonging (cf. Pilossof 2012). Thus, veterans in Zimbabwe were indigenous people reclaiming their land from the white colonial farmers, while in ancient Rome it was the poorer veterans who expropriated land belonging to fellow Romans or Italians after military campaigns. In Roman Italy, it was a matter of the Italians being against the Romans, or poor veterans[13] against rich elites (Dio Cass. 48.8), as argued by Brunt (1962). Discontent over land inequalities in both cases was motivated by the fact that the rich and the political elites accumulated vast tracts of land at the expense of the majority of the poor, in both cases creating the problem of a poor peasantry, a hungry and landless city mob, and, most importantly, a veteran phenomenon. Such a phenomenon lies at the centre of this book.

While the differences are appreciated, the concepts of 'veteran' and 'masculinity' are used in this book as key concepts in analysing the relations of military men in crisis situations of resource re/distribution, ownership and accumulation. These relations, I argue, generally involve two broad areas: relations of the action of the general upon his forces or vice-versa – and relations of control over the conferment or distribution of material benefits (e.g. App. *BC.* 5.47). Neither of the two areas is alien to the other. Control over power and material benefits (booty) in both societies was mediated by relations between the general and his men, and also by relations among the general's men. The Campus Martius violence at a meeting between Octavian and his soldiers for the division of land is a good example (App. *BC.* 5.16). I analyse the specificity and interconnections of these two broad areas as a framework for appreciating the political economy of masculinity and expropriation among military veterans, in environments plagued by military usurpation – or, perhaps I should say, in environments where veterans are a law unto themselves.

## The two worlds of veterans

It should be noted that in comparing the two sets of veterans in Rome and Zimbabwe, I do not claim that the masculinities of the two sets of veterans were a product of absolutely similar existential experiences and processes. The differences are important. They allow us a way of viewing how dispositions to violence induced by masculinities of war and colonization, experienced differently in separate historical and geographical contexts, may converge in the treatment of land as an object of power. I explore these differences below.

To begin with, Zimbabwe is embedded in a capitalist world and dependent on commerce and other economic relations with the world (Mlambo, McClymont and Zvoma 2017). Rome was not similarly pressured by a more powerful corporation-dominated global community, and so one might initially suppose that its economy was not subject to the same pressures of development as that of Zimbabwe. Deep-seated historical and political issues underlie Zimbabwe's land question (Moyo and Chambati 2013). A more traditional and limiting perspective on this question holds that land struggles and expropriations in Zimbabwe are simply the result of key political issues, such as the Zimbabwean contestation of British colonial policies, nationalism and decolonization, issues which might seem to have no place in a comparison with ancient Rome. While the political factors are present, a focus on these factors needs to be challenged and complemented, to avoid obscuring the role played by other motivations, and by the social identity of soldiers (in particular, an ideologically charged masculinity) and the modalities and dynamics of the violence of soldiers.

There is another difference. Zimbabwe, in contrast to the Roman Republic, was a victim of colonialism. The colonialists of the country that became Southern Rhodesia, and later Zimbabwe after independence in 1980, turned to agriculture, appropriating land from the indigenous people and, through legislation, ensuring that the people would become workers on the land (Auret 2009: 101). The guerrilla veterans fought to dismantle colonialism, and emerged from the colonial war exhibiting victorious masculinities, so as to challenge existing colonial and postcolonial social arrangements – by going after the land and property of not only white farmers but even fellow-citizens. In contrast to the colonized territory of Zimbabwe, Rome was a great power which itself colonized surrounding communities and territories. Veterans of first-century BC Rome were victorious in imperial wars. Those who won in foreign wars, and those who were victorious in civil wars fought between competing dynasties of power, also emerged to question the existing social and political order through the exhibition of victorious masculinities. Thus, although I am dealing with two distinct versions of masculinities that have each their own ideological significance – the masculinity of a colonist (ancient Rome) and that of victorious people in a colonized country (in Africa), I argue that the central quest in both societies by veterans was to gain land or other rewards of war by taking up and expressing peculiar masculinities. I thus seek to unpack and give nuance to the various contextual factors and how they intersect, to explain the construction, performance and appearance of land-based masculinities across time and space. I illustrate this issue below by examining the concept of colonization as an example.

In the case of ancient Rome, as the case of European colonization of Africa, the ideal of male dominance was linked to Roman supremacy in which a hegemonic version of civilization maintained the power of Roman gender ideologies by preserving Roman male power as inevitable. As such the notion of civilization construed a colonial masculinity, which was deployed to dominate and control territories and peoples. 'Civilization' may be understood as involving the following: improvement in material subsistence and standard of living; growth of social and political institutions; development of language and literature, philosophy and science, art and refinement, morals and religion (Morey 1903: 12–13). Contrast between the 'civilized' and the 'uncivilized' may apply to the three broad areas mentioned to, of material standard of living, social institutions and development. The Romans considered themselves to be more developed and more civilized than their subjects – an imaginative construction of their frontiers that materialized land as the object of Roman colonial power – a problem that later affected Rome when soldiers and generals returning from wars, even civil wars, went after land and property belonging to fellow Romans and Italians as the object of their power struggles. In the thinking of certain Romans, the Romans and people of other ethnicities did not inhabit the same kind of bodies (Montserrat 2000: 164). Greek men, for example, were regularly criticized for their effeminacy and lust (Juv. *Sat.* 2.93-99 and 3.58-80). Non-Romans were also un-Roman for reasons such as their dress, mannerisms, accents and behaviour, which set them apart as foreigners and different (ibid.).

The superior attitude adopted towards colonized peoples by Romans and its attendant effects are reminiscent of what was suffered by Africans. During the 1920s in Southern Rhodesia, the story of Julius Caesar's '*Veni, vidi, vici*,'[14] (I came, I saw, I conquered) had a wide currency as it provided a ready framework for situating the colonial settlers' claims to be 'civilized,' and reinforced a worldview in which the *Pax Britannica* was the direct descendant of the *Pax Romana* (Jeater 2005: 8). This framework worked as a means for the white settlers to justify their domination of the locals, in which they perceived themselves in the image of the civilizing and mighty Rome. This takes me to my claim: that there is something similar to a Roman masculinity in Zimbabwe.

## A Roman 'colonial masculinity' in Zimbabwe

Classical political motifs are significant in the lived reality of white farmers in colonial and postcolonial Zimbabwe. It is instructive to note that Africans were placed in the Classical age by the colonists[15] whose knowledge about the locals was informed by white ethnographic accounts about Black Africans informed by knowledge of classical literature (see Bullock 1927; Jackson 1905). Such twentieth century ideas are still persistent in twenty-first-century white writings about Africans and land expropriation. In these writings, the African is depicted as the barbarian at the gate and also as similar to the nymphs and shepherds of the classical pastorale (Jeater 2005: 9; cf. Pilossof 2009). These two models were used to justify the continuation of a direct rule model and to dominate the Black race (Summers 2013). The 'barbarians' model required only that the whites act as civilizers, bringing Africans into modernity, while the pastoral model placed on the white race the burden of preserving all that was best of the old world (Jeater 2005: 9; cf. Barker 2007).

The reaction of the white farmer to the destructive tendencies of the veteran who took over the farm the white farmer previously owned[16] is informed by the embeddedness of such beliefs and perspectives about Africans that characterized conversations about Black Africans between whites in Southern Rhodesia in the 1920s as they grappled to understand the indigenous Africans. The postcolonial white farmer, like his colonial counterparts (colonial administrators, missionaries etc.) used the Classics, as a lens to define and justify their relationship with Africans. Their imagining of local Africans was a form of re-appropriation, as it transposed a classical landscape upon the geography of Africa, such that the African was seen as inhabiting the Golden Age landscape. By alluding in his writings to the Classical myth of the Golden Age, Bullock portrayed the Golden Age of indigenous Southern Rhodesians as typical of hunter-gatherer societies when '. . . men found the kindly fruits of the Earth sufficient for all' (Bullock, cited in Jeater 2005: 10). The African was not only displaced physically from their land, but also displaced in the way they related with their colonial master, as if they were not living in their country of origin. As Jeater (2005: 8) puts it: 'Speaking with Southern Rhodesian Africans in the 1920s, administrators, farmers and missionaries did not clearly hear the local voices, but heard echoes from somewhere in the Mediterranean, sometimes between the birth of Homer and the death of Christ.' Theirs was a masculinity based on a view of themselves as superior to the natives, of a higher intellectual level, and more capable of protecting the environment. How could the inferior, barbaric and less gifted masculinity retain possession of a noble gift of nature? Colonial masculinity is built on the edifice of presumed superiority over indigenous masculinity in every dimension of life.

There certainly was some indirect influence of a Roman masculinity in Zimbabwe through British colonialism. Roman colonial administration was mirrored in British colonial policy in Southern Rhodesia.[17] In antiquity Britain was under the colonial subjugation of the powerful empire of Rome, and this inadvertently influenced the development of their imperial political culture from 55 BC to *c*. AD 500 (Webster 2003). Achille Mbembe's notion of the 'postcolony' identifies specifically a given historical trajectory of societies emerging from the experience of colonization and the violence which the colonial relationship involves (Mbembe 2001: 102). The postcolonial state may appropriate colonial models of masculinity for the project of nation building, as Lee Kuan Yew did in Singapore (Holden in Connell 2005: 76). The concept 'postcolony' in Mbembe's words:

> . . . rehabilitates the two notions of *age* and *durée*. By age is meant not a simple category of time but a number of relationships and a configuration of events—often visible and perceptible, sometimes diffuse, 'hydra-headed,' but to which contemporaries could testify since very aware of them. As an age, the postcolony encloses multiple *durées* made up of discontinuities, reversals, inertias, and swings that overlay one another, interpenetrate one another, and envelope one another . . .
>
> Mbembe 2001: 14

During the colonial era and its aftermath, domination has been all the more strategic in power relationships, because it was based on a mobilization of the subjective foundations of masculinity and femininity (Mbembe 2001: 13). The postcolony, he argued (my italics):

> . . . is a specific system of signs, a particular way of . . . re-forming stereotypes – not just an economy of signs in which power is mirrored and imagined self-reflectively. The postcolony is characterized by a distinctive style of political improvisation, by a tendency to excess and lack of proportion, as well as by distinctive ways identities are multiplied, transformed, and put into circulation . . . the postcolony is also made up of a series of corporate institutions and a political machinery that, once in place, constitute a distinctive *regime of violence*.
>
> Mbembe 2001: 102

Roman masculinist ideology was ruthlessly practiced in its Roman North African province established in 149 BC. Cheikh Anta Diop contrasts the two concepts of civilization and barbarism in view of the barbarism of the Romans in Carthage (Diop 1981: 126). David Konstan argued that in destroying Carthage, Rome was certainly displaying its muscle, and no doubt issuing an alert to any other power in the region (Konstan 2021: 65). The language of Roman masculinity often invoked such notions as *imperium* (dominion), *fortitudo* (strength) and *virtus* – the ideal of masculine behaviour for all men to embody – which can be translated to mean valour (Williams 2010: 139).

Europe's colonization of Africa, in particular Cecil John Rhodes of Britain, was not only linked to similar ideologies of masculinity, but to how Cecil Rhodes consciously mimicked Julius Caesar in his conquest of Southern Rhodesia. For example, the institution of Roman-Dutch law as the *locus standi* of jurisprudence in Southern Rhodesia calls to mind the Roman law itself to which ancient Britons were subjected.

At a figurative dimension, colonial epithets, many of which especially in the Roman Republic[18] are virtues, mirror the effects of colonization suffered by

Africans at the hands of European countries in the nineteenth century (cf. Coles 2020; Sinha 1995). One may here refer to theories of colonialism which border on issues of the supremacy of the white race over the African race. The mirroring of ancient Rome in British imperialism is not a matter of uncritical imitation. There was a general inspiration of British imperialism, especially in the person of Rhodes, by ancient Roman achievements. Southern Rhodesian Africans were the colonial *clientele* of the *Pax Britannica* which was itself ironically inspired by the *Pax Romana.* Cecil John Rhodes viewed the Southern Rhodesians using the lens of the classical imperative of 'I came, I saw, I conquered' (Suet. *Div. Jul.* 37.2; Jeater 2005: 8). This provided a political framework which led the British colonizers to reinforce a worldview involving Southern Rhodesian Africans in which the *Pax Britannica* was the direct descendant of the *Pax Romana* (Jeater 2005: 8). Parchami argued that the notion of the violent *Pax Britannica,* as borrowed from the model of the *Pax Romana,* was a supremacist discourse based on the idea of peace maintained by force as a belief in providential destiny (Parchami 2009: 11). In comparison with the view of an ancient Roman, moreover, Rhodes' view of the British Empire would have been coloured by his belief in the superiority of the English race,[19] reflected in his words: 'You are an Englishman, and have subsequently drawn the greatest prize in the lottery of life' (Greene 2020). The association of Rhodes with racism is well known, and some view him as having paved the way for apartheid by working to alter laws on voting and land ownership. British colonial administrative operations were militant, in which the colonists, just like Classical Romans, were figures sent out to the ailing/weak and barbaric world, to convert it to 'civil' politics. It was in this sense that a Roman colonial masculinity influenced the Rhodesian colonial masculinity.

The post-World War Two period created for African soldiers a paradoxical situation in terms of what it meant to be a victor as a soldier in a war fought by a world empire (cf. Mann 2006).[20] After the Second World War the domination of the Black race by the white was further entrenched. A soldier resettlement policy was promoted and implemented, that resulted in the appropriation of territory in the unalienated Crown lands and the displacement of the 'inferior Blacks'. This did lead to the ex-serviceman's scheme, through which Africans who took part in the Second World War also obtained land-holdings in the Mhondoro Reserves of Zimbabwe, and through which some who had served in Burma as part of the First Battalion of the Rhodesian African Rifles got a heroes' welcome. Nevertheless Africans were placed in 'suitable employment' as 'boss boys' – a reward with connotations of effeminacy – in spite of the fact that they not only fought alongside white soldiers but were equally heroes. As 'boys', they were ranked low in the pecking order of the colonial discourse of a masculinity and civilized bodies. In contrast to this feminizing stereotype, there is also a violent colonial idea of Black masculinity, which portrays guerrilla veteran-masculinity as backward. This implies an idea of the white as civilizer and the Black as not yet civilized.

With respect to the concept of civilization as a human quality among military veterans, there is need to reflect on an important difference between ancient Roman soldiers and the African guerrilla. The masculinity of Zimbabwe's guerrilla fighter is in this respect distinct from certain aspects of the Roman ideals, in that the Zimbabwe guerrillas did not always represent themselves as a refined and civilizing force, nor did they view whites as a 'barbarous tribe'. Unlike the Romans, they were not colonizers but the colonized. Their pride was not in civilizing achievements but in warfare itself – an element which would also have been valued by ancient Roman soldiers. For Zimbabwean war veterans, it was physical heroism rather than civilized refinement that was the object of pride. Zimbabwe's liberation guerrillas perceived their *mbiri yechigandanga* (glory of brutality) as an area of superiority to the white farmers.

This brings up the issue of masculinities of war. How did the experience of being a soldier of an imperial power shape masculinities of first-century BC Roman veterans? How did the Zimbabwean guerrilla veteran's experience of fighting colonists shape their masculinities?

Through its practice of conquest, Rome created colonies as homes for decommissioned soldiers and its population in general. This was not all. In the civil war between Caesar and Pompey there existed a paradoxical invasion of the Roman people by itself, followed by the violent consequence of expropriation (see App. *BC.* 2.140-141), and the subsequent proscriptions that took place under the second triumviral era of Octavian, Antony and Lepidus.

The Romans indeed set foot in North Africa, but not in Zimbabwe. Nevertheless, in a way, the Zimbabwean war veterans' disposition to violence share some common traits with the violence of colonial domination, which was itself influenced by ancient Roman practices, as can be discerned through Cecil John Rhodes' administration of Rhodesia, now Zimbabwe. Both colonial and Zimbabwean war-veteran masculinities are violent, in their logic and ways of expression.

There is however a difference between them, in the following sense. Colonial masculinity, in its own time, had mellowed, and basked in its conquest, hence its veneer of peacefulness and care for nature. The Zimbabwean veteran-masculinity, by contrast, is an outpouring of anger and pain suffered at the hands of the colonizer, and seeks to vanquish everything in its path: it is raw and recently released. Black Rage is an integral part of postcolonial masculinity.[21] This has manifested in the looting and inferno in South Africa[22] where it recruited violent femininities too: veteran-masculinity, when it gets to unleash its suppressed rage, sweeps everything in sight, with the danger of consuming even the self.[23] It must be understood in terms of the humiliation and structural violence of colonialism (cf. Gewald 2003) and the emptiness of independence, and claims even of ongoing humiliation after independence. Thus other citizens, and the reminders and spaces of colonialism/white monopoly capital were fair game, as were fellow veterans who did not exhibit the same level of rage against white capital.

Mugabe was aware of this form of colonial oppression and displacement from his vast experience with colonialism. Speaking on global platforms, the veteran of the liberation war in Mugabe loomed large as his speeches were characterized by a militant and combative language. Such statements as 'Zimbabwe shall never be a colony again', 'We defeated this monster of colonialism, bring it and we will defeat it again', 'Zimbabwe is not a British colony', 'Blair keep your England, and let me keep my Zimbabwe' punctuated his speeches at United Nations Assembly Meetings.

It may be observed that the classical heritage was clearly a part of the dialogical language used in the postcolonial politics and debates on global platforms by Mugabe. This manifested Mugabe's rough masculinity of speech as a former guerrilla leader in Zimbabwe's independence war. The African political elite took Latin up at school, which became a source of social mobility (Parker 2012: 26; Lambert 2011). The Classics, as part of the educational curriculum in Southern African institutions, enabled the rise to high echelons of power of a generation of Southern African political leaders, such as Nelson Mandela and Oliver Tambo. Notably, in Southern Rhodesia, Robert Mugabe was part of the generation influenced by the Classics owing to his study of Latin, which was a part of the curriculum of legal studies at Fort Hare University (Parker 2012: 26). In one of Mugabe's famous and bold speeches at a United Nations General Assembly Meeting in New York in 2007, Mugabe paused to quote from the Lord's Prayer in the Latin language (the first parts of the Lord's Prayer). Presenting George Bush as a 'god of war' for his role together with Tony Blair in invading Iraq – what has been dubbed 'new colonialism' (cf. Evans 2003) – Mugabe spoke thus:

> This forum did not sanction Blair's and Bush's misadventures in Iraq . . . The two rode roughshod over the United Nations and international opinion. Almighty

> Bush: perhaps some might regard him as their god. No, he is not my god. I have but one God. He is in heaven — *pater noster, qui es in caelis*. Indeed, he wants us to pray to him.
>
> United Nations 2007: 22

Mugabe resorted to 'prayer' during his speech as a way to emotionally influence the world's heads of state by playing the suppliant. His speech was delivered in the context of the West's 'meddling' in weaker nations' affairs, in particular Zimbabwe's land question whereupon he accused Britain, the European Union and America for oppressing his poor country to which he appealed for God's help via the Latin language.

An interview with a guerrilla veteran reveals, further, a rare example of the influence of ancient Rome on a modern African military landscape. This veteran recounted how he would sketch on the front of his books, an imaginary image of Julius Caesar, his favourite Roman ruler at school. Julius Caesar's exploits in the Gallic wars as he put it: 'inspired me to become fearless.'[24] For this guerrilla fighter, ancient Roman history was the only bit of history he had done for the brief period he lasted at school before he joined the liberation war. Amazingly, he could still remember some of Caesar's speeches to his men, which he was happy to recite for me during our interview at the University of Zimbabwe's Senior Common Room bar. It must be stated that this isolated experience is not in any way representative of tens of thousands of guerrilla fighters. Among my BA Classical Studies classmates in 2004, there was also one fellow student who gave himself the moniker 'General Sulla' after the Roman general Lucius Cornelius Sulla Felix. He even participated in land expropriations in his home province using that moniker, and (at the time of writing) he was serving as a prison officer. A few individuals who read Classical studies at the University of Zimbabwe spoke about the moral justification for land expropriations, citing the Gracchi during land review committee meetings in their home districts. This, in my view, played a part in mobilization of households to participate in the occupations of white farmlands in such communities. Certain individuals,[25] too, who read Classics at the University of Zimbabwe went to the extent of drawing inspiration from ancient Roman and Greek examples of land distribution as arguments to justify their involvement in occupations of white-owned farmlands and to encourage their peers to take part in expropriation of the white farmers in post-2000 Zimbabwe.

The presence of Roman-like masculinities among whites and Blacks in Zimbabwe testifies to the involvement of Classics in the country's relationship with its colonial master, Britain. During the era of colonialism in Southern

Rhodesia, Classics contributed to the forming of a stereotypical relationship between Blacks and whites – not just an economy of signs through which power was mirrored and imagined by the colonizer.[26] Classics influenced how whites related with Africans politically. It helped in the entrenching, institutionalizing and legitimizing of racial categories in which Roman-like masculinities are discernible.

## 'Colonial masculinity' and expropriation

In this section, I explore the construction of a colonial masculinity, laying emphasis on how client-army veterans tended to practice a 'colonial masculinity' over expropriated fellow-citizens. I call it a 'colonial masculinity' because that is exactly what it was called in existing Roman texts. Brutus in his speech to his forces which he had gathered to fight the Caesarean party pledged to confirm land expropriated from fellow Romans, which land he described as 'colonies' for the settled veterans. 'We shall at once pay them out of the public money the price of this land of which they have been deprived; so that not only shall *your colony* be secure, but it shall not even be exposed to hatred.' (my italics) (App. *BC.* 2.141, White 1913).

Appian described an episode where ordinary Romans and Italians in the city of Rome lamented and resisted expropriations by triumvirate veterans (App. *BC.* 5.12). That this violent behaviour of client-armies was virulent is supported by the Via Sacra incident and the Placentia incident, where Sulla punished certain soldiers for looting things they had come across (App. *BC.* 1.7.59). It was during the Via Sacra incident that Sulla and Pompey lamented the condition of the Republic (App. *BC.* 1.7.59) – a paradox of its kind as these generals had supported confiscations.

This Roman analogy is a good descriptive analogy to Zimbabwe's guerrilla veterans' disposition to confiscation which was characterized by violence unleashed against fellow Black citizens whose farms were also expropriated as if they were taken from the white farmers.

Such actions subjected Zimbabweans to colonial violence, a process that cast liberation war fighters in the image of the former colonial government. The looting reinforces a disposition by guerrilla veterans to a violent veteran-masculinity, which is built on entitlement and executive self-provisioning. To justify acts of looting, guerrilla veterans sing: '*Zvinhu zvese ndezva Mbuya Nehanda*'/ All resources in the country belong to the great grand ancestor

Nehanda, and behind that ideology there are men who are indirectly saying '*Zvinhu zvese ndezvedu*'/ All things belong to us guerrilla veterans. They merit, in their logic, the loot on multiple grounds: historically, religiously, culturally, ideologically, etc. Thus the logic of a masculinity of looting, so to speak, restores the equilibrium and upholds the order of nature where real men of valour have earned their turn to deserve their loot.

In Brutus' speech there is also rhetoric of hostility to a masculinity of looting. Land expropriation by Caesar, which is against traditional values of justice and property ownership was execrated. Brutus promises his party that they will retain ownership of their land and that loss of land will be publicly compensated (App. *BC.* 2.140-141). In fact in the speech of Brutus, there is a political stance of republicanism and property rights assumed. Brutus contrasts the benign policy of Roman colonization where innocent citizens retain their properties without confiscation, and even foreigners are taxed but don't have all their land taken. Brutus promised freedom and respect for property rights. Brutus was struggling for the lands of Romans wrongly seized by Julius Caesar to be restored to the rightful owners.

On the other side, Caesar in his rhetoric is concerned mainly with power but there is a side-effect of territorial gain as a result of power. In the quote below, Caesar is informed by Curio that he could rule the whole world if he plays his cards right. Crossing the Rubicon might be held to have territorial significance as being equivalent to an *invasion* of Rome. The speech goes like so:

> Ten years you fought the Gauls, yet how small a part of Earth Gaul represents! Win a few battles and Rome that subdued the world is yours. As things are, no long triumphal procession awaits you, the Capitol demands no laurels of yours be consecrated; rather gnawing envy denies you all, and your conquests of foreign lands will meet only with reprimand. Pompey, your son-in-law, resolves to topple you from power. You could rule not half the world, but the whole of it, alone.
>
> Luc. 1.271ff

The struggles for political hegemony in Rome by competing generals was sustained by a rhetorical interpretation of the Roman city in which a rival general and his forces were perceived as a colonizing or invading enemy of Rome as a hostile country. This narrative presented forces of competing generals as gallant and heroic protectors of Rome against each other where one party labelled the other a 'colonizing army'. Land expropriations by Caesar's party was a process of staking claims to territoriality. The passage below illustrates this point in which

Pompey accused Caesar of turning his army to invade Rome. In Pompey's speech quoted, he seems to be struggling not so much for land as for power and allegiance, although he is trying to save face on account of not being located on his own territory. Pompey's remark that a city is a matter of men rather than houses is part of the rhetoric to de-emphasize the territorial aspect because he is forced by circumstances of the civil war to remain outside the city, and the fact that he is not territorially in Rome is offset by a face-saving strategy of drawing attention rather to the issue of the men who support him, who seem to be his substitute 'city'. It goes thus (my italics):

> When all was in readiness Pompey called the senators, the knights, and the whole army to an assembly and addressed them as follows: 'Fellow-soldiers, the Athenians, too, abandoned their city for the sake of liberty when they were fighting against *invasion*, because they believed that it was not houses that made a city, but men; and after they had done so they presently recovered it and made it more renowned than even before. So, too, our own ancestors abandoned the city when the Gauls invaded it, and Camillus hastened from Ardea and recovered it. *All men of sound mind think that their country is wherever they can preserve their liberty*. Because we were thus minded we sailed hither, not as deserters of our native land, but in order to prepare ourselves to defend it gloriously against one who has long *conspired against it*, and, by means of bribe-takers, has at last *seized Italy by a sudden invasion*. You have decreed him a public enemy, yet he now sends governors to take charge of your provinces. He appoints others over the city and still others throughout Italy. With such audacity has he deprived the people of their own government. If he does these things while the war is still raging and while he is apprehensive of the result and when we intend, with heaven's help, to bring him to punishment, what cruelty, what violence is he likely to abstain from if he wins the victory? And while he is doing these things against the fatherland certain men, who have been bought with money that he obtained from our province of Gaul, co-operate with him, choosing to be his slaves instead of his equals. *I have not failed and I never will fail to fight with you and for you. I give you my services both as soldier and as general*. If I have any experience in war, if it has been my good fortune to remain unvanquished to this day, I pray the gods to continue all these blessings in our present need, and that I may become a man of happy destiny for *my country* in her perils as I was in extending her dominion . . .'
>
> App. *BC*. 2.50,51, White 1913

A speech of Brutus referring to Sulla and Caesar below goes thus (my italics):

> A large number did so, whereupon Brutus continued, 'It is a good thing, my men, that you have done to come here with the others. You ought, since you receive

> due honors and bounties from your country, to give equal honor in return to her who sends you forth. The Roman people gave you to Caesar to fight against the Gauls and Britons, and your valiant deeds call for recognition and recompense. But Caesar, taking advantage of your military oath, *led you against your country much against your desire*. He led you *against our best citizens* in Africa, in like manner against your will. If this were all that you had done you would perhaps be ashamed to ask reward for such exploits, but since neither envy, nor time, nor the forgetfulness of men can extinguish the glory of your deeds in Gaul and Britain, you have the rewards due to them, such as the people gave to those who served in the army of old, yet *not by taking land from unoffending fellow-citizens*, nor by dividing other people's property with newcomers, nor by considering it proper to requite services by means of acts of injustice . . .'
>
> App. *BC*. 2.140, White 1913: 185

In Brutus' speech, Caesar is also labelled as an invader of Rome. It goes like so (my italics):

> But Sulla and Caesar, who *invaded their country* like a foreign land, and *needed guard and garrisons against their own country*, did not dismiss you to your homes, nor buy land for you, nor divide among you the *property of citizens* which they *confiscated*, nor did they make compensation for the relief of those who were despoiled, although those who despoiled them had plenty of money from the treasury and plenty from confiscated estates. By the law of war, – nay, by the practice of robbery, – *they took from Italians who had committed no offence, who had done no wrong, their land and houses*, tombs and temples, which we were not accustomed to take away even from foreign enemies, but merely to impose on them a tenth of their produce by way of taxes. . . . They divided among you the property of your own people, the very men who sent you with Caesar to the Gallic war, and who offered up their prayers at your festival of victory. *They colonized you* in that way collectively, under your standards and in your military organization, so that you could neither enjoy peace nor be free from fear of those whom you displaced. The man who was driven out and deprived of his goods was sure to be watching his opportunity to step into your shoes. This was the very thing that the tyrants sought to accomplish, — not to provide you with land, which they could have obtained for you elsewhere; but that you, because always beset by lurking enemies, might be the firm bulwark of a government that was committing wrongs in common with you. A common interest between tyrants and their satellites grows out of common crimes and common fears. And this, ye gods, they called *colonization*, which was crowned by the *lamentations of a kindred people and the expulsion of innocent men from their homes*.
>
> App. *BC*. 2.140-141, White 1913: 487–9

Such was the working of a colonial version of masculinity turned against Roman territory and Roman citizens by client-armies – a process that partly contributed in Caesar's rise to dictatorship and Octavian's one-man-rule. Such conditions, involving how they became the most powerful men illuminate how territorial expropriation was used in Zimbabwe as Mugabe's strategy to retain power.

Mugabe, who was patron of the biggest war veterans' association in Zimbabwe, the Zimbabwe National Liberation War Veterans Association (ZNLWVA) played a pivotal role in the military struggle for land reclamation. Because of this role, he came back from the bush war possessing martial authority to execute the expropriation of white farms. The Roman scenario illuminates the Zimbabwean scenario, not only in the nature of the power he exercised, but in the manner in which Mugabe as patron of guerrilla veterans and Commander-in-Chief of the Zimbabwe Defence Forces exercised military power to grant land to his guerrilla veterans and to landless peasants. Since 1980, Mugabe was the most powerful person in Zimbabwe, whose power and authority in the politics of land redistribution proved this. He was Commander-in-Chief of the Zimbabwe Defense Forces and, like the Gracchi, he was as it were the first real Tribune of the people, which office he used as arbiter of Social Justice and Guardian of Economic Prosperity. In a sense, this power metamorphosed into a one man imperium, the imperium that was sustained by expropriation as a means to reward his foot soldiers, the guerrilla veterans.

The mechanics of appropriation of political fields and land expropriation by military veterans in the two societies are detailed in Chapter Six.

In the Zimbabwean context, I must at once state that the word 'colonization' has definite historical nuances. It would seem unfair to the guerrilla veteran if one were to say that he replaced the colonizer as the new colonizer. As Stathis Kalyvas notes: 'When exiting a conflict, individuals and communities do not revert to the status quo ante; they have been fundamentally transformed by the experience of conflict.' (Kalyvas 2012: vii–viii). Colonization's first victim was the guerrilla fighter himself. He reflects the violence of the oppressor and uses the same violence to hold the liberated masses in perpetual fear – claiming Zimbabwe as his prize. In Zimbabwe, violence was central to the creation and maintenance of colonialism, as well as to the independence and decolonization struggles that arose from within the colony (cf. Dwyer and Nettelbeck 2018: 3). Research has shown that colonial masculinities can be reproduced as a local cultural tradition long after the end of colonialism (see for example, Mbembe 2001; Connell 2005). The torture and destruction that accompanied colonial war was reproduced in Zimbabwean society by the 'liberators'.[27] The Zimbabwean veteran epitomizes a return from war which expresses the contradictions of a freedom born of force and violence. What made the return of guerrilla veterans from war problematic was their failure to settle peacefully in society, as their survival depended on violence and appropriation. As Connell has observed, decolonization and transition to a postcolonial world are likely to involve problems about masculinity and violence (Connell 2005: 76). Thus, despite the differences discussed, Connell's theory makes 'colonial masculinity' a legitimate category of inquiry even in the ancient Roman veterans' context.

The following section examines differences in the military traditions of the two societies – a closer analysis of military masculinities of the two worlds of veterans.

## The two military traditions

There is a marked difference between the view of battle scenes among ancient Rome and Zimbabwean veterans. One tends to see Roman veterans' masculinities as triumphant, even in adversity, whereas Zimbabwean veterans, although also triumphant, tend to evoke pity. As the Zimbabwe liberation struggle was being sold as one of extreme sacrifice, the guerrilla veterans promoted 'competitive victimhood' and a concept of sacrifice.

To illustrate the Roman and Zimbabwean attitudes, I may refer, on the one hand, to a passage by Pliny on ancient Roman battle, which generally represents the ancient Roman ideals of military *virtus*, and, on the other hand, to an ethnographic account offered by my wife concerning her father, a guerrilla veteran.

Pliny (*NH*. 7.38, Perseus Digital Library n.d.f) illustrated notions of heroism and triumphalism among Roman fighters during the Roman Republic, even amid the horror of losing limbs. The chapter is on valour (implying heroism) with lots of reference to military body-parts as follows:

> A minute enquiry by whom the greatest valour has ever been exhibited, would lead to an endless discussion, more especially if all the fables of the poets are to be taken for granted. Q. Ennius admired T. Cæcilius Denter and his brother to such a degree, that on their account he added a sixteenth book to his Annals. L. Siccius Dentatus, who was tribune of the people in the consulship of Spurius Tarpeius and A. Aterius, not long after the expulsion of the kings, has also very

numerous testimonies in his favour. This hero fought one hundred and twenty battles, was eight times victorious in single combat, and was graced with forty-five wounds in the front of the body, without one on the back. The same man also carried off thirty-four spoils, was eighteen times presented with the victor's spear, and received twenty-five pendants, eighty-three torcs, one hundred and sixty bracelets, twenty-six crowns, (of which fourteen were civic, eight golden, three mural, and one obsidional), a fisc of money, ten prisoners, and twenty oxen altogether. He followed in the triumphal processions of nine generals, who mainly owed their victories to his exertions; besides all which, a thing that I look upon as the most important of all his services, he denounced to the people T. Romilius, one of the generals of the army, at the end of his consulship, and had him convicted of having made an improper use of his authority.

The military honours of Manlius Capitolinus would have been no less splendid than his, if they had not been all effaced at the close of his life. Before his seventeenth year, he had gained two spoils, and was the first of equestrian rank who received a mural crown; he also gained six civic crowns, thirty-seven donations, and had twenty-three scars on the fore-part of his body. He saved the life of P. Servilius, the master of the horse, receiving wounds on the same occasion in the shoulders and the thigh. Besides all this, unaided, he saved the Capitol, when it was attacked by the Gauls, and through that, the state itself; a thing that would have been the most glorious act of all, if he had not so saved it, in order that he might, as its king, become its master. But in all matters of this nature, although valour may effect much, fortune does still more.

No person living, in my opinion at least, ever excelled M. Sergius, although his great-grandson, Catiline, tarnished the honours of his name. In his second campaign he lost his right hand; and in two campaigns he was wounded three and twenty times; so much so, that he could scarcely use either his hands or his feet; still, attended by a single slave, he afterwards served in many campaigns, though but an invalided soldier. He was twice taken prisoner by Hannibal, (for it was with no ordinary enemy that he would engage,) and twice did he escape from his captivity, after having been kept, without a single day's intermission, in chains and fetters for twenty months. On four occasions he fought with his left hand alone, two horses being slain under him. He had a right hand made of iron, and attached to the stump, after which he fought a battle, and raised the siege of Cremona, defended Placentia, and took twelve of the enemy's camps in Gaul. All this we learn from an oration of his, which he delivered when, in his prætorship, his colleagues attempted to exclude him from the sacred rites, on the ground of his infirmities. What heaps upon heaps of crowns would he have piled up, if he had only had other enemies! For, in matters of this nature, it is of the first importance to consider upon what times in especial the valour of each man has

> fallen. What civic crowns did Trebia, what did the Ticinus, what did Lake Thrasymenus afford? What crown was there to be gained at Cannæ, where it was deemed the greatest effort of valour to have escaped from the enemy? Other persons have been conquerors of men, no doubt, but Sergius conquered even Fortune herself.

In contrast to this I now pass on to an account related to the Zimbabwean situation. My wife's father is a guerrilla veteran of the liberation war. My wife recounts below how her father would never entertain questions regarding how he fought the war while sober. He would only talk about his war experiences when drunk:

> 'Dad would not tolerate any questions about his war-time experiences. The only time he said something was when under the influence of alcohol, but even then he never liked the subject of war. He never liked the memory of how he carried heavy artillery in the bush. The Sinoia battle[28] scene was one incident that he does not want to remember as they arrived at the scene a day after the bombardments to bury their dead fellow fighters and hundreds of civilians. His position with regards expropriation of land as compensation is motivated by that he suffered and now he deserves to be rehabilitated by keeping away from the horror subject of war.'
>
> Personal communication with the author's wife,
> 2 May 2020, Marlborough, Harare

This attitude of not wanting to refer to the subject of war is echoed in many liberation war songs. Many of the liberation war songs, although they point to the heroic sacrifice and cost of war, and although they give the veterans accolades as 'men among men', evoke pity as they emphasize suffering and victimhood.

An eyewitness account written by a former guerrilla fighter, Agrippa Mutambara (2014), contains a mixture of pity and nostalgic feelings of triumphalism. Mutambara in his account laments how many guerrillas fled for dear life leaving seven guerrillas facing bombardment at the battle of Sinoia in 1966. Mutambara himself also fled after he was immobilized for a few seconds, owing to fear of bombardment. This seems quite different from most Roman battle narratives in which the sense of pity and suffering is dwarfed by a fighter's valorous triumph over adversity.[29] This is notwithstanding accounts mentioning moments of cowardice in battle combat such as Horace's abandonment of his shield. Horace's account has however been attributed to influences of Greek lyric poetry among Roman poets. I however attempt to explain the difference in attitude when facing adversity in combat between ancient Roman soldiers and guerrilla veterans of Zimbabwe.

The explanation for this difference lies in that the ancient Roman society had a long, rich and strong war tradition and culture that exercised and immersed its men in warfare, unlike the culture to which Zimbabwean men would have been exposed at the time of Zimbabwean independence. A long interval had passed between 1896/7, when the Shona and the Ndebele had last fought against the BSAC, and the late 1960s, when the liberation war began to be waged. Of course, there may be other reasons for the difference in attitude. We can interview modern people who have been traumatized by warfare, but we cannot directly interview their ancient Roman counterparts. Moreover, modern attitudes toward slaughter are more sensitive, and war is widely condemned; this was not true in ancient Rome to the same extent.

That said, the two sets of veterans' claims for honours, land and other rewards largely invoked valorous exploits – and also pity in the case of Zimbabwe's guerrilla veterans – contingent on perceived distance – in time, place and status.

## Manoeuvring of dead bodies, bones and scars

Another marked difference between Roman and Zimbabwean veteran activity was that in Zimbabwe even *dead bodies* of veterans were exploited in their politics of restitution and reward. By contrast, a Roman veteran's appeal would be more likely to focus on his living body and its injuries. In the Zimbabwean case, the dead body of a guerrilla fighter became very important, leading to its fetishization in the country's historical memory (see Fontein 2009, 2010)[30]. Even the ancestral prophecies given by spirit mediums Kaguvi and Nehanda pointed to a masculinity of their bones which were said in the prophecies would resurrect to fight against colonial forces. As Chenjerai Hove (1988) depicted in his novel *Bones*, there was a strong bond between the body of the freedom fighters and the ancestors. Bones of dead guerrilla fighters were used as potent tools in the process of expropriating land from the white farmers. The dead bodies were exhumed, paraded and then reburied. By parading the bones of dead veterans, the bones were made to occupy and appropriate a political field (see Gell 1998; Latour 1999), on discussions about agency and materiality of objects). The scenes of such reburials were broadcasted on national television such that the bones became ubiquitous. This ritual practice of reburials by veterans was an effective way of using the bones of dead guerrillas to push the argument of restitution.

Manoeuvring of dead bodies of their dead comrades in both the physical and symbolic senses helped re-write national memory (Shoko 2006: 12). The reburials were symbolic acts that sought to dramatize the recovery of a masculinity of memory by the veterans and the decisive defeat of the colonialists (Mlambo and Chitando 2015: 18). In this process, the dead veterans were deployed to become combatants in the armed struggle to expropriate land from the white farmers, something different from the ancient Roman context of land rewards for military veterans. In ancient Rome only the living veterans occupied and appropriated farms and political fields in their struggles for land and other rewards.

There is, however, some connection between the politics of land allocation and the dead body of a leader and benefactor of veterans in the narrative of Julius Caesar's funeral. It was during the funeral of Julius Caesar, that the consuls were sent out to the colonies such as held allotments of land already assigned by Caesar, out of fear that they might begin an uprising, due to emotions aroused by Caesar's death (Dio Cass. 44.51.4). There is a sense in which Caesar's dead body had a physical presence (cf. Erskine 2002) in the eyes of the consuls judging by their panicky reaction. Caesar's dead body was the locus upon which the violence that erupted in Rome took place. The speech which Appian put in the mouth of Antony at Caesar's funeral aroused violent emotions (my italics):

> While they were in this temper and were already near to violence, somebody raised above the bier an image of Caesar himself made of wax. The body itself, as it lay on its back on the couch, could not be seen. The image was turned round and round by a mechanical device, showing the *twenty-three wounds* in all parts of the body and on the face, that had been dealt to him so brutally. The people could no longer bear the pitiful sight presented to them. They groaned, and, girding up their loins, they burned the senate-chamber where Caesar was slain, and ran hither and thither searching for the murderers, who had fled some time previously.
>
> App. *BC*. 2.147, White 1913: 499

Caesar's funeral triggered violence in Rome as the general populace got emotionally charged upon seeing their hero's disfigured dead body. Caesar had distributed land not only to his veterans, but also to the general populace, at a time when the senate was not willing, hence the popularity of Caesar with the masses as a munificent general. Plutarch (Plut. *Caes.* 68) described a tumultuous scene during Caesar's funeral when, upon seeing the wounded and disfigured body of Caesar, the multitude engaged in acts of arson against Caesar's assassins.

Caesar gave property to the whole populace, and not just the veterans. This brings us to the question of the power of the city plebs. We should not forget the issue of power residing in the cities, and of urban discontent as having been more politically dangerous than its rural equivalent. In the city of Rome, according to Appian, multitudes always sung the praise of those who spent their fortunes on the welfare of the public to please it (App. *BC*. 1.11).

The funeral of Julius Caesar shows also how a dead body was manoeuvred by Antony for the sake of political power. Antony manoeuvred Caesar's dead body to occupy a political high ground. It was in itself a process of appropriating Rome's political field left vacant by Caesar's death. Caesar's funeral was an occasion for stirring up clan violence – an opportunity to eliminate Brutus and company from the political field, which Antony, Octavian and Lepidus quickly appropriated. It was time to remove from positions those who Caesar had advanced to the magistracies of Rome and to the command of provinces and armies. The speech of Antony in Appian below shows how Caesar's dead body was exploited (my italics):

> Carried away by an easy transition to extreme passion *he uncovered the body of Caesar, lifted his robe on the point of a spear and shook it aloft, pierced with dagger-thrusts and red with the dictator's blood.* Whereupon the people, like a chorus in a play, mourned with him in the most sorrowful manner, and from sorrow became filled again with anger. After the discourse other lamentations were chanted with funeral music according to the national custom, by the people in chorus, to the dead; and his deeds and his sad fate were again recited. Somewhere from the midst of these lamentations Caesar himself was supposed to speak, recounting by name his enemies on whom he had conferred benefits, and of the murderers themselves exclaiming, as it were in amazement, 'Oh that I should have spared these men to slay me!' The people could endure it no longer. It seemed to them monstrous that all the murderers who, with the single exception of Decimus Brutus, had been made prisoners while belonging to the faction of Pompey, and who, instead of being punished, had been advanced by Caesar to the magistracies of Rome and to the command of provinces and armies, should have conspired against him; and that Decimus should have been deemed by him worthy of adoption as his son.
>
> App. *BC*. 2.146, White 1913: 497

The senate had even charged Lucius Piso (whom Caesar had made the custodian of his will) not to give Caesar's body a public funeral in order to avoid the eruption of violence. Nonetheless there was an outcry as the people wanted to accord the body a public funeral.[31]

The mention of funerals at this stage in the argument brings up the related issue of spirituality, to which I turn in the next section.

## Veterans, masculinity and spirituality

A fundamental difference relating to ancient Roman and African military masculinities is the spiritual aspect of being. Reference to effeminacy of the soul in the ancient Roman context concerns the element of control. Gleason mentions that speaking in a deep or masculine tone was associated in ancient times with having more *pneuma* (spirit) in one's physical constitution, thereby having more of the masculine qualities of dryness, lightness and warmth; your voice was an index of your self-control (Gleason 1995: xiii; see also Dio Cass. 46.22 on the effeminacy of both the soul and the body (τὴν μαλακίαν καὶ τῆς ψυχῆς καὶ τοῦ σώματος).

In a chapter dealing with Polemo's *Physiognomy,* Gleason mentions how masculinity and femininity were linked with looks, motion and voice, and how a masculine deportment was recommended in which there was not too much alteration of expression (Gleason 1995: 55, 57–8). Moreover, in Plutarch's life of Antony, it is mentioned how Mark Antony had a noble dignity of form. His shapely beard, a broad forehead, and an aquiline nose were thought to show the virile qualities peculiar to the portraits and statues of Heracles (Plut. *Ant.* 4). This implies that not only voice and gait but also certain physical features were associated with masculinity. Nor should we ignore the importance of clothing associated with masculinity; according to Coulston, '[to] strip a soldier of his belt was to humiliate him, in effect to militarily emasculate him . . .' (Coulston 2005: 91). The bodies of Roman soldiers were thus conceptualized as corporeal, flesh and blood bodies. They were not vested with spiritual significance in the sense of Zimbabwean guerrilla veterans.

This spiritual aspect of being was a strong belief among many precolonial African armies – something which led to many deaths of African warriors in wars against the colonial forces. Most believed to possess some spiritual prowess. As a result, they confronted the gun in the belief that the bullet was harmless.

The construction of masculinity by Zimbabwean veterans is connected more with their ancestors. In Zimbabwean traditional religion, there exists an inseparable relationship between religion, land and the people. In the traditional past, the land was intimately associated with the history of the chiefdom, with the ruling chief and with ancestral spirits who live in it (Shoko 2006: 5). Ancestral spirits known as *vadzimu* (singular *mudzimu*) are considered important in Shona society (ibid.). Ancestors are guardians of the land, and play the role of mediating between the Supreme Being *Mwari* (the Creator and Sustainer of the universe), and living beings. The first *Chimurenga* war that occurred in 1896/7 against the BSAC was inspired by spirit mediums of *Mbuya* (Grandmother) Nehanda, and *Sekuru* (Grandfather) Chaminuka and Kaguvi, who led the uprising.

The bodies of guerrilla fighters in Zimbabwe were thus not conceptualized as 'merely' corporeal, flesh and blood bodies. Instead, these bodies were vested with deep spiritual significance (Mlambo and Chitando 2015). Inscribed on them were memories of ancestral promises and oracles. The bodies of the war veterans were spiritual libraries, imbued with declarations by the great ancestor, Nehanda, who had defied death at the hands of the colonizers and had brazenly declared that her bones would be resurrected. The bodies of the guerrilla veterans were not autonomous, free-floating bodies like those of Roman soldiers. Instead, they were vehicles used by the ancestors to reclaim the land that was taken from them by force by the white colonizers. The practice of reverting to magical military powers was an old tradition of war medicines used during anti-colonial rebellions and precolonial wars.[32] This magical aspect is not emphasized in Roman military practice. The Roman soldier was an expert in war by virtue of his strength, skill and ability to use his body and weapons at his disposal.

Another spiritual issue relates to the object of prayer. A masculine element is present in Classical ideas of the gods. Roman commanders prayed for victory to the Roman god of war (Mars), and not to their dead ancestors, as in the case of the African armies. It was customary for the Romans to offer sacrifices to the gods before going into war. Livy summarizes the Roman army's dependence on sacrifices to the gods before battle (Liv. 8.9.1-11. see also Plut. *Rom.* 18.7). The difference with the African practice is that the Roman made a direct appeal to the gods, unlike the traditional African practice where prayers and offerings were done through the spirits of ancestors.

Unlike Zimbabwean guerrilla fighters who fought as agents of their ancestors, it seems from Liv. 8.9.1-11 that there was a sense in which Titus Manlius acted as an agent of the gods. The role of the gods as can be discerned in Lucan ascribes a spiritual dimension to Caesar's civil war against Pompey. The gods are said by Lucan to be on the side of Caesar's fighters who are presented as a force on a mission to overthrow tyranny.[33] The reason given why the gods were to be so favourable in this instance was that Caesar and his men were seeking to overthrow a tyrant (Luc. 1.350-1, Duff 1928: 28–9). Citing Lucan (1.343-49), Elaine Fantham (1985: 124) shows how Caesar, after protesting vigorously that they (him and his soldiers) are being cheated by the senate of their plot of land at home for security in old age, he appeals for *action* to recover their rights and guarantees them *divine* support. There is a sense in which Lucan's Caesar, like Zimbabwe's guerrilla fighters, views his struggle as a war of liberation with spiritual significance, although what comes first in Caesar's case is action seen separately from what the gods could do to help his forces. His soldiers are urged to act and the assurance of divine help comes later. In the context of the guerrilla veterans of Zimbabwe, however, these two factors cannot be separated.

In fighting Roman wars, there is a sense in which Roman soldiers were seen as fighting wars to defend ancestral tombs, as Plutarch indicated in his account of Tiberius Gracchus' speech (Plut. *Ti. Gr*. 9.5). Of course, as far as land and spirits were concerned, the Romans did believe in *manes*, and their land was also meant to be ancestral, as is the case with traditional African cosmology. There are similarities in the accounts of parallels with Classical times, involving Shona gods and spirits, proposed by white ethnographers who worked in Southern Rhodesia in the 1920s. Burbridge (in Jeater 2005: 11) made a comparison between the *manes* and the *mudzimu* (spirit) in Shona culture, while also quoting Plutarch to explain why Shona traditional healers used woodpeckers for healing.

The Romans worshipped Mars, the god of war who was particularly revered by the army. Mars, according to Grant and Hazel (1979: 219), had originally been 'a god . . . of agriculture'. They further go on to say (my italics):

> . . . though originally he had been a god ... specifically of *agriculture* ... His function appears to have developed as the Romans themselves evolved from an agricultural to a warlike nation. He had a highly developed cult at Rome, being considered, next to Jupiter, the greatest patron of the State; . . . He gave his name to the month of March (*Martius mensis)* on certain days of which the priesthood of the Salii danced a war-dance and sang ritual songs. It was appropriate to his agricultural function that his major festivals were held in spring and early summer.

It is instructive to note that the worship of Mars is a cultural reservoir loaded with historical and ideological expressions of meaning related to war, politics and agriculture. Grant and Hazel (1979: 219) further noted:

> Mars gave his name to the Campus Martius, a field where the Roman males practiced warlike skills. In the time of Augustus he was given the title *Ultor*, 'Avenger,' in memory of the emperor's part in the victory over Julius Caesar's assassins. Soldiers sacrificed to Mars before and after battle, in association with the goddess Bellona, who was variously described as his wife, sister or daughter.

Mars' renaming by Augustus to *Ultor*, the 'Avenger' of Caesar's assassins was an appropriation of the god in the politics of the warring factions in Rome – the fighting which involved victorious soldiers getting boons of victory such as land and money. For this victory they gave thanks to Mars afterwards in the form of sacrifices.[34]

The Romans also had Bellona, a goddess of war, similar to Enyo of the Greeks, who was an important cult figure among the Romans, nevertheless with little or no mythology. This goddess was identified in early times with Mars' wife Nerio (Grant and Hazel 1979: 70). We may contrast her with Zimbabwe's female ancestor, Nehanda who in her rank is in no way inferior to male ancestors such as Chaminuka and Kaguvi, whereas, in the case of Roman gods and goddesses, gender matters in the accrual of power.

However the 'ancestral' lands motif in Rome seemed to have been more of political importance – not having so much a spiritual/religious significance as in the case of traditional Africa (cf. McClymont and Mlambo 2016). For example, there is the idea of Roman soldiers abroad fighting for Italy with the home front, understood in terms of ancestral tombs, of which Tiberius Gracchus gave a class-related interpretation, not understanding 'ancestral tombs' in terms of a collective view of 'home' but exclusively in terms of the family tombs of the aristocracy and the better off. The quote below is revealing of how the rich alienated the poor from the ancestral tombs:

> The wild beasts that roam over Italy have every one of them a cave or a lair to lurk in; but the men who fight and die for Italy enjoy the common air and light, indeed, but nothing else; houseless and homeless they wonder about with their wives and children. And it is with lying lips that their imperators exhort the soldiers in their battles to defend sepulchers and shrines from the enemy; for not a man of them has an hereditary altar, not one of all these many Romans an ancestral tomb, but they fight and die to support others in wealth and luxury, and though they are styled masters of the world, they have not a single clod of earth that is their own.
>
> App. *BC*. 1.10[35]

This motif reveals different cultural meanings ascribed to land and the different spiritual and philosophical worldviews through which masculinities of soldiers were framed in the two societies.

The Romans had a more legal conception of landownership than the Africans. In Italy it was also the dispossessed who were asserting ancestral links, because the dispossessed were (mostly) indigenous owners, not colonial intruders as was the case in Zimbabwe. In some cases it was the Romans who took Italian lands.

## A 'female masculinity' in land struggles

Drawing on Connell's structural theory on the state of play of gender relations in a society, and on a comparison with the notion of an African 'female masculinity', I consider in this section the possibility of arguing for a related masculinity in ancient Rome, through exploring the dynamics of the Roman social structure, emphasizing a dialectical relationship between structural constraint and human agency.[36] This is especially pertinent when considering the prohibition of female participation in war in ancient Rome, and the agency they displayed in resisting the triumvirs in matters of gender, power and land or property more generally.

Ancient Greek and Roman societies had an arrangement which would not allow women on the battle front. There is an incident in Homer's Iliad where the goddess Aphrodite takes part in the battle, and is rebuked for doing so by Diomedes. Yet African women in general, and Zimbabwean female guerrillas in particular, have defied and rejected the notion of fixed, predetermined gender roles.[37] Amadiume (1987) discerned in an African context not only the social construction of identities, but the disruption of distinctions between male and female. Far from all being subordinate to men, women in precolonial Africa, Amadiume argued, were structurally allowed to play roles usually monopolized by men, even if that meant becoming classified as 'men' in the process. Sex and gender-identification did not necessarily coincide. This made precolonial Africa a place where 'masculinity' was possible without men –'female masculinity', as women assumed positions or characteristics usually regarded as the preserve of men. In the same fashion, Zimbabwean female guerrilla veterans performed masculine roles, as they took part in land expropriations along with male guerrilla fighters (West 2000).

During the war of independence, many female combatants were by 1977 part of Mugabe's Zimbabwe African National Liberation Army (ZANLA) forces (Lyons 1999). The bodies of such women were exorcized of their femininity and granted membership in the privileged masculine class, catapulted into higher levels of citizenship and transmogrified, so to speak, into men (Tendi 2020: 43 n.65 and 66), '*varume pachavo*' (women who have become 'real men') (cf. Mbah 2017). Many such women during the post-2000 land expropriations colluded with masculinist ideals in the manner in which they accumulated power and strength of character, as they took part in the expropriation of white farmlands (Mlambo 2014: 265). My sister was part of this women's movement which, in combat mode, invaded farms in and around Masvingo province. These women would move about carrying weapons. At political meetings conducted to mobilize villagers female guerrilla veterans would dance to liberation war songs along with their fellow male veterans, in ways that expressed masculine aggression. Women veterans would dance while wearing big boots colloquially known in the Shona language as *bhutsu mutandarikwa* (the long shoes). This shoe has a long history of association with violence from the days of Rhodesian police officers to the era of the liberation war. Guerrilla fighters used the 'long shoes' to kick sell-outs and to intimidate the masses, to get them to comply with the demands of the war. I shall explore the importance of these shoes in detail in Chapter Seven, where I discuss the symbolic importance of military boots in masculinity discourses, in comparison with the Roman *caligatus* worn by the triumvirate veterans in the city of Rome as depicted by Dio Cassius (48.12).

By contrast, there were in ancient Rome, outside of a mythological context,[38] no women soldiers. Nevertheless, in spite of women's exclusion from the military, there was among the Romans the idea of *virtus muliebris* (feminine power [or virtue]) (cf. McInerney 2003). As reported by Dio Cassius (48.12), there is also reference to a civil procedure conducted by triumviral veterans when they massed at the Capitol in Rome – a procedure involving the handing over of a document to the Vestal virgins, who symbolically were the very opposite of masculinity. Ironically the Vestal virgins had the symbolic role of protecting the *sacra* which were symbolically linked to the continued safety of Rome (Greenfield 2011). They had also their form of power which even Julius Caesar, to some extent, recognized. We learn through Suetonius (*Iul.* 83.1) that in 45 BC, Caesar was prudent enough, in the volatile political environment leading to his assassination, to rely on the fidelity of the *virgo Vestalis maxima* to keep his will safe from fraud. Caesar's gesture may be understood as a recognition of *virtus muliebris* in that the will kept by the *virgo Vestalis maxima* was considered the most authoritative copy (Greenfield 2011). As Greenfield observed, the Vestals were attested as the custodians of politically sensitive and personal documents during the late Republic, which placed them at the centre of politics (Greenfield 2011: 167). By this role, the Vestal virgins occupied a political field usually a preserve of man in Roman politics.

Dio's depiction of Antony's wife Fulvia girding herself with a sword and giving out instructions to soldiers is another example of women power in Roman political struggles (Dio Cass. 48.10.4). Fulvia was instrumental in the struggle against Octavian over the distribution of land to Antony's veterans as per the initial agreement between the triumvirs. Appian recorded a conversation between Octavian and Cocceius, where Octavian accused Fulvia and her male counterparts of waging war against himself and Italy: 'Manius and Fulvia and Lucius brought war against Italy, and against me as well as Italy . . .'(App. *BC.* 5.62, White 1913: 483). Fulvia's actions, in spite of the strictures of Roman society, confirm Connell's theory that masculinity is a place of gender struggle contested by both men and women. In this case, Fulvia is portrayed as capable of causing war in Italy, despite being a woman.

Although there is a near-total absence of 'manly' women in land struggles in ancient Rome, Fulvia's stance resonates with how female power is represented in the context of land struggles in Zimbabwe. A picture of a freeze in Figure 1 below depicts, as it were, the *virtus muliebris* of Zimbabwean women. Women were/are counted as soldiers in the quest for land ownership in Zimbabwe. Femininity in Zimbabwe, in a sense, metamorphosed into a hybrid gender, where certain women were described as more than women. The sculpture at the National Heroes Acre of a female soldier standing with two male soldiers in Figure 2 below illustrates this. This exaltation of female qualities of heroism and martialism was striking in the Zimbabwean context, where women appear not to be denied military honour.

**Figure 1** National Heroes Acre in Harare, Zimbabwe. The frieze shows both male and female guerrilla fighters in action during the liberation war. Wikimedia/Gary Bembridge.

**Figure 2** The statue of the Unknown Soldier at the National Heroes Acre in Harare, Zimbabwe. Jekesai Njikizana/AFP via Getty Images.

Masculinity in the context of the acquisition of land was not the monopoly of male fighters in Zimbabwe. In some respects, masculinity was interiorized within the image of femininity. For example, the image of *Mbuya* Nehanda and other female guerrilla fighters was associated with heroic, ethical and institutional values, something expressed in a state-associated femininity where Zimbabwe is represented as a mother via the image of *Mbuya* Nehanda (Togarasei 2020) – a view comparable in some respects with the treatment of Athena as the patron deity of Athens, and the very image of Roma, the city of Rome, as feminine. It must be stated that the image of the city of Rome as feminine does not acknowledge women as valorous men.

In contrast to the above examples of respect accorded to femininity in Zimbabwe, we may, looking at Roman history, cite an instance where a woman was treated by veterans not as a fellow-fighter but more as a currency used in a transaction of power and male honour. Appian records an account where Octavian's soldiers sued for the peace of Brundisium in 40 BC between Octavian and Antony by arranging for Octavian's sister to marry Antony, a patriarchal act through which issues of empire and power were mediated by use of a female body by the most powerful men in Rome. Soldiers from both camps were yearning for peace. The betrothal of Octavia to Antony saw Octavian and Antony embracing each other and as Appian records: '... shouts went up from the soldiers and congratulations were offered to each of the generals, without intermission, through the entire day and night.' (App. *BC*. 5.7, White 1913: 487). Thus the armies knew their relative strengths and the futility of fighting each other. During the entire 30s BC, Octavia played a critical security role for the empire. She also secured the treaty of Tarentum in 37 BC. Plutarch (Plut. *Life of Antony*. 35.2-3, Perrin n.d. cf. Liv. 1.13. 3.) captures how her role of maintaining peace between Antony and Octavian caused her to become a most wretched woman (my italics):

> Octavia met Caesar on the way, and after winning over his friends Agrippa and Maecenas, urged him with many prayers and many entreaties not to permit her, after being a most happy, to become a most wretched woman. For now, she said, *the eyes of all men were drawn to her as the wife of one imperator and the sister of another*: 'But if,' she said 'the worse should prevail and there should be war between you, one of you, it is uncertain which, is destined to conquer, and one to be conquered, but my lot in either case will be one of misery.

Octavia's plea with Octavian highlights how she was made the female object of the public gaze: 'The eyes of all men were drawn to her as . . . wife . . . and sister . . .' In the transactions of power, Octavia's role was not only one of victimhood, but one of yielding to 'penetration' by the public gaze, and of subordination while facilitating a patriarchal agenda of the *tresviri*. Her role in the public/political space of Rome was one of motherhood in a patriarchal context, to secure peace for Roman citizens by protecting them from her husband and brother (cf. Plut. *Rom.* 19).[39] Octavia's national duty in this marriage was defined by patriarchal captivity and control – it involved the duty of reproduction and of caring for her husband, Antony, which amounted to caring for the matter of the fragile peace in Rome.

The cornered Octavia, manoeuvred by the *tresviri*, expresses womanly victimhood and patriarchal normativity in the Roman society. By suing for peace – a transaction which involved Octavia as the sacrificial victim – the veterans paved the way for Antony and Octavian to partition the whole of the Roman empire between themselves (App. *BC*. 5.7, White 1913: 487) – a process in which the two generals' veterans looked forward to their promised reward in the form of lands. After the conflict of Antony and Octavian was over, Octavia faded into the background. Cato protested and criticized such marriages and labelled them intolerable as they had the effect of prostituting the supreme power. Powerful men were helping one another to powers, armies, and provinces by means of women (Plut. *Life of Caesar.* 14.6).

In cases where women are prominent in resisting Roman patriarchy, they are represented mostly as weeping and mourning over the confiscations of their lands and other properties. A typical example is a case where rich women made an appeal to the triumvirs against taxation of their lands, houses and other properties. Appian recorded the following (my italics):

> The triumvirs addressed the people on this subject and published an edict requiring 1,400 of the richest women to make a valuation of their property, and to furnish for the service of the war such portion as triumvirs should require from each . . . The women resolved to beseech the women-folk of the triumvirs. With the sister of Octavian and the mother of Antony they did not fail, but they were repulsed from the doors of Fulvia, the wife of Antony, whose rudeness they could scarce endure. They then forced their way to the tribunal of the triumvirs in the forum, the people and the guards dividing to let them pass. There, through the mouth of Hortensia, whom they had selected to speak, they spoke as follows: 'As befitted women of our rank addressing a petition to you, we had recourse to the ladies of your households; but having been treated as did not befit us, at the hands of Fulvia, we have been driven by her to the forum. You have already deprived us of our fathers, our sons, our husbands, and our brothers, whom you accused of having wronged you; if you take away our property also, you reduce us to a condition unbecoming our birth, our manners, our sex. If we have done you wrong, as you say our husbands have, proscribe us as you do them. But if we women have not voted any of you public enemies, have not torn down your houses, destroyed your army, or led another one against you; if we have not hindered you in obtaining offices and honors, — why do we share the penalty when we did not share the guilt? 'Why should we pay taxes when we have no part in the honors, the commands, the state-craft, for which you contend against each other with such harmful results? 'Because this is a time of war,' do you say? When have there not been wars, and when have taxes ever been imposed on women, who are *exempted by their sex among all mankind? Our mothers did once rise superior to their sex and made contributions* when you were in danger of losing the whole empire and the city itself through the conflict with the Carthaginians. But then they contributed voluntarily, *not from their landed property, their fields, their dowries, or their houses, without which life is not possible to free women,* but only from their own jewellery, and even these not according to the fixed valuation, not under fear of informers or accusers, not by force and violence, but what they themselves were willing to give.
>
> App. *BC*. 4.32-33, White 1913: 195–7. see also Dio Cass. 47.14

The women are being asked to surrender portions of their property for the war effort. It is assumed that the war effort takes precedence over their own plans for their property, and that the male triumvirs can take command of the women's property for male/violent purposes. The loss of property is deemed unbecoming to a woman's birth, manners and sex. Thus ownership of property is a sign of a woman's rank and dignity as a woman. Because the women did not share in the violence of their male relatives, they do not see that they should share in the punishment.

At the same time, they do not see that their property should be taxed, since they have no part in political activity. They are looking at both possible rationales for property confiscation – punishment or taxation. They take the view that 'taxation without representation is tyranny', an issue that arose in the history of American democracy. This view of taxation without representation entails that civic responsibility – yielding up private property for the common good – is linked with civic rights. The women are being subject to civic obligations without civil rights, whereas the two should go together.[40]

The triumvirs are angry that women should hold meetings when men are silent.[41] Appian says (my italics):

> While Hortensia thus spoke the triumvirs were angry that *women should dare to hold a public meeting when the men were silent*; that they should demand from magistrates the reasons for their acts, and themselves not so much as furnish money while the men were serving in the army. They ordered the lictors to drive them away from the tribunal, which they proceeded to do until cries were raised by the multitude outside, when the lictors desisted and the triumvirs said they would postpone till the next day the consideration of the matter. On the following day they reduced the number of the women, who were to present a valuation of their property, from 1,400 to 400, and decreed that all men who possessed more than 100,000 drachmas, both citizens and strangers, freedmen and priests, and men of all nationalities without a single exception, should (under the same dread of penalty and also of informers) lend them at interest a fiftieth part of their property and contribute one year's income to the war expenses.
>
> App. *BC*. 4.34, White 1913: 199

An issue arises of whether the overruling of private property rights by the common good still applies when it is a matter of a faction of society fighting another faction, rather than the whole community fighting its enemies. The triumvirs did not like to explain themselves to women. Maybe they did not like to explain themselves to anybody? Their voice was in their sword – a violent rather than a reasoning masculinity.[42]

The politicians refused at first to discuss the situation rationally but responded with violence against the women, the lictors being asked to expel them. This was met by further violence by the multitude outside, and so was counterproductive. There was then a modified proposal where they compromised by asking less women to present an evaluation of their property, while men of all kinds were to lend some money at interest and also give a year's income, informers remaining a threat in this situation.

Hence Roman men and women had a different relationship to land and property, both depending on it for dignity, but with women in a less fair or advantageous position. Whether women were badly off in absolute terms in earlier times is another question. Hortensia seemed to indicate that women did not have the same tax burden in earlier ages.

> τί δὲ ἐσφέρωμεν αἱ μήτε ἀρχῆς μήτε τιμῆς μήτε στρατηγίας μήτε τῆς πολιτείας ὅλως, τῆς ὑμῖν ἐς τοσοῦτον ἤδη κακοῦ περιμαχήτου, μετέχουσαι;
>
> App. *BC*. 4. 33

> But why should we pay tax on property, who have a share neither in the governmental office nor in honour nor in the generalship nor, generally, in the citizenship which is fought for among you, for so much evil already?[43]

This example of resistance shows how women may become powerful, and how they could struggle to attain higher levels of a 'female masculinity', in spite of societal strictures. There was not much latitude for Roman women to achieve a higher gradation of masculinity especially in the context of war and the acquisition of land. In some ways Zimbabwean women were better off: at the same time, one need not exaggerate the degree to which women fared well in Zimbabwean politics and society. It is true that these women fought in the war of independence, and that they were also foot-soldiers in the acquisition of land from white farmers; but, as Connell argues, the African liberation movements in power have celebrated male 'founding fathers', while having an ambiguous relationship with women's liberation movements (Connell 2005: 76). During the liberation war, there were cases where female fighters were not seen as equals with their male guerrilla fighters. Research has indicated that the performance of masculinity by male guerrilla fighters during the liberation war involved, among other things, bedding several female fighters (by consent or otherwise) (Tendi 2020).

## Conclusion

This chapter explored the concept of 'veteran' as one of the conceptual domains of the present study – and examined some differences between the two cultures of ancient Rome and Africa. The masculinity of veterans was differently understood in both societies on account of different relationships to the global context, to colonization and to spirituality. The masculinity of ancient Rome had a divine element insofar as soldiers had an association with male gods. By contrast, Zimbabwean masculinity among war veterans did not involve association with gods, although war veterans attached importance to the dead and to the ancestors. The view of man and woman in both societies was also different, with the Zimbabwean idea of the war veteran including an element of female participation.

The following chapter explores the nexus of war, masculinity and land acquisition or ownership.

3

# Land Ownership, Masculinity and War

*For it seemed to both sides to be the simplest method to give to the troops which had fought with them the possessions of the unarmed. But, contrary to their expectation, great disturbance resulted and the matter began to tend toward war.*

Dio Cass. 48.6, Cary 1914

*'Violence is the resort at the moment. It's a war and we've changed our strategy. They [white farmers and their managers] are being beaten, yes, but you have to know why, they have been caught up in the crossfire. They are the ring-leaders and they are sponsoring people to protect their interests.'*

The words of a Zimbabwean war veterans' spokesman
cited in Buckle 2001: 37[1]

## Introduction

In the previous chapter I discussed the fundamental cultural differences in land-based masculinities in ancient Rome and an African context, with attention being given to the specific areas of spirituality and the experiences of women. I explored the concept of 'veteran' and its nexus with land and other rewards of war, which were conceived as remuneration or rewards of valour for military veterans. In this chapter, I explore how notions of masculinity based on martial honour in patriarchally organized societies can provide a basis for understanding the cultural logic and social processes of reward distribution among military veterans, in which masculinity, gender-ideologies and power influenced how land ownership and dispossession was conceived in the two societies. I therefore explore how, in the two societies, patriarchy and war worked as the loci for discursive constructions of ideals of power, in which land expropriation and the possession or dispossession of land can be analysed and contextualized. I argue that in both societies patriarchy led to power being obtained by more powerful men, which in turn produced ideologies of gender within a hierarchical male-dominated structure. I explore how in both societies – if I may here borrow some convenient expression from Solomon-Godeau (1997), which seem apt for my study – there was a gendered binarism of language in which the word 'male' connoted the positive qualities of heroic and manly ideals, in opposition to terms negatively associated with the feminine. My main purpose of comparing the two patriarchal societies is to investigate the cultural logic of ownership of land and dispossession in Roman society in general, and the dominance of masculine ideals in the acquisition of land by client-armies in first-century BC Rome in particular. A key argument of the chapter is that in both societies the political and philosophical rationalization of ideal masculinity supported expropriation in a manner that repressed and repudiated effeminacy. As Witzke noted, in Rome "... female sexual status was ideologically linked to the male body politic of Rome from its inception, from the city's foundation by the children of the disinherited and raped Rhea Silvia to the rape of the Sabine women, violently snatched for the 'proper' propagation of the city through their virgin bodies." (Witzke 2016: 251)

## Male power, land and a 'masculinity of the polis'

A 'masculinity of the polis'[2] influenced the behaviour of military veterans in ancient Rome and Zimbabwe. As far as the ancient polis is concerned, Arendt, cited in Willis (2011: 22) argued:

> The organization of the *polis*, physically secured by the wall around the city and physiognomically guaranteed by its laws – lest the succeeding generations change its identity beyond recognition – is a kind of organized remembrance. It is as though the wall of the *polis* and the boundaries of the law were drawn around an already existing public space which, however, without such stabilizing protection could not endure.

The polis of the Greeks was based on separate cities as states. In both Rome and Zimbabwe, the state extended beyond the walls of a single city. Yet in both cases, although we do not have a walled city, we do have a politically significant area for which the veteran were deemed to provide stability and protection. The politics of power in the two worlds of veteran applied to a space which provided stability and peace through the war efforts of fighters. This space calls to mind a more abstract sense of the word *polis*, that of not the walled city but the body of citizens or the state (Liddell and Scott 1889: 654). The war veterans were concerned about the space relating to their own citizens or state. The politics of power in both worlds claimed Rome and Zimbabwe respectively as prizes of war for the victors.[3] Thus, the veterans in both Rome and Zimbabwe, in their attitudes to land acquisition and appropriation of political fields, displayed what might be called a 'masculinity of the polis' related to *polis* in the sense of the civic community, and reminiscent of ancient attitudes towards the *polis* as an actual walled city.

In the two societies, the men who fought for their country are celebrated and do feature as martial, patriotic and self-sacrificing. A Roman example is that of Dio's narrative of Pompey's self-sacrifice to the Roman state since boyhood (Dio Cass. 36.25.2). Cato also pointed out that Rome's fighting men possessed the qualities of valour and self-sacrifice (Cat. *Orig. frg.* 51). Narratives in ancient Roman texts and in the war history of Zimbabwe, involving men who fought in war, interlace inexorable patriotic values with heroicized masculinity, as they relate severe and bloody war scenes in which the fighters took part. These patriotic values were virtues.

There was also in first-century BC Rome, a rhetoric that presented Roman generals and their client-armies as fighters for the freedom of Rome and defenders of Rome's citizens from tyranny. This rhetoric treated the client-armies as symbols of national patriotic values (cf. Milne 2009). When Sulla marched against the city of Rome, envoys from the Senate asked him why he was leading an army against his country. 'To deliver her from her tyrants,' (App. *BC*. 1.57) he replied. Similarly, Augustus boasted of having raised an army to champion the liberty of the Republic when it was oppressed by the tyranny of a faction (*RG*. 1). The end of the civil war between Antony and Octavian was tidily controlled by Octavian, the man who emerged victorious and who not only saved the city and restored the Republic but also founded Rome anew (Breed, Damon and Rossi 2010: 10). In re-writing the story of his own civil war, Augustus portrayed Antony as a villain and the embodiment of unpatriotic values, who corrupted Rome's manly values by getting married to an Egyptian woman, Cleopatra.

We can note that politics in both cases was understood so as to link the state and civic virtue with masculinity. The social systems conformed to the masculinity of the polis,[4] and the decisive determinations of male power were understood in the military terms of founding and defending one's country. In talking of the masculinity of the polis in connection with Rome, one may also point to references in ancient texts. For example, Polybius refers to the valiant acts of men who fought for the Italian nation and also for the Roman state:

> διὸ κἄν ποτε πταίσωσι κατὰ τὰς ἀρχάς, Ῥωμαῖοι μὲν ἀναμάχονται τοῖς ὅλοις, Καρχηδόνιοι δὲ τοὐναντίον. ἐκεῖνοι γὰρ ὑπὲρ πατρίδος ἀγωνιζόμενοι καὶ τέκνων οὐδέποτε δύνανται λῆξαι τῆς ὀργῆς, ἀλλὰ μένουσι ψυχομαχοῦντες, ἕως ἂν περιγένωνται τῶν ἐχθρῶν. διὸ καὶ περὶ τὰς ναυτικὰς δυνάμεις πολύ τι λειπόμενοι Ῥωμαῖοι κατὰ τὴν ἐμπειρίαν, ὡς προεῖπον ἐπάνω, τοῖς ὅλοις ἐπικρατοῦσι διὰ τὰς τῶν ἀνδρῶν ἀρετάς· καίπερ γὰρ οὐ μικρὰ συμβαλλομένης εἰς τοὺς κατὰ θάλατταν κινδύνους τῆς ναυτικῆς χρείας, ὅμως ἡ τῶν ἐπιβατῶν εὐψυχία πλείστην παρέχεται ῥοπὴν εἰς τὸ νικᾶν. διαφέρουσι μὲν οὖν καὶ φύσει πάντες Ἰταλιῶται Φοινίκων καὶ Λιβύων τῇ τε σωματικῇ ῥώμῃ καὶ ταῖς ψυχικαῖς τόλμαις· μεγάλην δὲ καὶ διὰ τῶν ἐθισμῶν πρὸς τοῦτο τὸ μέρος ποιοῦνται τῶν νέων παρόρμησιν. ἓν δὲ ῥηθὲν ἱκανὸν ἔσται σημεῖον τῆς τοῦ πολιτεύματος σπουδῆς, ἣν ποιεῖται περὶ τὸ τοιούτους ἀποτελεῖν ἄνδρας ὥστε πᾶν ὑπομένειν χάριν τοῦ τυχεῖν ἐν τῇ πατρίδι τῆς ἐπ' ἀρετῇ φήμης.
>
> see Polyb. 6.52.6-11, Perseus Digital Library (n.d.a)

> For, as the Romans are fighting for country and children, it is impossible for them to relax the fury of their struggle; but they persist with obstinate resolution until they have overcome their enemies. What has happened in regard to their navy is an instance in point. In skill the Romans are much behind the Carthaginians, as I have already said; yet the upshot of the whole naval war has been a decided triumph for the Romans, owing to the valour of their men. For although nautical science contributes largely to success in sea-fights, still it is the courage of the marines that turns the scale most decisively in favor of victory. The fact is that Italians as a nation are by nature superior to Phoenicians and Libyans both in physical strength and courage; but still their habits also do much to inspire the youth with enthusiasm for such exploits. One example will be sufficient of the pains taken by the Roman state to turn out men ready to endure anything to win a reputation in their country for valour.

There are also the founding narratives of Rome, which contain representations of heroic and masculine individual deeds. Marius was hailed as the Third Founder of Rome, on account of the peril which he averted from the city, a danger which was viewed as comparable to that of the Gallic invasion.[5] This tradition was passed on to the men who participated in Roman wars as soldiers. The acquisition of territories by force and the building of cities by Roman men was deemed masculine, implying a show of strength by men possessed of patriotic fervour (cf. Takacs 2009: xix).

The logic of a masculinity of the polis also applies to the Zimbabwean world of veterans, as it relates to the making/founding of the modern Zimbabwean state through the heroic fight for political independence from British imperialism, a fight which included the post-2000 expropriations of white-owned farmland by guerrilla veterans. Heroic individuals who took part in the war were recognized and celebrated as 'makers' of Zimbabwe. Something comparable to a masculinity of the polis emerged from that positioning as 'makers' or 'founders' of Zimbabwe in which much blood was shed. Zimbabwe is presented in liberation war songs in such a way as to suggest that only males fought in the independence war. One such song says: '*Zimbabwe Ndeyeropa baba, Zimbabwe ndeyeropa ramadzibaba*' (Zimbabwe is from blood, father; Zimbabwe is from the blood of the Fathers) (Chitando and Tarusarira 2017).

The masculinity of the polis secured the legacy and honour of a fighter who took part in the honourable deed of fighting for the fatherland. Modern research also attests to the interconnection of the dynamics of war, masculinity and nation building (cf. Nagel 1998). Something like a 'masculinity of the polis' had the same agenda in both worlds of veterans: justifying the veteran's access to the 'spoils of war' in which terms land for the veteran was framed. We see Caesar in Lucan's epic promising not to punish his soldiers for attacking their homeland (Luc. 7.261-262). The tribune Curio openly tells Caesar that since they are now exiles of their homeland, they must take Rome as *a spoil of war* if they wanted to be citizens again. '*at postquam leges bello siluere coactae, pellimur e patriis laribus patimurque volentes exilium; tua nos faciet victoria cives.*' (Luc. 1.276). [But after the laws were compelled into silence by war, we were driven from our native homes and suffered exile willingly; your victory will make us citizens].[6] Caesar's emotive account of Pompey's injustices at Rome (Luc. 1.303-32) is followed by the complaint that the rewards of war (*praemia belli*) are being snatched from him and from his men by Pompey (Luc. 1.340-341. cf. App. *BC*. 5.3, White 1913: 381). Thus, the civil war between Caesar and Pompey has Rome as the greater prize (*pretio maiore*) – greater than the whole of Gaul which Caesar had conquered (Luc. 1.282). Lucan shows Caesar's soldiers pledging their loyalty. They have been to the farthest ocean for him and wish only to follow him; for him they will kill kinsmen, plunder temples and take cities by storm, be it Rome herself that they sack (Fantham 1985: 124).

Zimbabwe's guerrilla veterans expropriated land and property belonging both to whites and to fellow Blacks. In their scheme of operation, Zimbabwe was perceived as their trophy because they took part in a war to claim it from colonial Britain. Research has shown that soon after independence, owing to indiscipline, boredom and declining living standards, some Zimbabwe People's Revolutionary Army (ZIPRA) guerrillas became involved in lawless activity involving banditry in the country's southern and north-west regions (Tendi 2020). Some ZANLA guerrillas also continued to engage in banditry in the north-east and eastern parts of Zimbabwe (ibid.), where they raided and terrorized villagers. This continued at a later date, as many guerrilla veterans did not show an inclination towards peaceful behaviour. For example, during the 2008 elections, Mugabe raised the issues of land and injustice as part of his election campaign, despite the fact that over 95 per cent of white farmers had left the countryside (Pilossof 2009). When the election result did not go in his favour, expropriations of the few white farms remaining were carried out by the war veterans in a role akin to that of following a political agenda (ibid.). Mugabe and his hordes of veterans clearly held Zimbabwe to ransom as they felt entitled at their prize – Zimbabwe.

## An adult-masculinity, land ownership and dispossession: A Roman perspective

Appian and Dio Cassius mentioned the insecurity (involving landlessness) of Caesar's soldiers after the prolonged civil war against Pompey (Coles 2020 cites, App. *BC*. 2.94, Dio Cass. 42.30, 52). Nevertheless, I note that there is a better way to demonstrate the importance of land ownership by Roman military veterans.

Since my approach uses cultural analogies to shed light on military men and the phenomena of violence and land expropriation, I refer to African culture to explore common occurrences of the phenomena. I investigate some of the ways client-army veterans perceived their physical bodies, by exploring the connection between an 'adult-masculinity' and the problems of access to land. My starting point is the examination of what I call an 'adult-masculinity' – a term inspired by my reading of Appian's *Bellum Civile*. 12.128. This exploration of the self-perception of client-army veterans allows for an investigation of the symbol of the veteran and the meanings and configurations of masculinities generated whenever their bodies were deployed in fields of operation – i.e. fighting on battlefields, occupying territories, expropriating estates and engaging in politics generally. I first state what the ancient Roman texts seem to suggest vis-à-vis the problems of access to land and manliness, and then contrast the Roman material with what obtains in contemporary Africa. This will assist in ascertaining and understanding client-army soldiers' martially and patriarchally motivated behaviours and beliefs in respect to the ownership of land in the challenging contexts of war.

It is necessary to explore some of the ways in which client-army veterans perceived themselves as the Roman sources suggest. I investigate the relationship between an 'adult-masculinity' and the issues surrounding the possession of land. There is a sense in which adulthood without land was not thought of as a manly adulthood. For example, the self-perception of Octavian's soldiers as mature adults was dependent on an understanding of their physical bodies as the bodies of men and not of women, as the bodies of grown up adults as opposed to the bodies of children. The tribune Ofillius challenged Octavian, who had distributed honours and prizes to some of his legions, stating that crowns and purple garments were playthings for boys (παισὶν ἀθύρματα[7]), that the rewards for soldiers (στρατοῦ . . . γέρα = lit. gifts of honour of an army.[8]) were *lands* and money. (App. *BC*. 5.128, White 1913: 589–91). Appian recorded that the veterans of Antony and Octavian demanded cities *as prizes for their valour*.[9] (App. *BC*. 5.128; see Liv. 25.31.8–9 on giving of cities to soldiers for plunder).

Thus the idea of a soldier, or a warrior/fighter, as other societies may call them, captures some fundamental aspects of human organization and human symbolism. There is a link between the fighter/warrior and the idea of adulthood, and in turn, a link between the fighter/warrior and the concept of manhood (Mazrui 1977: 75; cf. Ocobock 2017). A boy in Roman political culture possessed no *virtus* and was not a man in the sense that the Latin word *vir* denotes (McDonnell 2006). Slaves were regularly referred to as *puer* (boy) as they were not capable of possessing *virtus* (valour/courage) (ibid.). Roman generals engaged in political rhetoric in which the imagery of the bodies of boys was used in masculinity-discourses and struggles for political and military power. Sulla tried to deny Pompey, who was only 26, a triumphal reception at Rome, calling him a 'beardless youngster' (not yet an adult man, who could grow facial hair) (Eyben 1993: 48–9).[10] The visible growth of facial hair was one of the cultural markers in the ancient world of being masculine (Montserrat 2000: 179). This resonates with beliefs on achieving manhood in traditional African societies, which involve physical growth and a mature male body, usually characterized by growing a beard (Morrell 2006). Pompey's lack of a beard thus rendered him infantile, a position he challenged by forcing Sulla to approve his first military triumph. Because Pompey challenged the insult of being called a boy, he triumphed at the unprecedented age of 26. This vindicates Connell's assertion that masculinities are produced in the process of social interaction in which actors exploit the resources and strategies available to them in their specific social settings (Connell 2001a; 2001b). In this case, Pompey exploited military hardware to defy the social norms defined by the physical feature of possessing a beard. In this case, a socially constructed masculinity became secondary to a martial-based masculinity.

One might also argue that a male adult is someone who has a capacity to earn his own living by owning and maintaining his own land or homestead (Mazrui 1977). Mazrui (1977) mentions cases where this is true of most African countries such as Uganda, Somalia, Kenya, Ethiopia and many others. In the logic of Mazrui, adults are sometimes to be differentiated from elders. In this sense, while boys are not yet adults, elders have grown past active adulthood. They are no longer at the peak of their physical powers. Julius Caesar's soldiers were aware of this distinction. Exhausted by too many wars, at Placentia, they simulated old age and bodily weakness as a strategy to be discharged and to compel Caesar to give them more rewards (Dio Cass. 41.35.2, Cary 1914: 61–3). It is from the ranks of adults that full warriors are recruited. In ancient Rome active military service was between the age of 17 and 46 (Keppie 1983: 36). Therefore self-reliance was something built into the concept of a soldier because of its link with the notion of adulthood (Mazrui 1977: 75). There was a sense in which those in the military strove to prove their capacities to do things that could not be done by children, if Ofilius' and Sulla's examples are anything to go by.

I may refer also to the insults traded between Pompey, Metellus Pius and Sertorius: for example, the portrayal of Metellus as an old woman and Pompey as merely Sulla's pupil (that is, a schoolboy) (Plut. *Sert.* 19.6, *Pomp.* 18.1, 18.4. see also Eyben 1993: 48–9). In this regard, the two were represented as women or boys and not as real men. The young Octavian was also at one point a victim of his youth. In Dio 50.18, we see Antony attacking and demeaning him as an unfit general because of his bodily weaknesses compounded by his youthfulness (my italics):

> ... yet in no respect are they also lacking as in the *youth* and inexperience of their commander ... He is a veritable *weakling* in *body* and has never by himself been victor in any important battle either on the land or on the sea. Indeed, at Philippi, in one and the same conflict, it was I that conquered and he that was defeated.

Suetonius also provides a narrative in which the senate's disregard of and disdain for Octavian as a boy was linked to its unwillingness to pay veterans led by a boy. Suetonius captures this perception as follows (my italics):

> When Augustus heard that Mark Antony had been taken under Lepidus's protection and that the other military commanders, supported by their troops, were coming to terms with these two, he at once deserted the aristocratic party. His excuse was that some of them had contemptuously called him *'the boy'*, while others had not concealed their view that, once publicly honored, he should

> be done away with-to avoid having to pay *his veterans* and himself what they expected.
>
> Suet. 12. 11-12; cf. Dio Cass. 46. 41.5

Octavian was spurred to act by the senate's decision to refuse to give land to (his) veterans, on the pretext that they were led by a boy. Octavian himself acknowledged that he raised an army when he was only nineteen years of age (*RG.* 1). In the eyes of the senate, Octavian was a boy and by association, his veterans were not taken seriously.

Yet for the poet Horace, even a boy's masculinity should not be despised, for a young warrior can be toughened by war. Horace refers to a Roman boy hardened by the environment, who was trained in warfare and could outmatch any opponent (*Carm.* 3.2 cited in Takacs 2009: 52). 'Let a boy toughened by military campaign take gladly to and learn thoroughly pressing dearth, and as a formidable horseman, with a spear, vex the ferocious Parthians.'[11] This does not mean of course that the young will always prevail, particularly if they have less experience. The poet Vergil in the Aeneid states that Pallas, a younger and inexperienced warrior, was killed by Turnus, a more experienced and seasoned fighter (Verg. *Aen.* 8.51-54).

## Masculinity, land ownership and dispossession: Transcultural perspectives

Having explored Roman ideas of masculinity to some degree, I now consider how owning or not owning land or property was experienced by Roman men in general, which includes client-army soldiers. I compare veterans' experiences of ownership of land and their responses to landlessness in an agrarian setting in order to catalogue human behaviour, responses, instincts and societal beliefs vis-à-vis landed property ownership and the forces at play in processes of acquiring, defending or fighting for landed property. The goal of this endeavour is to understand the function of concepts of masculinity vis-à-vis land or property ownership during the era of client-armies.

I start by exploring how the nexus of land/property and housecraft was theorized by Aristotle. Such a nexus as Aristotle alludes to existed in ancient Rome, as it does in contemporary Africa. Since Aristotle's views form the basis of my analogical treatment of the issues at hand, I cite him at some length in order to illustrate his exposition of nation, statecraft, housecraft, homestead and the gendered power relations that existed in his society. It must be noted that the work known as the *Economics* is only dubiously attributed to Aristotle; nevertheless I find it useful to the present task because it belongs to his school and is, in my view, good evidence. His exposition goes thus (my italics):

> By a Nation we mean an assemblage of houses, lands, and property sufficient to enable the inhabitants to lead a civilized life. This is proved by the fact that when such a life is no longer possible for them, the tie itself which unites them is dissolved. Moreover, it is with such a life in view that the association is originally formed; and the object for which a thing exists and has come into being is in fact the very essence of that particular thing.
>
> From this definition of a Nation, it is evident that the art of Housecraft is older than that of Statecraft,[12] since the Household, which it creates, is older; being a component part of the Nation created by Statecraft.
>
> Accordingly we must consider the nature of Housecraft, and what the Household, which it creates, actually is.
>
> The component parts of a household are human beings, and goods and chattels. And as households are no exception to the rule that the nature of a thing is first studied in its barest and simplest form, we will follow Hesiod and begin by postulating 'Homestead first, and a woman; a plough-ox hardy to furrow.' For the steading takes precedence among our physical necessities, and the woman among our free associates. It is, therefore, one of the tasks of Homecraft *to set in order the relation between man and woman*; in other words, to see that it is what it ought to be.
>
> Of occupations attendant on our goods and chattels, those come first which are natural. Among these *precedence is given to the one which cultivates the land*; those like mining, which extract wealth from it, take the second place. Agriculture is the most honest of all such occupations; seeing that the wealth it brings is not derived from other men. Herein it is distinguished from trade and the wage-earning employments, which acquire wealth from others by their consent; and from war, which wrings it from them perforce. It is also a natural occupation; since by nature's appointment all creatures receive sustenance from their mother . . .
>
> *Oec.* 1.1343a, Perseus Digital Library (n.d.b)

The terms 'housecraft' and 'statecraft' are translations respectively of οἰκονομική and πολιτική which may be rendered as 'economics' and 'politics'. For Aristotle, economics is the science of setting up a household. A household is made of human beings and goods or chattels. Family members are members of the household. The woman is viewed as a chief associate in the household, which presupposes that we have a householder, and a woman who is his associate. The householder for Aristotle is thus a male and the male is head of the family. This is confirmed in the *Politics* where it is said, 'Again, as between the sexes, the male is by nature superior and the female inferior, the male ruler and the female subject.' (Aristot. *Pol.* 1254b, Perseus Digital Library n.d.c).

Aristotle indicates, in the citation from the *Economics* above, that among tasks relating to goods and chattels, agriculture takes precedence, and is deemed superior to trade and war.

In an African traditional household we also have a male-headed household and a lifestyle where agriculture has pride of place. In Africa, as in Aristotle's set-up, there exist an arrangement where a male–female relations and a land-owning ethic are linked in one institution.

> Male-headed families are the ideal family model in Zimbabwe. Within these families, the male has ultimate decision-making power. He controls all forms of property-including his wife, who in some groups is also regarded as his possession. The male does not necessarily live permanently with his family, a situation that often results in a division of the family unit. Such households are headed by men who either work away from home or have a polygamous family that is dispersed. Occasionally, the assumed male head supports the family inadequately. He simply makes the major decisions and owns whatever property has been in the family that is managed by his wife or wives. The women, with help from their children, develop and maintain property that is officially in their husbands' names. The men cut costs by making the women work and using child labor, supposedly in the interest of the family. Culturally, men have been given the prerogative of manipulating the system so that much work falls on the shoulders of the women and children.
>
> Riphenburg 1997: 34

Although women in Africa can work on a piece of land, most of the continent's female farmers work on land under rights dependent on or ancillary to those of males (Shipton 1994: 350, Goheen 1994), though many writings also depict women as investing much energy and creativity to gain more control over land (cf. Bassett and Crummey 1993).

Max Weber argued that tradition was a source of authority (Weber 1972). When Robert Mugabe was regarded as father of the nation, the philosophy behind such a title assumed that, according to the African tradition, a father has the power to defend, protect, punish and redistribute resources to the family. At the micro-level, the idea of being a father in many African cultures entails being the head of the family. To be a father means to be most senior, and hence the family patriarch. Duties of the father include being the primary provider of the material needs of the family, from shelter to food, and also being protector of the family against threatening forces of whatever nature (Lesejane 2006: 175). In its representation, fatherhood in most African states is manifested as a violent patriarchy.

We find a traditional idea of fatherhood also in Roman culture, and the Roman *paterfamilias* (the Latin term for 'father of the family' or the 'owner of the family estate') may be viewed as a head of household in a similar set-up to the one described by Aristotle. Roman historians have viewed Roman paternal authority as the very basis of Roman social order and stability (Cantarella 2003: 282). The *paterfamilias* possessed the power of life and death over his children and was in charge of all the household's finances, property and lands. As in Africa, there is a male head of a household and a male-centred community associated with property, especially land; the family and land together make up a household. It is instructive also to note that Augustus' favourite title, which was put on the chariot statue in the centre of Forum Augusti and which he used to close the *Res Gestae* (35), was *'pater patriae'* given by senate, equites and people in 2 BC, with connotation that all citizens were his dependents.

The common factor in the three societies seems to be a male-ruled collection of persons (a man and his family) and a various kinds of property (land and other things) which are closely associated with one another and in physical proximity. It would appear that the owner of the land and the male head of the family are the same person in all three societies, ancient Greece, ancient Rome and the African society as represented by Zimbabwe and other patriarchal African examples. I set out to explore, through a close analysis of Roman texts and narratives from Zimbabwe, the problems of land/property ownership vis-à-vis concepts of manliness and how these may be understood to have given form to masculinities that manifested in connection with war veterans' relation to land/property ownership.

The text box of responses from Zimbabwe's guerrilla veterans, juxtaposed with Roman reflections below, capture views on how veterans from the two worlds felt manly or not by virtue of owning or not owning a piece of land or a homestead, and touch on the question of whether not owning land was experienced as effeminacy. This juxtaposition allows for exploring the issues of confiscation, landlessness and dispossession, as experienced by Roman males in general and by client-army soldiers in particular, and also by those whose land they confiscated. The mirroring conducted in the text box aims at giving a glimpse of responses to landlessness in the world of Zimbabwean and Roman veterans, followed by a detailed interpretation of the Roman material.

'I am a war veteran and according to Shona culture, it is the husband that feeds the wife/wives and children. A landless man is a man-less man. *Ungaita baba vasina munda here?*/ Can anyone be a father without owning a field to farm on?' (Personal communication with a war veteran A) (Zimbabwe)

On the one hand the rich who had *lost their land* collected together in groups and made lamentation, and accused the poor of appropriating the results of their tillage, their vineyards, and their dwellings. Others said that the graves of their ancestors were in the ground, which had been allotted to them in the division of their fathers' estates. On the other hand *ex-soldiers* (*settlers*) were lamenting that they had been *reduced (by their landlessness) to extreme penury, and from that to childlessness, because they were unable to rear their offspring.* They recounted the military services they had rendered, by which this very land had been acquired, and were angry that they should be robbed of their share of the common property. (My italics) (App. *BC.* 1.10.) (Ancient Rome)

'Without land in life, one doesn't mean anything to his family; I want to say that it's land that means everything to a man. *Kana usina chunhu uri mukadzi*!/If you don't own property you are a woman.' (Personal communication with a war veteran B) (Zimbabwe)

His (Cicero) property was confiscated, his house was razed to the ground, as though it had been an enemy's, and its site was dedicated for a temple . . . 'Are you not ashamed Cicero.' He said, 'to be weeping and behaving like a woman? (Dio Cass. 38.17-18, Cary 1914: 235, 237.) (Ancient Rome)

'Without possessions, especially land, a man has no meaningful existence. In fact one is as good as dead. We were killed when the Smith regime deprived us of our ancestral lands, and I feel like I continue to die without land.' (Personal communication with a war veteran D) (Zimbabwe)

'You don't represent anything when your wife sees other men owning land while you have nothing *except being called a war veteran*. I do farming on useless sandy soils while the elite have good and productive farmland.' (Personal communication with war veteran E) (Zimbabwe)

Even the men who have obtained their discharge still follow the standard *under the name of veterans another word for protracted misery*. A few, indeed, by *their bodily vigour have surmounted all their labours; but what is their reward*? They are sent to distant regions, and, under color of an allotment of lands, they are settled on a barren mountain, or a swampy fen. War of itself is a state of the vilest drudgery, without an adequate compensation. The life and limb of a soldier are valued at ten pence a day; out of what wretched pittance he must find his clothing, his tent-equipage, and his arms; with that fund, he (the soldier) must bribe . . . intense cold in winter, and the fatigue of summer campaigns; destructive war, in which everything is hazarded, and peace, by which nothing is gained, are all the soldier's portion (Tac. *Ann.* 1:17, Arthur Murphy, 1908: 20). (Rome)

'When a man is not respected, they say "This is not a man, it's a woman". *We veterans are mocked and looked down upon by society.* What brings dignity and respect is what you have. I would rather own land.' (Personal communication with a war veteran F). (Zimbabwe)

Caesar showed his readiness to submit to arbitration, and the others promised to be there but did not go, either because they were afraid or because they thought it beneath them; at any rate, they were wont to *make fun of the veterans*, calling them among other names *senatus caligatus*, on account of the military boots they wore . . .[13] (Dio Cass. 48.12) (Rome)

In the responses given by Zimbabwe's guerrilla veterans and the Roman reflections juxtaposed with them, I observe that there is a sense in which a piece of land or homestead on which a family was created and raised remained symbolic of achieved manhood and was viewed as the seat of male power. Being a 'real man' came with what one owned, above all, land. Having no land was experienced as weakness and a loss of male identity, resulting in crisis. If a man lost his land, he was reduced to the inferior status of a woman.

Such a feeling or sentiment could also be seen at play also among white farmers who had their lands confiscated by Zimbabwe's liberation war veterans. War-related trauma played a role among white farmers, as many of them testified to feeling ransacked, besieged and even emasculated. A white farmer and Rhodesian war veteran who fought on the side of Ian Smith during the liberation war, now living in the city of Harare underlined this when he said: 'before the expropriations, I was a man.' (Personal communication, October 2018.)[14] It is instructive to mention that some former white farmers, especially those with military training, attempted to take back their farms in an effort that testifies to the invocation of their war skills to regain their former status of dominance and influence (see Pilossof 2009: 624). Nevertheless, farming had turned into an increasingly precarious occupation for the white men who suffered extreme violence from the guerrilla veterans. In the end, farming for the former white farmer came to be considered hazardous work that bore the stigma of weakness and defeat. This also applied to some guerrilla veterans who expropriated land during Mugabe's reign. While the official position in Zimbabwe is that land expropriation is over, it continues to unfold and new victims continue to be created. There is an internal contest of militant/martial masculinities between hostile factions of guerrilla veterans. Masculinity is not given once and for all, but must constantly be fought for and asserted. The birth of the so-called 'second republic' and/or 'new dispensation' created a new group of 'accumulators' who were not in government before the coup of November 2017 and therefore feel that now is their time to use the machinery of the state to acquire the lands they always coveted. These lands are being acquired by evicting white commercial farmers, war veterans who were settled during Mugabe's time as well as erstwhile members of Mugabe's regime who are at loggerheads with the new regime. These current dialectics of land expropriation in Zimbabwe are revealing of the southern African country's troubled past, violent present and uncertain future.

Similar human feelings of dispossession can be recovered by analysing some texts of ancient historians to demonstrate the effect of expropriation on victims of veterans, and how their reaction was productive of images of effeminacy. Appian reveals this palpable feeling of anxiety with overtones of emasculation among landless Roman war veterans who bemoaned their childlessness, which they attributed to being landless. Appian depicted the landless as having lamented that their state of landlessness had reduced them from security to penury, and from that to childlessness, because they were unable to rear their offspring (App. *BC.* 1.10). Appian indicated how fatherhood in a social rather than a biological sense was affected by being landless. These are two distinct aspects of masculinity at play here.

Effeminacy – or being a eunuch (although in this case, childlessness was not a result of biological impotency) – was something the Roman society looked down upon as a sign of being powerless. Such a construction of gender was the logical product of a patriarchally structured society where the ability to procreate was important in defining both sex and gender, and loss or denial of the reproductive functions placed certain individuals outside the logic of conventional, family-derived social categories (Montserrat 2000: 158). We may recall the farmers who lost their farms during the confiscations of the second triumvirate, and took up arms to join Sextus Pompey, who was leading a resistance movement. It is no coincidence that in this era a Roman man's identity remained tightly entwined with the notion that precarious manhood could be best demonstrated and won on the battlefield (Stewart 2016: 13), after one had lost their seat of male power as owners of a farm. Octavian even alluded to the possibility of a return of the expropriated farmers with the help of Sextus Pompey whom they had joined to repossess their farms which he had given to his soldiers: 'Octavian . . . began to excite the colonized soldiers against the latter, representing that Antony intended to bring back Pompeius with the owners of the lands which the soldiers now held, for most of the owners had taken refuge with Pompeius.' (App. *BC.* 5.53, White 1913: 465). I referred earlier to Appian's depiction of the landless lamenting their state of landlessness which had reduced them to childlessness, because they were unable to rear their offspring (App. *BC.* 1.10). One might have their paternal and biological masculinity intact, but still feel unmanly owing to landlessness – hence the need to fight. I am not saying this was the sole concern among the followers of Sextus, as security itself could have been another reason for taking up arms.

Intrigues for power signal how veterans and different male actors were caught up in this struggle for resources which in the end produced discourses productive of gender images and meanings. This shows that a veteran-masculinity (made up of soldierly bodies, arms of war, etc.) was a different kind of male power, which by itself was woefully inadequate, as veterans had to fight to gain land and a homestead – sources of a different kind of male power. This situation can be compared to that of third- and fourth-century Roman citizen colonists, who remained *proletarii* (unqualified for military service) because the two *iugera* of land they received was inadequate to make them to *assidui* (qualified farmer-soldiers on account of affording military equipment) (Roselaar 2009).

Being without land and children and the inability to rear one's offspring are also culturally problematic in some African societies. In Northern Kivu in the Democratic Republic of Congo, to be landless is more or less equated to being unmanned. Manhood, male power and social coherence are achieved through creating and maintaining a homestead on which a family can be raised. These norms have not changed, despite displacement and economic circumstances that have made the acquisition of a homestead difficult or unlikely for many in Northern Kivu owing to the perpetual presence of insurgent warfare (Lwambo 2011: 4).

There is, however, a problematic aspect in the status of landowner possessed by a war veteran. Often, war veterans failed to work the land properly, since they weren't really fit to be farmers – an issue which shows how veterans were actually victims of their own ideology in both societies. Some Zimbabwean war veterans I interviewed had chosen town life and abandoned their newly acquired plots. They indicated that they left their fields lying fallow because they had no aptitude for farming.[15] Some guerrilla war veterans resorted to renting out their plots to white farmers. In Praeneste, Latium, Sulla's landless veterans re-sold the plots assigned to them to private citizens (Cic. *Agr.* 2.78, 3.14, *Cat.* 1.8). Can we then say that veterans sometimes exchange masculinity for money and leisure? Human feelings of hopelessness, disempowerment, dispossession and above all emasculation from different cultures across time and space are manifested across a wide range of human experience.

Nevertheless, the problem of losing land is revealing of the effects of emasculation as a constant feature in ancient Rome. An evicted owner's reaction to expropriation, I suggest, may be quite informative of the effects of emasculation, as represented by Dio Cassius below.

## Dio Cass. 38.17-18

Dio Cass. 38.17-18 suggests that being dispossessed of one's land or property more generally was experienced as weakness and a loss of male identity. The belief that a man who fails to control his own grief, loss, desires and fears is less than fully masculine occurs in many texts (Cic. *De. Offic.* 1.71, Cic. *Fin.* 2.94; Hor. 3.2). In Dio (38.17-18, Cary 1914: 237) we learn how Cicero, having lost his property and banished from Rome, is found weeping by Philiscus, who rebukes him for 'weeping and behaving like a woman', and growing 'faint-hearted'. The word here corresponding to the English 'would grow … faint-hearted' is μαλακισθήσεσθαι, from μαλακίζω, which means to become weak or effeminate (Liddell and Scott 1876: 424). This suggests that the sadness which would result from deprivation of property or exile could be construed as weak or effeminate, and that loss of property could be perceived in ancient Rome as emasculation, although this lack of maleness would not appear to obtain if Cicero were to react to his fate in the more manly way which Philiscus would prefer. It is important to note that from the viewpoint of Stoic philosophy what feminizes Cicero was the fact that he wept about his loss, and not the loss of land itself (cf. Rubarth 2014).

We also find Antony's lawyer Quintus Fufius Calenus describing Cicero as being effeminate. The words used are μαλακία (Dio Cass. 46.2, Cary 1914: 42) and γύννις (Dio Cass. 46.3. Cary 1914: 42). μαλακία means softness or effeminacy: 'softness, tenderness: of men, effeminacy, weakness', (Liddell and Scott 1876: 44), while γύννις means 'a womanish man, weakling' (Liddell and Scott 1876: 47).[16] The argument between Cicero and Calenus involved, among other things, the issue of granting land to Caesar's veterans. It is also imperative to consider the end result of the quarrel between Cicero and Calenus. When Calenus prevailed over Cicero, Caesar's adherents voted that Caesar's soldiers and those who had deserted Antony should be given land, and that Caesar be given back his money with which he had equipped the army on account of Rome (Dio Cass. 46.29.4). What is evident here is the gendered self-presentation of the triumph of a hyper-masculinity over male effeminacy. Masculinity is in this passage located within the broader context of the gendered ideology of land rewards for veterans. Cicero and Calenus were debating issues of power as if they were issues of gender, in which the materialization of power depended on land. Gender is the primary source of the figurative language with which power relationships, intertwined with land rewards for veterans, were articulated.

In the following section, I explore the role of heroic honour in the making of a war veteran's body. First-century BC Roman generals and their hordes of veterans operated in a civil war environment where losers' properties and land were confiscated by the winners. Masculinity-discourses involving war veterans' participation in battles produced images of masculinized bodies (heroized masculinity), set apart from the bodies of non-fighters, something which generally characterized modes through which veterans expropriated land.

## Honour and heroicized masculinities

In ancient Rome, masculinity was regarded as a quality associated with Roman greatness, and was central to the construction of the ancient Roman image. Vergil shows us the centrality of this notion in Rome. In the sixth book of the Aeneid, there is a list of the heroes who contributed to Rome's greatness over the centuries (Verg. *Aen.* 6.756-859). According to McDonnell (2006: 14), the awarding/granting of honours during the Republic, the meaning of valour was associated with physical courage.

In most African countries that attained independence from colonialism, honour is indeed a dominant value.[17] At the Zimbabwe's National Heroes' Acre (a place of burial for liberation war heroes and heroines), the dead heroes and heroines were adorned with decorations of military valour (Mugabe 2001: 158–77). The heroes and heroines were remembered for their contribution to Zimbabwe's great independence, including old heroes of earlier struggles against colonial occupation like Chaminuka, Kaguvi and Nehanda.

Following Plato, one may call the culture of such societies, and the character syndrome in which honour and eagerness for glory are excessively developed, timocratic (Cornford 1914: 266). The term 'timocracy' comes from the Greek word for honour (τιμή). Plato's speech below represents an Athenian's view of a typical Spartan when referring to timocracy and the timocratical character. His description, it must be noted, not only applies to ancient Athens, but to the kind of culture and character we have in mind when speaking of honorific cultures or the honorific syndrome among people of different cultures (Conford 1914: 266). Over and above the desire to rise or to become the most powerful, the timocratic character has the following traits: 'He must be ambitious for office ... (and must) base his claims on his exploits in war and the soldierly qualities he has acquired through his devotion.' (Cornford 1914: 266, cf. Plaut. *Truc.* 495). I apply this Platonic theory of honour to the politics of rewarding veterans in both societies.

For example, Zimbabwean history shows how precolonial wars, the liberation war and the third *Chimurenga* became important sites for the historical evolution of ideals of heroism and masculinity – a process which masculinized the national history.

The construction of war masculinities was a long process. In post-independence Zimbabwe, the defining characteristics of masculinity have rested in the hands of liberation war veterans and the ruling ZANU-PF party, who essentially defined masculinity in their own image. They maintained control over the image and definition of the masculine. Other male citizens, especially those who did not fight in the liberation war, were regarded as powerless and less patriotic. The liberation war veterans constituted a small part of the Zimbabwe population, but they supplied the dominant image of masculinity. Even dissenting voices within the veterans movement and the veterans who left the party or were expelled, were considered undisciplined and as having eventually became cowards and effeminate – something that resonates with the Roman *disciplina militaris*, a method of social control of soldiers which inculcated a masculine *habitus* into soldiers, both through sexual propriety and the avoidance of effeminacy and also through a general disposition of the body and mind (Phang 2008).

It is worthwhile discussing contemporary Zimbabwe's conception of a hero in direct contrast with that of ancient Rome. I begin with Robert Mugabe's use and definition of the word 'hero', whose use became part of the methods of practicing politics in Zimbabwe. It goes like this (my italics):

> Our notion of *heroism* thus comes directly from the bloody resistance to British imperial expansionism and the challenges, which come with foreign domination. These *heroes* we have here at the National Shrine and elsewhere in and outside the country come from the tradition of resistance and tell through their lives the story of our struggle in its various constitutive facets; trade unionism, urban protests, nationalist politics ... and of course *liberation soldiery.*[18]
>
> Our essence as a nation indeed lay in our people's resistances of domination, foreign domination that now asserted itself over our land. The 1893 and 1896–7 struggles, the second and third Chimurenga are dramatic episodes in the story

> of our nation, episodes that have given a tragic ring to our Independence and freedom, giving us as they do a sense of loss and of inhuman cruelty by one imperious race to another. But the same episodes have also given us a sense of sacrifice, of purpose, of unity and cohesion, of achievement, indeed of heroism and ownership . . . This indeed is our land . . . we fought and died for it!
>
> Mugabe 2001: 136

In ancient Rome, military talents and ambition gave birth to heroicized masculinities in the practice of politics. Military service was the preliminary to a political career (Polyb. 6.19.4). Competing generals ended up in civil wars and military and political usurpations (Cic. *Att.* 16.31). According to Barton, the values of the ancient Romans, especially during the Republic, were overwhelmingly those of a warrior culture (Barton 2001: 11). Ideals of honour determined the behaviour of fighters. It was a competitive environment where competing dynasties of power wrestled to attain powerful positions in Rome's socio-political and economic life. We should note that a successful Roman man was competitive yet disciplined. Discipline provided the mechanism for the behavioural controls (Takacs 2009: 6–7), which were unfortunately no longer in force during the client-army era. The client-armies and their generals had lost discipline, which led to violent struggles. In order to account for the cultural motivation that gave war veterans in the two political landscapes an attitude of entitlement and expropriation, I contrast the two views of heroism and honour and how they functioned.

## Heroism, entitlement and expropriation

When making land expropriations, war veterans drew on socially sanctioned and popular imagery of power as militant heroism, bravery (see App. *BC.* 1.69), and valour, as incidentally manifest in the socio-economic and political structures of their societies. Veterans in post-war societies usually have a character syndrome in which masculinity, and past war achievements, are excessively developed.[19] There is usually in existence a cult of military prowess which heroicizes masculinity and glorifies war and the war hero.[20] Honour is not only a recognized but also a desired phenomenon, as indicated by frequent reference thereto in the speeches of fighters recorded in narratives of war. With specific respect to masculinity, anthropologists and ethnographers concur in their observations that it appears in most cultures as something to be acquired, achieved and initiated into – often involving painful rites and rituals.

This can be made clearer through Bourdieu's theory of habitus. Habitus, as he defined them, are: 'systems of durable, transposable *dispositions,* structured structures predisposed to function as structuring structures, that is, as principles of the generation and structuring of practices and representations which can be objectively "regulated" and "regular" without in any way being the product of obedience to rules . . .' (Bourdieu 1977: 72). I am here focusing on war veterans' habitual inclination to being treated with honour as valorous men. Their habitual practice thus refers to a disposition which emphasizes the special place of the body in Bourdieu's elaboration of habitus, which gives prominence to mastery of the body (Bourdieu 1977). For Bourdieu 'dispositions' are 'cultivated' through interaction with 'a whole symbolically structured environment', and these 'cultivated dispositions' become 'inscribed in the body schema and in schemes of thought'.[21]

Thus, my context of the notion of honour is clarified by Bourdieu's reference to the Kabyle 'sense of "honour"', a phrase that stresses the dual location of honour in the mind and in the flesh.[22] The mastery of the body is essentially the successful in-corporation (literally, the taking into the body) of particular social meanings, inculcated through various bodily disciplines oriented to mundane practices such as 'standing, sitting, looking, speaking, walking' (Cowan 1990). Thus veterans were predisposed to notions and behaviours of honour, whereby they expected to be regarded with honour and respect.

The merit and honour of war among fighters in most post-war societies, including Rome and Zimbabwe, to a certain extent, determined the distribution of land/rewards and indeed prescribed and influenced the attitudes and behaviours of the fighters (see Dio Cass. 41.28.1, 43.14.1, 48.9.1-2, App. *BC.* 1.9, 5.2.12, and Plut. *Ti. Gr.* 9.5). An example from a Rhodesian colony makes this claim more palpable. Some contents from a letter written by pioneer war veterans demanding their rewards for fighting to create the Rhodesian colony demonstrates circumstances that often push military veterans to stand for their honour.

> It is with pain and regret that we are *forced to stand up for our honor* and services rendered to this colony for the past 53 years. We shall be unworthy of our names and citizenship if we keep silent any longer. We have been waiting with patience for the authorities and public in general to recognize our sacrifices to this colony but so far it has been in vain and as we are seeing the sun of our lives set we feel aware that the dishonor and shame will be left on the land of our sacrifices. We now appeal to you as the representative of the King in this country to give us justice before we pass on . . .[23] (my italics)

The notion of heroism in the first-century BC Roman Republic was deployed by veterans as a strategy to claim land rewards. In fact, leaders of veterans found themselves trapped into shouldering the responsibility of providing for their men's welfare. This precarious situation obtained on account of the demands or strictures implicit in the notion of honour. Claims for honour had to do with previously made promises. Appian recorded that soldiers demanded the cities which had been selected for them before the war as prizes for their valour (App. *BC.* 5.2.12). Failure to provide the acreage promised to one's band of fighters would have meant a breach of the code of honour. Cicero described the extravagant promises of Antony to his veterans, promises of town houses and acreage wherever they preferred (Cic. *Phil.* 8.9).

It follows that generals earned honour by keeping promises. The Roman Senate lost the support of Julius Caesar's veterans by reneging on the promise they had made to pay them after they defeated Antony. The young Caesar, Octavian, to keep his honour, and hence to safeguard his ambition of becoming the strongest man in Roman politics, became a ruthless plunderer, in order to pay the veterans. Suetonius says (my italics):

> After the capture of Perusia he took vengeance on many, meeting all attempts to beg for pardon or to make excuses with the one reply, 'You must die.' Some write that three hundred men of both orders were selected from the prisoners of war and sacrificed on the Ides of March like so many victims at the altar raised to the Deified Julius. Some have written that he took up arms of a set purpose, to unmask his secret opponents and those whom fear rather than good-will kept faithful to him, by giving them the chance to follow the lead of Lucius Antonius; and then by *vanquishing them and confiscating their estates* to pay the rewards promised to his veterans.
>
> Suet. *Aug.* 15, Rolfe 1913: 137–9

Also in keeping with his veteran alliance, which had enabled him to rise to power Octavian '. . . abandoned the cause of the nobles without hesitation, alleging as a pretext for his change of allegiance the words and acts of certain of their number, asserting that some had called him a boy, while others had openly said that he ought to be honoured and got rid of, to escape the necessity of making suitable recompense to him or to his veterans.' (Suet. *Aug.* 12, Rolfe 1913: 141). Octavian claimed to fight and free the state, but another objective was: '. . . to strive for the *honours* of my father.' (my italics) (Cic. *Att.* 16.16.3).

To appreciate this view, we may refer to Pitt-Rivers' observation that honour is a sentiment that is manifest in conduct, which then is evaluated by others, thus yielding reputation (Pitt-Rivers 1968: 505). As William Miller noted:

> . . . in an honor-based culture there was no self-respect independent of the respect of others . . . unless it was confirmed publicly. Honor was then not just a matter of the individual; it necessarily involved a group, and the group included all those people worthy of competing with you for honor.
>
> Miller 1993: 116

According to Gilmore, honour encompasses the entirety of masculine components of public reputation (Gilmore 1987: 126). Honour is both internal to the individual and external to him – a matter of his feelings, his behaviour, and the respect he receives (Pitt-Rivers 1968: 505). These aspects of behaviour may be related in such a way that honour felt becomes honour claimed, and honour claimed becomes honour paid (ibid.). In competing for precedence, one needs power to defend one's honour (Pitt–Rivers 1968). It is one's sense of honour that often drives one to acquire the instruments of power in the first place (ibid.).

Ideals of honour had a powerful material impact on the lives of veterans. Notions of honour were central not only in the working of a veteran-masculinity in both societies, but also in the dynamics of power relationships between generals and their forces. The following passage from Seneca sheds a light on this point:

> But the truly wise man and the aspirant to wisdom will use different remedies. For those who are not perfected and still conduct themselves in accordance with public opinion must bear in mind that they have to dwell in the midst of injury and insult; all misfortune will fall more lightly on those who expect it. The more honorable a man is by birth, reputation, and patrimony, the more heroically he should bear himself, remembering that the tallest ranks stand in the front battle-line. Let him bear insults, shameful words, civil disgrace, and all other degradation as he would the enemy's war-cry, and the darts and stones from afar that rattle around a soldier's helmet but cause no wound. Let him endure injuries, in sooth, as he would wounds — though some blows pierce his armor, others his breast, never overthrown, nor even moved from his ground. Even if you are hard pressed and beset with fierce violence, yet it is a disgrace to retreat; maintain the post that nature assigned you. Do you ask what this may be? The post of a hero.
>
> Basore n.d.

The above passage demonstrates the importance of notions of honour among military men, and also spells out some characteristics of such men as they posed as heroes in society. A veteran would always try to distinguish himself from a new recruit, to prove that he had earned his honour. Veterans developed a masculinity distinctive from that of new recruits by heroicizing their masculinity. Cicero made some incisive observations regarding some of the qualities that distinguished a veteran from a new recruit, involving for example the ability to endure pain or to despise wounds (my italics):

> Why is it that there is this sensible difference between a *raw recruit and a veteran soldier*? The age of the young soldiers is for the most part in their favor; but it is practice only that enables men to bear labor and despise wounds. Moreover, we often see, when the wounded are carried off the field, the raw, untried soldier, though but slightly wounded, cries out most shamefully; but the more brave, *experienced veteran* only inquires for someone to dress his wounds . . .
>
> Cic. *Tusc.* 2.16, Yonge 2005

> But this precept which is laid down with respect to pain is not confined to it. We should apply this exertion of the soul to everything else. Is anger inflamed? is lust excited? we must have recourse to the same citadel, and apply to the same arms. But since it is pain which we are at present discussing, we will let the other subjects alone. To bear pain, then, sedately and calmly, it is of great use to consider with all our soul, as the saying is, how noble it is to do so, for we are naturally desirous (as I said before, but it cannot be too often repeated) and very much inclined to what is *honorable*, of which, if we discover but the least glimpse, there is nothing which we are not prepared to undergo and suffer to attain it. From this impulse of our minds, this desire for genuine glory and honorable conduct, it is that such dangers are supported in war, and that brave men are not sensible of their wounds in action, or, if they are sensible of them, *prefer death to the departing but the least step from their honor*. The Decii saw the shining swords of their enemies when they were rushing into the battle. But the honorable character and the glory of the death which they were seeking made all fear of death of little weight. Do you imagine that Epaminondas groaned when he perceived that his life was flowing out with his blood? No; for he left his country triumphing over the Lacedaemonians, whereas he had found it in subjection to them. These are the comforts, these are the things that assuage the greatest pain.
>
> Cic. *Tusc.* 2.24, Yonge 2005

Seneca (Sen. *Of Consolation: To Helvia* 3, Stewart 2021. [1900]) also explored the theme in a way that clarifies the distinction insofar as the disposition of a veteran and a new recruit were concerned::

> The last wound is, I admit, the severest that you have ever yet sustained: it has not merely torn the skin, but has pierced you to the very heart: yet as recruits cry aloud when only slightly wounded, and shudder more at the hands of the surgeon than at the sword, while veterans even when transfixed allow their hurts to be dressed without a groan, and as patiently as if they were in someone else's body, so now you ought to offer yourself courageously to be healed. Lay aside lamentations and wailings, and all the usual noisy manifestations of female sorrow: you have gained nothing by so many misfortunes, if you have not learned how to suffer. Now, do I seem not to have spared you? nay, I have not passed over any of your sorrows, but have placed them all together in a mass before you.

## Conclusion

This chapter has explored the connection of masculinity, patriarchy, heroic honour, land ownership through expropriation and war in ancient Rome and Zimbabwe. Past war experiences and glories, in conjunction with cultural beliefs regarding what it means to be a man, have the effect of building the veteran up to larger-than-life proportions. There is a definite honour associated with masculinity. Such an aggrandized picture of the war veteran determines the ways in which war veterans position themselves in society, and how in turn the veterans mediate their masculine dispositions. In addition, the comparison of human feelings of dispossession and the cultural responses to landlessness in societies separated by two millennia reveal how a sense of masculinity is tied up with ownership or retention of land.

The chapter has also examined cross-cultural dynamics, involving notions and beliefs surrounding how manhood was attained in traditional African societies and in ancient Rome, laying emphasis on the concept of an adult-masculinity and how the concept helps in shedding light on land ownership in the two societies (cf. Morrell 2006). I have noted that although veterans and their generals in both societies had more power because of their soldierly bodies and the material resources of their profession, like weapons, this power was not wholly adequate. Of course, bodies and weapons served as 'resources', to use the terminology of Connell (Connell 1995), by which masculinity was constructed and enacted. However, after the end of wars in which they fought, war veterans still felt unmanly as long as they did not own a piece of land or a means of livelihood. And because of their wounds too, discourses on masculinity and effeminacy emerged.

Since war veterans develop a self-imagination with a disposition to violent claims to land, the following chapter explores how that behaviour sometimes exceeds limits or boundaries by exhibiting a certain 'madness' that characterizes violent actions of expropriation. Such behaviour of war veterans in the two societies raises the question of whether their 'madness' was provoked by war or by ideals of masculinity in the context of expropriation.

# 4

# Warfare-madness, Violence and Expropriation

> *On every side they brandished their swords, and menaced the centurions and tribunes at one moment, the whole Senate at another. Their minds were maddened by a blind panic, and, unable to single out any one object for their fury, they sought for indiscriminate vengeance.*
>
> Tacit. *Hist.* 1.82, Hadas 1942: 468–9

## Introduction

The Thirty Years' War (1618–48) was infamous for its avaricious bands of mercenary soldiers, who laid waste to entire regions searching for bounty (Stearns 2012: 367). In Africa, incidents of rape and killings during the Congolese war[1] and the Rwandan genocidal civil war (1994) are a matter of historical record (Stearns 2012: 31, 366). We may reference here the horrendous eye witness accounts of white farmers and ordinary Zimbabweans who suffered gruesome violence at the hands of Zimbabwe's guerrilla veterans (Barker 2007; Buckle 2001). My reading of equally impenetrable horrors of violence and murders in Lucan's account of the civil war between Caesar and Pompey creates images of soldiers plagued by warfare 'madness'. I investigate how armed madness may be framed in terms of the political economy of masculinity.

In the previous chapter I raised the question of the violent behaviour that the self-imagination of veterans was likely to cause in society. To address the question of the violent mad behaviour of military veterans, this chapter focuses on the horror of violence, examining war veterans' disposition to violence, to explore whether their masculinities were inherently 'mad,' or whether the 'madness' was instigated by war in the context of expropriation in ancient Rome and Zimbabwe. 'Madness' here refers to, among other things, unbridled anger, forms of inexplicable violent action, fanatical and crazed disposition to violent behaviour.

Is the 'madness' of warfare linked to behaviour driven by masculinity? To what extent does a 'madness' of warfare complicate or clarify our efforts to understand episodes of expropriation in the two military contexts? I therefore aim to interpret and analyse Roman texts relating to madness in wartime, contrasting Roman narratives with narratives of violent madness from a modern military context, to gauge the extent to which the madness of warfare in military contexts of expropriation can be productive of images and meanings of masculinity and gender.

I start off the present task by examining the role of combat qualities of former soldiers and how these qualities affect civilians in post-war situations. Using the ancient Roman notions of *intentio* and *ferocia* as ideas that can help explain violence by veterans even in a modern post-war society, I proceed to explore the relationship of masculinity and a certain 'madness' of war that characterize the two worlds of veterans.

## Combat qualities

Hannah Arendt spells out the dangers and unpredictability of human actions (Arendt 1988). The numerous processes set off by human initiative can easily rage out of control. What more the dangers and unpredictability of actions initiated by military men? As an example of this, we may point out that a single war veteran's actions or a group of them can set things in motion without anyone foreseeing the effects of their initiatives, let alone controlling what happens when their initiatives get entangled with other groups' initiatives. Tacitus frequently terms common soldiers a *vulgus*, a mob prone to irrationality as well as avarice and violence (Phang 2008: 156). Hannah Arendt's view allows us to question the place of collective ideologies of masculinity in explaining behaviour characterized by a certain 'madness' of military veterans which they exhibited in expropriation and violence. I explore how this 'madness' had to do, in each case, with collective emotions, ideologies, culture, greed and grievance, thereby providing a perspective on the soldier's life during the instability of war and post-war situations (cf. Kalyvas 2006).

Well trained soldiers in ancient Rome demonstrated a high degree of *impetus* (onslaught, energy) in combat – qualities which were deployed against Roman citizens during and beyond the immediate aftermath of battles for supremacy, and were hard to distinguish from *furor* (madness) and *ira* (rage) (Phang 2008). Referring to the political and social economy of Roman soldiers, Phang observed that: '*disciplina* inculcated a masculine *habitus* into soldiers through a general disposition of the body and mind, and promoted a state of *intentio* or "readiness" that powered soldiers as fighters ... Also instilled in Roman soldiers was individual motivation that formed an individual *habitus*. Individual *habitus* internalized courage and aggression/*ferocia*.' (Phang 2008: 8, 46). This aggression tended to manifest itself when least expected. A good example was the Campus Martius incident of a confrontation between Octavian and his troops described by Appian as follows (my italics):

> Having been called, about that time, to the Campus Martius *for a division of the land*, they came in haste while it was still night, and they grew angry because Octavian delayed his coming. Nonius, a centurion, chided them with considerable freedom, urging decent treatment of the commander by the commanded, and saying that the cause of the delay was Octavian's illness, not any disregard of them. They first jeered at him as a sycophant; then, as the excitement waxed hot on both sides, they reviled him, threw stones at him, and pursued him when he fled. Finally he plunged into the river and they pulled him out and killed him and threw his body into the road where Octavian was about to pass along. So the friends of Octavian advised him not to go among them, but to keep out of the way of their *mad career* (μανιώδει φορᾳ). But he went forward, thinking that their *madness* (τὸ μανιῶδες) would be augmented if he did not come.
>
> App. *BC*. 5.16, White 1913: 403–5

Greek words μανιώδει φορᾳ and τὸ μανιῶδες for madness are forms of μανιώδης meaning mad or literally 'like a madman' (Liddell and Scott 1889). Thus, aggression or brutality was the spirit that Roman soldiers cultivated. In the passage above, the madness of Octavian's soldiers was linked to the division of land and other rewards which Octavian later distributed to his fighters. This brutality and *intentio* had consequences also on aristocratic estates and properties which were expropriated. The Roman *intentio* can be illustrated by referring to violent dispositions among Zimbabwe's guerrilla veterans.

The following section explores how the Roman notions of *intentio* and *ferocia* can be explained by viewing the violent dispositions of guerrilla veterans of Zimbabwe. From the late Roman Republic onward, the *ira* or *ferocia* of soldiers was associated with mutiny, civil strife, and civil war (Phang 2008: 47). This behaviour was associated with a certain 'madness' and a violent masculinity linked to the payment of rewards to soldiers in the form of land, money or booty etc. Livy (28.24.8), recounting the story of a mutiny of Scipio's soldiers in Spain, observed: *Flagitatum quoque stipendium procacius quam ex more et modestia militari erat* (As a result, the pay was demanded in a manner more empty-headed than what suited the custom and modesty of a soldier).[2] The 8,000 soldiers of Scipio at Sucro, as Livy presented it, mutinied due to a predisposition to fighting and looting, which they were not able to do due to the peace prevailing at the time. I therefore argue that one way of explaining expropriations is to view them as a manifestation of contagious 'madness' among veterans, but a 'madness' which must be viewed in the light of masculinity and gender. The victims of the violence and madness of Roman soldiers found in Lucan reveal significant aspects of the Roman client-army soldiers' involvement in such acts. Fagan observed that 'ancient anecdotes and fiction can act as mirrors that reflect social attitudes, assumptions and realities, even if the immediate context is highly dubious or even fantastical.' (Fagan 2011: 469–70). I would argue that like the themes of hyper-masculinity and violence seen in modern Zimbabwe, Lucan's work reflects the civil war violence committed by Caesar's men. Zimbabwean guerrilla examples allow analysis of the tumultuous and fervid passions and actions of fighters which may be useful to re-imagining the Roman textual narratives.

## The notions of *intentio* and *ferocia* as reflected among Zimbabwean veterans

There is an African proverb which goes: 'Anger and madness are brothers!' Zimbabwe's guerrilla fighters were never fully demobilized after the independence war of the 1960s and 70s. Poor, hungry and angry, the veterans were ever ready for re-mobilization, in line with their ideological and political values in Mugabe's scheme of things. Since land expropriation in Zimbabwe was characterized by a radical and deeply rooted nativist economic nationalism (Ndlovu-Gatsheni and Willems 2009: 945) which had emerged from the liberation war, the theme of *intentio* played out clearly. The guerrilla veterans positioned themselves as 'soldiers posing on parade' (Mlambo 2018: 172) and resorted to military occupation tactics to expel white farmers from their farms. Since white farmers remained on the farms even after independence, guerrilla fighters believed that they were at war with the white farmers.

*Ferocia* is also visible in guerrilla veterans behaviour. Visual images in the Zimbabwean media can demonstrate the manifestation, through a warlike madness, of gender ideals and a violent masculinity, a view which is heuristically useful in viewing madness among Roman veterans.

Figures 3 and 4 show a manifestation of the madness of warfare of guerrilla veterans, which left a trail of destruction on many farms. This kind of madness has been variously revealed through the lens of the media. In the global media,

**Figure 3** Guerrilla veterans invading Liz McClelland's farm in Redacre Raffingora, Zimbabwe, in 2000. Peter Jordan via Alamy.

**Figure 4** The burning car of slain Zimbabwean farmer Martin Olds is left outside his farm in Namyandlovu some 50 kilometres (31 miles) west of Bulawayo, Zimbabwe, on 18 April 2000. A group of some forty armed war veterans attacked Olds' farm on 18 April 2000, killing Martin Olds as he tried to escape his burning farm. Costa Manzini/AFP via Getty Images.

the guerrilla veterans were made to fit the stereotype of thugs and criminals (Smiley and Fakunle 2016). To be fair, the contested images of the war veterans were being played out in both the domestic and global media. On the domestic front, some critics and newspapers projected negative images of the guerrilla veterans (Willems 2004). They were presented as bloodthirsty, rugged and dangerous. However, the state-sponsored media celebrated the guerrilla veterans as masculine, brave, principled and inspired individuals who were taking back land from former colonizers.

The dominant narrative was of the chaos and terror that the guerrilla veterans were wreaking on the commercial farms. The guerrilla veterans were depicted as marauding beasts who were hounding white women and children off their lands, while assaulting and murdering their husbands. In some instances, there 'were sympathies extended to kinsmen affected by the violence,' (Ndlela 2005: 81) and this influenced the way in which events were covered. Of course, the guerrilla veterans themselves were quite willing to feed this particular narrative. In some instances they set up imaginary roadblocks with the sign, 'War Veterans Ahead'. The idea was to portray the war veterans as members of a fiery and unrelenting and ubiquitous movement.

In the dominant independent media coverage, the guerrilla veterans were presented as a real threat to the lives of white farmers, as well as to the economic well-being of the country. They were cast as hungry, not knowledgeable about farming, and instigating disaster for Zimbabwe. The narrative of guerrilla fighters as threatening and intimidating had a negative impact on tourism and other sectors of the economy (Zhou 2010). Overall, the guerrilla veterans were associated with danger, aggression and economic collapse.

The purpose of my examination of visual images of the guerrilla veterans' mad and violent dispositions is to build my imaginative reconstruction of Julius Caesar's Pharsalus fighters as depicted by Lucan. I argue that built within certain social manifestations of masculinity is a certain strand of madness – a transgression of boundaries or an extreme expression of behaviour that can be linked with murder, sexuality, wanton expropriation – themes that dominate Lucan's *De Bello Civili*. I thus examine the role of masculinity and the madness of war in contexts of expropriation. Images of violent madness from another society are not necessarily counter-intuitive in our efforts to put into perspective what ancient terminologies such as *ferocia* and *intentio* meant in their Roman setting and context. These images are in my case used as aids to re-imagine Caesar's ferocious men. The images enhance my re-imagination of what a mad veteran looked like, and the actions he is likely to have performed.

I proceed with an examination of experiences of guerrilla veterans in Zimbabwe which transformed them into violent men with animalistic tendencies.

## Wantonness and madness among Zimbabwean war veterans

Having detailed notions of madness and masculinity in ancient Rome and how the Zimbabwean context of veterans could be analytically beneficial to an understanding of the Roman context, this section examines the Zimbabwean world of veterans, in much detail, vis-à-vis notions of madness, masculinity and a disposition to violence and confiscation.

The beginning of this wanton behaviour may be attributed to expectations for rewards of valour after the liberation war. This expectation was motivated by greed, anger and grievance. An interview granted by one veteran who preferred to be called Wevhu (not his real name, and which means son of the soil) revealed that veterans were sometimes motivated by promises of mansions belonging to white men during the war of liberation. Thus white men were proscribed by nationalist leaders, something which actually materialized 20 years after the liberation war. A similar situation as happened in Rome. Appian recorded that the rich were proscribed because they had handsome villas (App. *BC.* 4.5). He also tells us that '. . . the soldiers demanded the cities which had been selected for them before the war.' (App. *BC.* 5.2, 12). Such anecdotes find resonance with what the guerrilla veteran revealed in an interview. He spoke thus:

> We knew about the beautiful farms and mansions. I was a commander of a section of guerilla fighters during the liberation war. Part of the promises that motivated my men included land redistribution, and of course the open encouragement for our men to take whatever they could take from the white men.[3]

One veteran, Mabhunumuchapera (a code name which literally means 'White men you will all perish'), remembered how, during the war, they used to send the *anamujibha* (baggage carriers) to raid cattle from surrounding white men's farms, which they slaughtered for meat.

> We frustrated the enemy. We took the enemy's wealth during the war. We told ourselves that after the war we were going to take more cattle for ourselves and for our parents and relatives. This third *Chimurenga, chikomana* (young man), is the fulfilment of the promise. We have indeed taken not only the land but also

> the cattle of our ancestors which the white farmer had appropriated. *Hauzvizivi here kuti zvinhu zvose ndezvambuya* Nehanda (Do you not know that all things belong to our ancestors? (literally Grandmother Nehanda).[4]

I asked him why they took the cattle which did not belong to them. He retorted:

> *Iye murungu paakauya munyika medu muno akauya nen'ombe here? Akabva nen'ombe kumhiri kwemakungwa here? Ko minda yavakarima vakabva nayo kumusha kwavo here?Ucharangarira here* (the Ndebele war of dispossession? They dispossessed us because Rhodes was bragging that they had the maxim gun and we did not.) *Takatora minda ende ticharamba tichitora. VaMugabe vanogarotaura wani kuti ndizvo zvatakarwira.* (Did the white man bring any cattle here? Did he bring the land from abroad? We took the farms and we are not going back. Mugabe always says that we fought for the land).'[5]

I also extracted some information from the life history of one veteran, which can shed some light on this issue of promises. He wrote:

> I was not part of those who invaded farms but I got my plot after the fast track land reform program. I understand why my colleagues did what they did because at the time and even now no one cared how we fared as guerrilla veterans. All we had were promises we were given when the war ended. So it was time to take the task of rewarding ourselves into our own hands though at times I regret the violence that occurred when it happened, but it was necessary.[6]

In Zimbabwe, war veterans appropriated their hero status in wanton militant form devoid of any discipline. This is captured in many songs that were performed during the post-2000 mobilization crusades. The songs are a typical performance of madness, and they justify the guerrilla veterans' access to the spoils of war in the form of land, money and other rewards. One such a song goes: '*Mukaona ma war vets achitora minda, mukaona VaMugabe vachitora minda, ndicho chitenderano naVaMugabe*' (When you see war veterans expropriating the land, it is a fulfilment of the promise between them and Robert Mugabe). This is also captured in another song loaded with words of masculinity and violence. The song goes: '*Mbiri yechigandanga ndiyo mbiri yatinayo*' 'The glory of brutality is our fame'. War veterans were very wanton and were never brought to book for their behaviour. In another song, the war veterans warn civilians to be warry of their violence lest it visits them. The song goes thus: '*Chenjera, chenjera, vanamukoma vanorova, chenjera, Vanorova nematanda chenjera chenjera …*' 'Beware of guerrilla fighters, they beat with logs, Beware

Beware . . .' On top of beating civilians, guerrilla veterans also boasted of their greedy and a sharp appetite for meat in a song which goes: '*Gandanga haridye derere mukoma haridye derere, gandanga haridye derere mukoma, rinorutsa!*' 'A Guerrilla does not eat okra, it causes him to vomit!' The performance of such songs served a purpose of justifying the veteran's access to the spoils of war. The songs served to summon combat-related masculinities, providing the war veterans with an opportunity for generating fresh militant masculinity to brutalize their victims and to get what they wanted (Chitando and Tarusarira 2017). While these songs sum up the mentality of guerrilla war veterans, it must be stressed that their irrational behaviour of wantonly beating up people also tapped on combat-related masculinity.

Zimbabwe's guerrilla fighters experienced severe trauma during the war. Blessing-Miles Tendi described an account of a ZANLA commander Josiah Magama Tongogara's bruxism which appeared to have been brought on by a series of traumatic incidents during the war (Tendi 2020: 97). In an interview with Felix Muchemwa quoted by Tendi, Tongogara would walk around slapping his forehead very hard and grinding his teeth, while talking to an imaginary person he thought wanted to kill him (ibid.). During land invasions in the 2000, the same guerrillas committed rape and murder as has been documented in Human Rights reports (Meredith 2002). This mad behaviour has continued as most guerrilla veterans in recent years have not shown an inclination towards peaceful behaviour (Maringira 2017). In some respects, the guerrilla veteran's madness is an external physical expression of the conflict within, which his return from war causes in him – spilling over of his inner bitterness as he lashes out indiscriminately in a trance. This violent disposition is an essential part of his character and make-up. The following narratives contextualize the madness.

It was narrated to me that near Bindura town in Northern Zimbabwe, a guerrilla veteran came across a ZANU-PF political mob assaulting a suspected Movement for Democratic Change (MDC) supporter – a political party whose supporters were accused of not supporting land occupations by the guerrilla fighters. Symbolically, the war veteran saw in this MDC supporter a reincarnation of the colonial/Rhodesian soldier and decided to remobilize and to marshal his masculinity towards conquering his victim. The oral testimony of an eye witness reveals a gruesome act of violence that one can only expect to see in a vampire movie – a result of a madness of warfare and its manifestation in situations when military men unleashed violence as a means to fight to get what they wanted. The oral testimony goes thus:

> This particular veteran had been injured during the war of liberation in a gun battle. The community knew that he had a bullet lodged in his body. Doctors had actually told him that the bullet could not be extracted from his body because it sat precariously close to one of his ribs. So he had lived in misery ever since. Upon finding ZANU-PF supporters assaulting the said victim, the ex-soldier got very excited. He actually cried out, '*Sudurukai. Imbomirai kumurova neshamhu. Ndoda kuita wekuruma nemazino angu kuti anzwe kurwadza kwandinoita ini zvangu pachangu.*' / Move over, you guys and stop hitting this fellow with sjamboks! I want to bite him with my teeth. I actually want him to feel how painful I am!' Upon which the guerilla veteran knelt down and unstrapped the trousers of the MDC supporter and brought it down and proceeded to bite the victim's buttocks, spitting out chunks of buttock flesh and biting again . . . This time not spitting out! He was eventually restrained by the rowdy members of ZANU-PF who found this act rather weird.[7]

By removing his victim's trousers the war veteran was, matter-of-factly, emasculating his victim. This act demonstrates what masculinity is about. It is about being the top dog, as well as *kurwadza* (to be felt and to be known to cause pain and to dominate one's victim). This and related violent behaviour by veterans reveal how they marked and conquered their territory, leaving a mark on the bodies of their victims and in communities to signify command.

Then there are also stories that have widely circulated in many social circles in Zimbabwe. The stories are about guerrilla veterans (supported by members of the Zimbabwe National Army)[8] during the 2008 presidential run-off campaign[9] who went around capturing MDC supporters and asking them, 'Do you want long or short sleeved shirt?' If the victim said, short sleeve, then the guerilla veterans were said to hack off the victim's arm. If the victim said, long sleeve, then they chopped off the victim's wrists. Godfrey Maringira's anthropological historical survey (Maringira 2017), demonstrated that some post-independence soldiers (except for generals – who were liberation war fighters – and other partisan commanders who publicly supported Mugabe and ZANU-PF) who are not veterans of the liberation struggle (the more recent recruits) were professionals who refused to be used by Mugabe and his ZANU-PF party to violate civilians. Maringira's findings validate to some extent my submission that liberation guerrilla veterans developed a distinct masculinity and mentality over time – quite different to that of post-independence soldiers.

Having discussed the dangerous effects to society of mad and marauding guerrilla fighters, I move on to examine a wide variety of Roman texts. I argue that issues of rape, desecration of temples, killings and expropriation mentioned in such sources can be placed in real life contexts as extraordinary occurrences during and after the war. The purpose of this endeavour is to demonstrate that notions of masculinity and warfare-madness in first-century BC Roman Republic were aspects of behaviour and actions of client-armies experienced by the communities of their times. That such acts of violent madness are a historical factuality in historical and existing post-war contexts allows us to perceive the Roman narratives and anecdotes as part of a cultural discourse of violence. My interpretation mainly of Lucan's passages in the following section is an attempt to give the actions of Roman client-armies a reading informed by masculinity and gender discourses. This perspective allows for an appreciation of the history of client-armies to have been not just about politics and military power, but that it was also about the impact of Roman soldiers' madness on society at large. The following section attempts to make meaning of the grim detail of acts of rape, murder and desecration of temples and destruction of cities found in Lucan's *De Bello Civili.*

## A 'madness' of warfare in ancient Roman texts

This section is an investigation of the 'madness' of warfare in Lucan's epic poetry. Ancient Roman texts are replete with narratives of a madness of war. Polybius (1.37, 6.52) depicts Roman soldiers' violence as motivated by anger. The boundary between soberness and a certain impulsiveness to violent behaviour can be very thin in military contexts. I may refer here to the example of Pompey's disposition as recorded by Plutarch (my italics):

> He [Caesar] asked the people whether they approved of his laws and, when they said they did, he called upon them to give him their help and to defend him against those who were threatening to resist him with their swords. This they promised to do, and Pompey actually added that, if it was a question of swords, he could produce a sword and a shield as well. The nobility were deeply offended by this mad and *boyishly* impulsive remark of Pompey's . . . the people, however, were delighted with it.
>
> Plut. *Caes.* 14, Warner 1958: 256–7

Pompey's reaction is said by Plutarch to be boyish. The meaning here is of impulsiveness, like a kid who does things on the spur of the moment without thinking.[10] The observation I make is that during the processes of performing masculinity, the performer may sometimes exhibit or betray puerile characteristics. The crossing of the boundary between a masculinity performed by an adult and that of a juvenile shows that masculinity performances may manifest a similar energy in different forms. What we can see is an army general behaving like a juvenile with the potential of deadly consequences to civilians. Although as Pompey was poised to exhibit aggressive behaviour to get land for his veterans, his reaction in this case may not be interpreted as a 'macho' stance since his reaction is said by Plutarch to be boyish (μανικὴν καὶ μειρακιώδη φωνὴν = mad and boyish discourse). Pompey's behaviour reveals a combination of traits of madness and masculinity. He exhibited an infantile reflex, deficient of self-control – rendering a reading of the passage taking masculinity along with madness more suitable.

Lucan's *De Bello Civili* insinuates rape and murder during the civil war between Caesar and Pompey. Such cases bring to the fore the relationship between masculinity and crime (Messerschmidt 1993; Meredith 2002). Lucan showed how men have risen beyond the limits of legal power (Luc. 2.175f., 2.565)[11] and, especially in the case of Caesar, advocate their own ability to create legality out of crime (Luc. 2.203).[12] Efrossini Spentzou (2018: 268) calls this Caesar's contagious sublime excess, which everything and everyone in touch with him was 'absolved from limits'. Through an examination of Lucan's *De Bello Civili*, supported by historical texts from across different contexts it is possible to explore the interface between masculinity and a veteran behaviour characterized by unreasoning furor and blind rage (see Woodman 2006; Saddington 2009). There are numerous medical metaphors in modern society about violence as a symptom of "social pathology," violence as a "disease" that "is difficult to predict" that comes in convulsions, spasms, and seizures (Kalyvas 2006: 33). Contagious madness is also captured in Sallust's description of Catiline's mental condition in physical terms (Sall. *Cat.* 15.4-5) – the Catilinarian conspiracy was described by Sallust as a vile pestilence. Cicero's description of Saxa and Cafo (Antony's veterans) as country boors (Cic. *Phil.* 10.22) captures the barbaric nature of a madness associated with the actions of Antony's men. Ancient historians have mentioned this sort of behaviour; we have noted that Plutarch referred to Pompey's speech as mad and boyish (Plut. *Caes.* 14, Warner 1958: 256–7).

Livy, for instance, referred to the mutiny at Sucro as a result of a plague of mental disorder (Aranita 2009: 36). Appian's Campus Martius incident mentioned earlier, involving the division of land for Octavian's soldiers, is also revealing of this aspect of a behaviour of madness. A close examination of Lucan's *De Bello Civili* also reveals profound facets of military brutality that can be augmented. The grim detail that Lucan dramatically portrays is typical material that catalogues the mad behaviours of soldiers in and outside combat situations. The manner in which Lucan's poetry inserts itself into domains where military violence was carried out, domains where acts of wanton rape and desecration of temples were carried out, and where vulgar conversations among soldiers took place, reveals the penetrating and invasive nature of his poetry as a source of the historical reconstruction of military life – a broad and deep approach to events which cannot normally be found in other sources. Lucan's poetry causes its readers to imagine; and I argue that the imaginary re-creates the real. This aspect gives depth to historical analysis. Thus, drawing upon Kirstein's (2017: 191, 195) interpretation of the text as part of a cultural discourse on violence, I ascribe a literary and metaphorical interpretation of gender to behaviour driven by an armed madness.

The kind of behaviour described in Lucan manifested itself in most cases as a problem of ill-discipline in the armies. It is in this context that insubordination is understood as contagious disease (Aranita 2009: 37). Plutarch ascribed the ill-discipline in the army to Sulla who corrupted his soldiers with excessive booty and allowed them to live in luxury *contra morem maiorum* (Plut. *Sull.* 12.7). A description of indiscipline of the Roman army in Africa (as they plundered farmlands and farmsteads, selling cattle and slaves for imported wine) was recorded by Sallust (*Iug.* 44) in what summarizes how *mos militaris* among soldiers had been eroded. This ill-discipline is dramatized by Lucan's words put in Julius Caesar's mouth: 'Deny a strong man (meaning his veterans) his due and he will take all he can get.' (Luc. 7.257-8).

In Lucan's account of the mutiny of Caesar's veterans at Placentia (Luc. 5.237ff, Graves 1956) it is possible to explore references to their disposition to a certain madness of warfare. In speculating on the cause of the mutiny, Lucan gives two possibilities:

> . . . seu maesto classica paulum
> intermissa sono claususque et frigidus ensis
> expulerat belli furias: seu praemia miles
> dum maiora petit damnat causamque ducemque,
> et scelere imbutos etiam nunc venditat enses.
>
> Luc. 5.244-248

> Either the leaving off of the trumpets with their sorrowful sound or the confined and frigid sword had expelled the madness of war; or the soldier, while he sought greater rewards, condemned both the general and his cause, and offered his crime-stained sword even now for sale.
>
> The Latin edition of Lucan used is that of Haskins 1887

The first possibility has connotations of martialism and masculinity. The trumpets and sword are alluded to, which form part of the atmosphere of war; and Lucan also mentions *furias* or madness, alluding to the feelings of violent warfare. But in the reference to *frigidus ensis* there seems to be some sexual symbolism. The term *frigidus* may be traditionally explained as *nullo sanguine calefactus* (warmed by no blood). Haskins (1887: 164) and Lewis and Short (1879: 780) interpret the phrase in this specific passage of Lucan as meaning 'inactive' or 'idle'; but *frigidus* is also a term related to sexual enthusiasm: Ovid refers to a *non frigida virgo*, a maiden 'glowing with love' (Lewis and Short 1879: 779). *Frigidus*, like the English *frigid*, refers to females who lack sexual enthusiasm. So the phrase *frigidus ensis* may be understood as connoting an effeminate state: the adjective is one applicable to women, and it suggests that the sexuality relating to the *ensis*, presumably a male sexuality, is chilled. The sexual overtones imply a view of war as masculine, and of refraining from war as feminine or effeminate.

The second possibility ventured is mercenary, suggesting that the veterans were holding out for greater financial compensation. The term *venditat* suggests that primarily financial rewards rather than rewards of valour are sought in the second of the alternative possibilities presented by Lucan. Yet there may be overtones of a martial ethic not wholly forgotten. The word *praemium*, reward, is related to *praeda*, meaning 'booty' so that its derivation suggests the booty of war (Lewis and Short 1879: 1423 cf. 1416). In Luc. 5.308 there is a reference to *praemia Martis*, the rewards of Mars, showing that the connection of *praemium* with war is not forgotten by Lucan.

## Sex, rape and the desecration of temples in Lucan (Luc. 5.305-308)

That the warlike feelings of the veterans might have a sexual aspect is suggested by 5.305-308:

> non illis urbes spoliandaque templa negasset
> Tarpeiamque Iovis sedem matresque senatus
> passurasque infanda nurus. volt omnia certe
> a se saeva peti, volt praemia Martis amari.
>
> Luc. 5:305-308

He would not have denied them cities and temples to spoil, and the Tarpeian seat of Jupiter, and the mothers and young women of the senate who would suffer unspeakable things. Certainly he was willing that all manner of savage things be sought of himself; he was willing that the rewards of Mars be loved.

In the translation of Graves (1956: 115), the unspeakable things to be suffered by the *matres senatus* and the *nurus* are understood as sexual; he uses the words, '... outrage the mothers and daughters of senators'. This seems to refer to acts of males on females, acts of violence associated with soldiers which are also expressive of masculinity.

We may note that certain other expressions in the passage seem to have sexual associations. The passage says Caesar 'would not have denied' his men various things; yet we may talk of a sexual desire being 'denied' or 'not denied'. In fact, the *matres* (mothers) and *nurus* (young women) suffering *infanda* are grammatically objects of *non . . . negasset* (would not have denied) along with the *urbes* (cities) and *templa* (temples), so that there is a sort of zeugma linking non-denial of women to soldiers with non-denial of objects of attack to soldiers. So *non negasset* signifies as one side of its double meaning the non-denial of women to soldiers for sexual purposes, and the fact that the same verb covers non-denial of women and cities/temples leaves open the possibility that the non-denial of women and of temples/cities are analogous.

The term *spolianda* (to spoil) is derived from the verb *spolio* which can mean to rob someone of clothing (Lewis and Short (1879: 1745); Lewis and Short cite examples where *spolio* can be applied to *pudicitiam* (shame) and *dignitatem* (dignity), and a use by Cicero of the phrase *spoliare et nudare* (to strip and denude), applied to monuments. So the word *spolianda* can have sexual connotations. The soldiers are not just attacking but 'stripping bare' cities and temples. The fact that *templa* are mentioned as well as *urbes* makes the spoliation an act of desecration insofar as it applies to temples. Polybius explains that laws of war oblige one to destroy the enemy's 'forts, harbors, cities, men, ships and crops, and other such things, by which one's opponents are weakened and one's own affairs and assaults are made more powerful and render such act just' (Polyb. 5.11.3); but the desecration of temples and statues of the gods without any advantage to oneself one can only call 'an act of insane temper and rage' (Polyb. 5.11.4).[13]

The following images are evoked by Lucan's words in order: spoiling, with the possible sexual connotation of stripping; desecration; non-denial, a concept with a possible sexual connotation; a girl, Tarpeia; then the mothers and young women of the senate; then, unspeakable sexual things. The sexual overtones are at first ambiguous and debatable, but then female images are brought in, followed by an obvious association with sexuality when Lucan speaks of *infanda*. It is as if there is a pattern of deeper sexual association.

In line with this pattern, we may ask whether *saeva* has a sexual association. *Saevus* is of course an adjective used with wild animals (Lewis and Short (1879: 1651); the connotations of the word are mostly of violence, but it may be pointed out that wild animals are not paragons of sexual discipline, so a certain whiff of sexuality may attach to *saeva* given the recent use of *infanda*. The *saeva* may be referring to the madness of war, *belli furias*, mentioned in Lucan. 5:246. Could there be a connection between madness and sexuality? We know from the story of Sophocles in Cicero that Sophocles viewed the sexual desire of his youth as a wild and furious master (*domino agresti ac furioso*) (Cic. *De. Sen.* 14.47, Falconer 1930). So wildness and fury had for Sophocles and Cicero an association with sexuality; and thus the term *saevus*, unmistakably connoting wildness and fury, may possibly connote sexuality.

Then comes the reference to *praemia Martis*, the rewards of Mars. Mars is the god of war; but, as we know from Homer's Odyssey, his rewards included sex with Aphrodite. So although the primary meaning here is that of the rewards of war, a possible sexual connotation is not absent. Finally, there is the word *amari*, to be loved; definitely a word associated with sex even in our modern culture. So the images or ideas of the passage present us with the following associations in order: despoiling, with possible sexual meaning; desecration; non-denial, with possible sexual meaning; a girl; mothers; young women; unspeakable sexual things; wildness and fury, with possible sexual meaning; rewards; a masculine war god with a mythological history involving adultery; and finally, love, with a possible sexual overtone. Some of the potentially sexual expressions, taken in isolation, might not have a clear sexual meaning; but the fact that these expressions are part of a sequence of ideas and images involving *infanda*, unspeakable things, raises the question of whether it is simply a coincidence that certain images can be sexually interpreted, or whether the sexual associations are related to the meaning of the *infanda* expression, and a theme of sexuality runs through the passage. Yet regardless of how far we can see sexual meaning in the passage, we may still see in the reference to *infanda* a sign of warlike spirit expressed in a masculine and sexual fashion, and argue that the martial attitude of war veterans is portrayed in Lucan as linked to masculine sexuality and masculine madness.

After the above-quoted passage in Lucan. 5.309 we have a phrase which likewise can be interpreted so as to link militarism with sexuality: *militis indomiti*, 'of an untamed soldier'. The term 'untamed' of course can apply both to warlike violence and to lust. In suggesting that there is a sexual meaning to 5.305–309, I am not suggesting that the sexual connotations are the only connotations. Warlike or violent imagery is certainly present here, and the hypothesis of a double association of the veterans with sex and violence in the passage is not to be ruled out.

Line 5.309 contains the phrase *mens sana*, a healthy mind, an expression which contrasts with the savagery of the passage. It also calls to mind another contrast, namely, the contrast in Stoic philosophy between the mind and the lusts of the body, between reason and passion. This is a contrast which is echoed in the writings of the historian Sallust, who speaks of the mind as the ruling element in us, shared with the gods and distinguishes it from the body, shared with the beasts (Handford 1963: 175), and who, having indicated that the soul is the guiding and controlling principle in humans, warns against allowing base desire to enslave it (ibid., 33). This may lead us to ask whether Lucan as a Roman is influenced by the Stoic idea which contrasts the reason with the passions. If he is, then the linkage of violence and sexual passion is not surprising, for both of these are 'passions' which Stoic philosophy alike seeks to eliminate.

Thus the reason why Lucan links violence with sexuality in his description of Caesar's veterans could be that he views both lust and violence in terms of the Stoic category of 'passion' and therefore links them together. So, although the association of violence and sexuality in Lucan's veterans seems at first sight to support the idea that the veterans of Caesar were inspired by a martial ideal linked with masculinity, there is need to ask whether Lucan's philosophical spectacles rather than the facts of history caused him to link violence and sexuality as he does. Or maybe there is an element of both history and philosophical interpretation. Where Lucan is concerned my conclusions remain open to nuances.

## Conclusion

In this chapter I explained the problem of the 'madness' of masculinity in Ancient Rome and Zimbabwe. Analysis of Lucan's texts revealed a lot of warfare violence, rape, desecration of temples and wanton destruction of property. I argued that a messy relationship between masculinity, warfare-madness and expropriation could explain such actions by veterans in the two societies. This warfare 'madness' is the total disregard for control, limit and decorum. The 'madness' is palpable in its unrestrained acting out of unbridled desire to accumulate and subjugate other men, women, wealth, land and power as the two societies have shown.

Using the two concepts of 'hegemonic' masculinity and 'homosociality', the following chapter explores the materialization of masculinity ideals in the two societies. I analyse the processes through which war veterans stuck together under their generals as men characterized by martial qualities for the achievement of material goals. The two concepts thus allow us to give nuances to the analysis of the working of masculinity among veterans and their leaders, with attention paid to their competition for land, power, honours and other rewards. The purpose of this endeavour is to explain power relations within and among groups of military men. The two concepts therefore seek to uncover more flexible meanings of masculinity of greater descriptive utility in discussing episodes of expropriation and violence in first-century BC Rome.

# 5

# Veterans and the Prize of Valour: Masculinity and the Homosocial Strategy

*The task of assigning the soldiers to their colonies and dividing the land was one of exceeding difficulty. For the soldiers demanded the cities which had been selected for them before the* war *as prizes for their valour . . .*

App. *BC*. 5.12, White 1913: 395

## Introduction

In the previous chapter, I focused on the behaviour of veterans as characterized by a madness of warfare. I gave an interpretation of masculinity and gender in relation to the mad behaviour of violence and expropriation revealed by comparative evidence in ancient Rome and Zimbabwe. Yet in the light of such a madness, it is easy to overlook the importance of masculinity in the fashioning of the relationships and activities of fighters and their leaders. This chapter considers masculinity as a category that in fact presided over the distribution of land and other rewards and the sharing of power between generals and their veterans.

I explore the complex interactive relationships of interdependence between client-army soldiers and their generals – relationships in which masculinity discourses massaged and challenged the troops' valorous self-imagination, at the same time constructing a real heroic world in which their fantasies were reconceived into realizable dreams[1] by the spurring of the troops into action in fighting for victory and its accompanying benefits. I apply the notion of what I call 'mythology of masculinity and domination'[2] to the relationship between a commander and his troops – through analysis not only of speeches but also of other bodily skills and qualities through which masculinity was expressible. Such an analysis allows for examination of the cultic figure of the general as a hero with many facets (cf. Campbell 2004).[3] Mary Beard (2007: 226) referred to an argument by Scheid and other scholars pointing to the oscillation of the general between divine and human status (Beard further cites Wissowa (1912: 126–8); Strong (1915 64–5) and Versnel (1970: 62), cf. Plut. *Ant.* 4. see also Martin 1987). The point of mentioning this example is not to suggest that this was a dominant motif in the portrayal of army generals of the late Roman Republic, so much as to show that masculinity in ancient Rome could be, to some degree, mythical.

I thus seek to make visible a world of power relationships between generals and their fighters, fashioned by masculinity discourses involving fighting, disputes for land and other rewards. I argue that client-army fighters' relationships with their general, and their predisposition to a mad violence, was governed by a masculine ethos through which they organized themselves in relationships defined by a martial ethic, fear, respect, conflict and ruptures to achieve their goals, material or non-material (see, for example, Tacit. *Hist.* 1.84).[4]

I also seek to explain the fighters' group solidarity using the concept of homosociality and hegemonic masculinity (see Connell 1995; Hinojosa 2010). The purpose of such an investigation is to discover how the fiction of masculinist identities among client-army veterans elided or reduced individual differences, and functioned in such a way as to prioritize group solidarity.[5] By contrasting the two societies of Rome and Zimbabwe, I seek to explore common factors and varied manifestations of masculinity among fighters and their generals, in environments where disagreements, struggles for power and rewards of war often threatened the existence of entire groups. I have a particular interest in what I call 'lateral' and 'vertical' masculinities.

The main purpose of this chapter is to demonstrate how masculinity functioned as a governing ethos among fighters and their leaders, and how this made transactions for rewards dynamic and complex. I only partially refer to relationships and activities of Zimbabwe's guerrilla veterans, for an explanatory analysis of the function of masculinity that could be applicable to the Roman situation – and I rely mostly on my interpretation of Roman texts to illustrate my argument.

## Defining homosociality and hegemonic masculinity

Minimally, my application of the term 'homosociality' exploits it as a concept to understand men's collective attempts to uphold and maintain power and hegemony – a power-seeking or power-retaining masculinity (Sedgwick 2015). It is a mechanism and social dynamic through which I seek to explain the maintenance of hegemonic masculinity by veterans, using comparative evidence from the client-army era and modern military situations. The concept of homosociality according to Hammaren and Johansson (2014: 2) refers to 'how men, through their relations with other men, tend to bond, build closed teams, and defend privileges and positions'. I seek to explore how this was the case with client-army soldiers. In research into hegemonic masculinity among men who were joining the American military, Hinojosa discovered that they regarded themselves as superior to other men.

> The men positioned themselves as more ... physically able, emotionally controlled, martially skilled ... than civilians, members of other branches, different occupational specialties, and of different rank. In claiming these characteristics as qualities possessed by themselves, pre-active duty service men construct a masculinity that is symbolically dominant over others.
>
> Hinojosa 2010: 179

Connell understood hegemonic masculinity as a cultural dynamic by which a group claims and sustains a leading position in social life (Connell 2005: 77)

My understanding of client-army soldiers is thus based on the manner in which they organized themselves as a social cohort, indifferent to certain property rights issues, guided by personal attachments and motivated by hopes of material benefits (Brunt 1962). Being members of the cohort community signalled a new self-consciousness among soldiers. Commenting on the status of the post-Marian army, Mommsen wrote: 'His only home was the camp, his only science war, his only hope the general.' (Mommsen 1895: 188). Veterans were commonly men who had lost their property or never possessed any. According to Brunt (1962: 75–6),

> ... they had little prospect of continuous and remunerative employment in civil life after discharge, and it is also clear from the conduct of the troops who served under Sulla, Pompey, Caesar and the dynasts who struggled for power after Caesar's death that veterans were apt to feel more loyalty to their commander than to whatever government could claim legitimate authority at Rome.

Veterans, in general, represent a special social group, since they are not only generally indigent,[6] once hostilities have ceased, but are also trained in war (cf. Dio Cass. 36.26.4) and often have group solidarity, to defend each other. An incident in Rome between Octavian and his veterans illustrates this point succinctly. Appian (*BC*. 5.15, White 1913: 401–3.) described the incident as follows (my italics):

> Once in the theatre when he was present, a soldier not finding his own seat, went and took one in the place reserved for the knights. The people pointed him out and Octavian had him removed. The soldiers were angry. They gathered around Octavian as he was going away from the theatre and demanded their comrade, for, as they did not see him, they thought that he had been put to death. When he was produced before them they supposed that he had been brought from prison, but he denied that he had been imprisoned and related what had taken place. They said that he had been instructed to tell a lie and reproached him for betraying their *common interests*.

This group solidarity almost always caused veterans to exercise their power to defend their interests and to dominate weaker groups in society. Conditions of poverty made them dangerous as they 'could be hooked indiscriminately by the political bait of either a Marius a Sulla or an Octavian.' (Gabba 1976: 27).

It was because of their group solidarity that Julius Caesar would not allow his veterans to settle in the immediate neighbourhood of the old landowners, to avoid 'hereditary enmity' between them (App. *BC*. 2.94). Suetonius also recorded that Julius Caesar avoided assigning land to his veterans side by side (Suet. *Div. Jul.* 38.1). The reason why Julius Caesar avoided settling his veterans in concentrated groups (preferring to settle them in small groups throughout Italy (Dio Cass. 42.54.1) was to prevent them from distressing their neighbours, and even from plotting revolts as happened during the reign of the emperor Tiberius (Tac. *Ann.* 4.27). The practice of violence seemed to have bound the veterans together. Each individual veteran formed a violent link in a chain, a part of the great structure of violence in society. Veterans had group identity and, as a social cohort, acted, when they could, in ways that promoted their hegemonic masculinities over weaker groups in society.

The section below on Zimbabwe makes clearer the logic of a violent link between individual veterans who form a group in society.

## Homosociality and hegemonic masculinity: The Zimbabwean context

I proceed now to a discussion of how homosociality and hegemonic masculinity operated among Zimbabwean guerrilla veterans, for the purpose of contrast with ancient Rome. In conformity with the basic nature of homosociality, veterans in Zimbabwe refer each other as fellow comrades. The word 'comrade' was used to refer to a fellow fighter in the liberation struggle, and the same appellation is used among veterans after independence. All the epitaphs of the veterans of the liberation struggle buried at the national burial place, called the National Heroes' Acre, bear the prefix 'Cde', for Comrade (see Chung 2006).

Zimbabwe's guerrilla veterans and their former leader Robert Mugabe (1980–2017) were comrades, having suffered together during the liberation war. In spite of differences during the liberation war,[7] they shared the same anti-colonial resistance and regarded imperialism and everything perceived to represent it as the ultimate enemy. The guerrilla veterans had strong bonds, captured in the powerful Shona expression, '*komuredhi ishamwari yeropa*' (a comrade is a blood friend) – an expression that speaks of the redemptive power of blood in nationalist discourses. Whatever differences they may have had with their general were minimized on the basis that they shared the same commitment towards fighting for the fatherland. What is more, there was a strong notion among the guerrilla veterans, especially soon after independence, that violence had redeeming qualities for societies that waged liberation struggles. In what speaks to a homosocial order of guerrilla veterans, Frantz Fanon, commenting on the violence waged against colonialism by Africans, stated the following about colonized people:

> The practice of violence binds them together as a whole, since each individual forms a violent link in that great chain, a part of the great organism of violence which has surged upwards in reaction to the settler's violence in the beginning . . . The mobilization of the masses, when it arose out of the war of liberation, induced into each man's consciousness the ideas of a common cause of a national destiny and a collective history.
>
> Fanon 1965: 73

This takes me to reflect on the role of blood and violence in establishing bonds of friendship in ancient Roman wars.

In Roman military practice, the Latin term *commilito*, signifying 'a comrade', 'companion in war' or 'fellow soldier', (Lewis and Short 1879) was favoured by great commanders who had earned the right to use the title through their own active campaigning, and who wished to flatter their armies by an egalitarian and affectionate address (MacMullen 1984: 443–4). Julius Caesar, as presented by Lucan (1.299-302), called his fighters fellow allies in war, on account of their common suffering for ten years during the Gallic wars in which much blood was shed: '*bellorum o socii, qui mille pericula mecum,*'/ *ait,* '*experti decimo iam vincitis anno,/hoc cruor Arctois meruit diffusus in Arvis? volneraque et mortes hiemesque sub Alpibus actae?*' (He said: O allies in war, who have faced a thousand dangers with me, and are now victorious in the tenth year, is this what the blood shed in the northern lands has deserved, and the wounds and deaths, and the winters spent by the Alps?)[8] According to Suetonius (*Aug.* 25.1), Augustus, during the civil war, addressed his troops using this name: '*neque post bella civilia aut in contione aut per edictum ullos militum commilitones appellabat, sed milites.*' (After the civil wars neither, in a public meeting or through an edict, did he call any of the soldiers 'fellow soldiers'– but [only] soldiers).[9] (cf. Luc. 5.358 and Suet. *Div. Jul.* 67.2).

However, there is need to highlight the tension between veterans and their leaders. This view is key also to unpacking the nature of relations between Roman veterans and their generals, which were not always cordial. The generals also feared and acknowledged the power of their soldiers. Amidst the Placentia mutiny as put across by Lucan, Caesar knew that drawn swords belonged not to the general but to the soldiers (Luc. 5.254).

The guerrilla veterans of Zimbabwe did not get the land without a struggle against not only former white farmers, but also their leaders. They did not participate in land expropriation only as troops taking orders from their commanders. The role of Zimbabwe's guerrilla veterans as trained soldiers, their organizational skills were valuable resources that their generals and patrons recognized and dreaded. I shall briefly comment on each one of these resources, as I highlight the extent to which the guerrilla veterans became a formidable force that even their generals had to transact with, using high levels of tact and vigilance (Mlambo and Chitando 2015), something which I will contrast with the Roman generals' relations with their veterans. However, to highlight the differences and sometimes the adversarial relationship between the guerrilla veterans and their commander is not to deny the homosocial relationship that existed between them.

The guerrilla veterans had many grievances against their general Mugabe, as they felt used and abandoned. In August 1997, they drowned out Mugabe's speech at the National Heroes Acre and demanded to be compensated for their wartime sacrifices to the nation. With his back against the wall, Mugabe conceded, as he was wary of his guerrillas' military abilities and sought to placate them (Mlambo and Chitando 2015). The army, police and intelligence operatives did not dare arrest the guerrilla veterans during their demonstrations and even during the expropriations in which they committed wanton and brutal killings of white farmers, destruction of property and ransacked farmhouses. Their war experience and training became a powerful resource at both the practical and ideological levels. Practically, it enabled them to deploy their military skills in the farm invasions. Ideologically, it gave them an 'untouchable' status, as they had the aura of victors, having fought the Rhodesian forces. So veterans could collaborate with their commander (Mugabe) in the process of farm expropriations on the basis of their military experience, and clearly sometimes Mugabe looked helpless as the situation with the guerrillas escalated. This reminds us of Octavian's crisis with his veterans echoed by Appian: 'Octavian knew that these citizens were suffering injustice, but he was without means to prevent it, for there was no money to pay the value of the land to the cultivators, nor could the rewards to the soldiers be postponed . . .' (App. *BC*. 5.15, White 1913: 401–3).

For Mugabe, things got worse as the veterans of the original independence struggle who remained in the Zimbabwe National Army and those who remained outside finally combined to oust their commander from power in a military coup in November 2017. This illustrates how war veterans may be motivated by wartime sentiment to unite in order to achieve their goals. It may be suggested that Mugabe's dethronement by liberation war veterans was to some degree motivated by perceived effeminate tendencies, since he wished to have his wife Grace Mugabe succeed him. Zimbabwean guerrilla veterans condemned Grace Mugabe for Mugabe's loss of masculinity, a factor that led the veterans to unite to unseat their former commander.

This reminds us of a Roman parallel in which Antony lost most of his forces as a result of his flirtation with Cleopatra, deemed a sign of effeminacy in Dio Cassius' account (my italics):

> '. . . what is there about him that anyone should dread? His physical fitness? But he has passed his prime and become effeminate. His strength of mind? But he plays the woman and has worn himself out with unnatural lust . . .' *His reputation with the soldiers? But even of them have not condemned him? A sign of this is that numbers daily come over to our side.*'
>
> Dio Cass. 50.27.8, Cary 1917: 495

This demonstrates how veterans deployed ideas of gender to invoke positions of power and weakness in their relations. In the following section, I examine the relationship between Roman client-army soldiers and their generals using the two notions of homosociality and hegemonic masculinity.

## Homosociality and hegemonic masculinity: The Roman context

Dio Cassius (41.29.1, Cary 1914: 51) referred to the relationship between a general and his forces as a 'society of men', (*σύστημα ἀνθρώπων*).[10] Ramsey MacMullen (1984) examined evidence from inscriptions and the ancient Roman texts in detail, shedding light on the concept of the Roman legion as a society. The concept of homosociality allows for an examination of charged power relations, whose material base was land, money and other rewards, and also security from acts of impunity, between fighters and their generals. Some forms of friendship and dutifulness between soldiers were idealized by Roman authors (Ward 2016: 317). The soldier's amity was not an affection or internal disposition merely, but a formal alliance with a semi-contractual character, a kind of treaty between persons (Wills 1966: 33). The two notions of *amicitia* (friendship) and *pietas* (dutifulness) were actually martial virtues. Client-army soldiers and their generals shared these values and, as MANLY men, pledged to act together for a shared cause.

An important idea when dealing with the notion of gender among the ancient Romans is its relation to power and powerlessness (Montserrat 2000: 154). Thus, part of my analysis of the working of masculinity among client-army soldiers and their generals, and between rival generals (in their struggles for power, land, honours and other rewards), takes cognizance of the fact that hegemonic masculinity – if I may here borrow some convenient expressions from (Montserrat 2000: 154), articulated different positions, involving either power, domination and control, or loss of control, powerlessness and subordination. Octavian, addressing his veterans, reveals such a scenario of power and powerlessness. As Appian presents it, Octavian spoke thus (my italics):

> You know, too, he said, the reason why Antony was lately vanquished. You have heard what the Pompeiians in the city did to those who had received certain gifts from Caesar. What confidence can you have of keeping the *lands* and money you have received from him, or what confidence can I have in my own safety, while the *relatives of the murderers thus dominate the Senate*? . . . I see only one path of safety now for both of us: if I should obtain the consulship by your help. In that case all my father's gifts to you will be confirmed, *the lands that are still due* to you will be forthcoming, and all your *rewards* will be paid in full . . .
>
> App. *BC*. 3.87, White 1913

Dio recorded an even more threatening speech by Octavian to his soldiers whom he made to think that Anthony's scheme with the Egyptian Queen Cleopatra was bent on robbing them of their properties and entire possessions.

> '... against Sextus also, to win Sicily only, and against this very Antony, to win Mutina only, you carried on similar struggles, and so zealously that you came out victorious over both. And now will you show any less zeal against a woman who has designs upon your possessions, and against her husband who has distributed to her children all your property'
>
> Dio Cass. 50.28, Cary 1917

The strategy used here bordered on a rhetoric that exploited the fundamental emotions of collective identity for self-interested political and material ends. Octavian's veterans feared that a change in the political order would inevitably lead to the reconfiguring of power that would reverse the land settlements for veterans. Such fears combined, with their homosocial affection for Caesar, made them irreconcilable with those who murdered their general, and instead they chose to lend their *gravitas* to Octavian. To demonstrate their affection with Caesar, says Suetonius (my italics), 'The musicians and the masked professional mourners, who had walked in the funeral train wearing the robes that he had himself worn at his four triumphs, tore these in pieces and flung them on the flames, to which *veterans who had assisted at his triumphs* added the arms they had then borne.' (Suet. *Div. Jul.* 84, Graves 1956: 47). These fears, one can argue, became deeply rooted in the collective psyche of veterans in the late Roman Republic, and it explains their attachment and loyalty to their generals as opposed to the government.

What characterized the transactions of power between competing generals and their hordes of fighters was the currency of active masculinities and the attendant marginalization of feminized masculinity. It is possible to deal with the issue of power relations among soldiers because their behaviour brings them into prominence in most narrative accounts of the ancient sources. Such narratives tell a story of a society of men undergirded by a masculinist ethos as a means to attain and maintain hegemony. Thus, hegemonic masculinity during the client-army era was constructed in relation to subordinated and marginalized masculinities as well as in relation to femininities. Acts of resistance by those who were expropriated or by women were suppressed and subdued by a masculinity which strengthened hegemonic gender ideals. For example, Appian and Dio Cassius, in their presentation of *virtus muliebris,* displace femininity to the margins of the narrative field. Dio presents Octavian disdainfully dismissing the decadence and corruption of Cleopatra's Egypt and her ally Antony, linking it to a malign femininity, or a perverse and depraved masculinity. The roles of Cleopatra (Dio Cass. 50. 24) or Fulvia (Dio Cass. 48.12), for example, are only significant insofar as their involvement in the struggles for territorial control, land and power determined the relations between male protagonists (Antony and Octavian) who are narratively coupled, constituting the active players in the narrative (Dio Cass. 48.12). In the same narrative, veterans espoused the cause of Octavian and had the final verdict in which they condemned Fulvia (Antony's wife) and Lucius (who were fighting for the right to also divide land to their forces together with Antony's veterans as per the previous arrangement between Octavian and Antony) as guilty of wrong-doing. Homosociality, however, did not necessarily depend on the outright elimination of women, but rather, on the more powerful bonds that united men to one another and which collectively operated to secure the subordinate position of women. That is the reason why women were exchanged in marriage by generals of the First and Second Triumvirate for the sake of their power. Homosociality upheld hegemonic masculinity and patriarchy.

The society of Roman veterans, was also characterized by a relationship which allowed veterans to entertain hopes of owning an allotment of land, money and other rewards, as such promises were material and forward-looking (App. *BC.* 1.86 with Brunt 1971: 301). For example, Julius Caesar quelled discontent among his soldiers by nourishing an expectation of imminent enrichment, and by making a specific statement of intent on the provision of land (Keppie 1983: 49). In 47 BC, he discharged some of his veterans, and at once gave them land as a surety of sincerity, and as a foretaste of the rewards all would get as promised after the end of the war (Plut. *Caes.* 51.1). Another example was the case of Octavian and Antony and their forces. The duo promised veterans land, houses and wealth in their bid to defeat Brutus. The two leaders found themselves having to offer more frequent and more substantial incentives to the soldiers (Saddington 2012: 126). As a result, the most beautiful parts of Italy were marked up for their veterans. Appian captures this as follows:

> To encourage the army with expectation of booty, they promised them, besides other gifts, 18 cities of Italy as colonies cities which excelled in wealth in the splendor of their estates and houses, and which were to be divided among them, just as though they had been captured from an enemy in war.
>
> App. *BC.* 4.3, White 1913: 145

Promises made to war veterans by their generals marked the generals' ambition to provide for the welfare of their veterans and also the limits of their power to fulfil such promises. Dio Cassius explains such a difficulty with respect to Octavian (Dio Cass. 48.8.1-5). For the leaders of the veterans to be able to deal with their veterans' demands for land, they needed personal and political authority. One of the problems that arose was that the demands of the veterans were not simple or uniform, as they were made for various reasons, not all of them equally valid or beneficial to society, and leaders sometimes made promises they either could not or did not wish to keep, in order to curry favour with their forces, or for temporary convenience.

What is important to note are the ways in which such promises were negotiated between generals and their veterans. Veterans, through their martial relationships and bonds, constructed power blocs to negotiate, fight, acquire and protect their privileges and gains (see Feldherr 1998: 104–5; Roller 2009).[11] Generals too depended on land to create relationships with their forces. Marius, for example increased his political power from the position of *patronus* that he assumed in relation to the settled veterans. Sulla's return and the civil war that followed ended the domination of the *populares*, cemented by his settled veterans (Smith 1955: 106). After the death of Julius Caesar, Octavian's army was joined by his father's veterans who encouraged him to take the name of Julius Caesar. Their interests were of course in preserving their lands, which were threatened after the assassination of their general in 44 BC. Octavian's idea of building his power around his father's veterans further buttressed the supremacy of familial and patriarchal masculine bonds in securing the legacy of his father and securing the future of his power. Julius Caesar had great hopes in Octavian, loved him and cherished him, intending to leave him as successor to his name, authority and sovereignty (Dio Cass. 45.1.2). In fact, the war against Caesar's murderers was one in which familial, patriarchal and homosocial bonds manifested a violent masculinity, as Octavian was avenging the death of his father (Dio Cass. 45.12), Antony the death of his friend, and Lepidus the death of his general.

## Homosociality, land and the Roman army

To demonstrate the homosocial order of the client-armies, I start with an exposition of how the Roman state had completely lost control of the army, whose loyalty was now invested in individual generals. During the first-century BC, soldiers were identified with their leaders, for example as *milites Caesaris* or as *milites Cn. Pompei.* (Cic. *Att.* 1.18.6). The Roman Republic disintegrated into contending and hostile groups in which the senate fought for power and privilege, and great individuals fought for personal power (Smith 1955: 87). The state was replaced by groups whose aims were expressible in material terms – land, booty, money, etc. Plutarch tells us that by the time he left Spain, Caesar was being saluted by his soldiers as 'Imperator' because he was rich and also because he had made them rich (Plut. *Caes.* 12).

Octavian went to soldiers recently settled by Julius Caesar in Casillinum and Caiatia (where Caesar had confiscated the lands of the locals for his men) and offered each 500 denarii to join him – more than two years' salary (Saddington 2012: 126). The senate could normally promise a pension to the army. Thus individual Roman generals entered politics to assure a grant of land for their bands of veterans, hence becoming more popular than the senate.

Military service during the Roman Republic increasingly drew the legions farther from Rome for lengthy periods of time. During the middle to late Republican period, soldiers who served together for many years adopted collective nicknames, and legions acquired their own identities – fixed insignia, designations – and proclaimed loyalty to specific commanders (Ward 2016: 312). Dio Cassius recorded that Sulla became what he was because he held command of the armies for so many years in succession, while Marius became what he was because he was entrusted with so many wars in succession (Dio Cass. 36.31.4). This created a sense of community among soldiers fighting under an individual general. Caesar's soldiers actively encouraged bonds of friendship and loyalty within his legions, and praised those who aggressively fought beyond their unit in order to protect or avenge comrades and superior officers (Ward 2016: 318).

In the following section, I explore how transactions for land and other rewards between client-army soldiers and their generals can be understood in terms of vertical and lateral masculinities.

## Vertical and lateral masculinities

Vertical or hierarchical homosociality, I argue, should be seen as a means through which generals and their forces strengthened power and created close bonds to maintain and defend hegemony. Vertical masculinity was characterized by a certain measure of power and control emanating from the general – down through the hierarchy – to his forces. Thus, vertical masculinity functioned from above, when generals issued orders to their forces and whenever they had the prerogatives of the law into their hands, and not vice-versa (cf. Dio Cass. 41.35.1).

However, a certain bond of friendship, as Dio Cassius would say, was necessary to keep generals and their soldiers together – the absence of which resulted in soldiers deserting their generals.[12] This may be viewed as a lateral form of masculinity, based on friendship rather than superiority and subordination. Dio records that men create friendships based on two factors: influence or prestige, and advantages to be gained (Dio Cass. 36.30.2, 36.30.5, 36.39.3). He describes how in 47 BC, for example, Julius Caesar attached to himself members of his party by bestowing offices, and retained the loyalty of those who had fought for him by means of land allotments and money (Dio Cass. 42.51.3). The Placentia mutiny offers an example of securing the goodwill of soldiers by providing land. Dio recorded that in their mutiny at Placentia, the soldiers' hope was to obtain from him (Caesar) anything and everything, seeing as he stood in so great need of them (Dio Cass. 41.26.1, Cary 1914: 47; see also Luc. 5.244-248). Caesar in his speech to his soldiers at Placentia even stated: 'Most of you obey my orders very scrupulously and satisfactorily . . . and in that way have acquired so much land as well as wealth and glory . . .' (Dio Cass. 41.28.2, Cary 1914: 51). This was lateral cooperation where a general offered something to his men in return for loyalty and support as opposed to issuing commands and instructions.

Generals also often used the support of their veterans for their political ends, without which they achieved nothing.[13] It was a centurion who forced the senate to give the under-age Octavian the consulship (Suet. *Aug.* 19). On the other hand, the veterans were willing to be used by their general, expecting land and other rewards, in return. This may also be well illustrated by Appian's description of the Sullan dictatorship (my italics):

> And there were 120 000[14] men throughout Italy *who had recently served under him in war* and had *received large gifts of money and land from him* . . . all of whom rested upon Sulla's safety their hopes of impunity for what they had done in *co-operation* with him.
>
> App. *BC.* 1.104

This homosocial relationship is also reflected in Appian's description of Octavian's relationship with his veterans. In his address to his men, Octavian reminded them that his securing of the consulship through their help, would also secure land allotments for them (App. *BC.* 3.87). Thus, the long-term mutual obligation and reciprocity between generals and their forces was characterized by a vertical and a lateral masculinity, which established a homosocial relationship. The homosocial relationship was also fraught with challenges as I explain below.

## Ruptures

In this section I observe that ruptures within the relationship of a general and his troops are also important in understanding how masculinity worked. Sometimes generals and their forces had a relationship that in certain moments, suffered a breach (cf. Dio Cass. 48.8.1-4). It was during such moments that veterans demonstrated their muscular arrogance, agency and resistance when demanding their dues. Dio tells us that Caesar's Campanian legions 'had much to say about the toils and dangers they had undergone and much about what they had hoped for and what they declared they deserved to obtain.' (Dio Cass. 42.53).

As the citation from Dio illustrates, client-army soldiers were reliant upon a political language of claims that reconceived the wars in which they fought as the standard against which the expropriations and their rewards were to be understood and justified. By 'political language', I mean the words, images, ideas and expressions of sentiment that composed a common rhetoric animating inconsistent relations of power that existed between generals and their forces – a relationship that was both cooperative and adversarial, on account of the issues of indiscipline and of disputes over unfulfilled promises of land allotments and other rewards (see Dio Cass. 42.52). It was a language that existed within a terrain marked by violence, mutiny, rejection and bitter struggles. The language was composed of claims, demands and contestations. It was also a language of struggle, recognition and obligation on the part of war veterans and their generals.

Ruptures in these relationships are an important aspect of veteran masculinity. Sometimes relations between veterans and their generals were fraught with misunderstandings and unexpected coincidences. In 67 BC, during a campaign against Tigranes the Armenian, the Roman general Lucius Lucullus was unable to control his soldiers, as they were always revolting, and finally deserted him. Dio Cassius says Lucullus was among other things, strict in his punishments, and did not understand how to win his troops over by persuasion, or by mildness, or by being friendly through conferring honours or bestowing wealth – all of which are necessary for forces on a campaign (Dio Cass. 38.16.2).

A more favourable outcome is seen in the case of Caesar. Caesar chronicles the mutiny at Vesontio where he demonstrates the control he could exert over his troops (Caes. *BG*. 1.39-4). Martin Helzle argued that Caesar's speeches in Lucan throughout are militaristic based on the higher frequency of imperatives, violent language, and military vocabulary[15] when compared to the speeches of Pompey and Cato, the other two major characters in Lucan's *Pharsalia* (Helzle 1994: 121–2). Using the example of the Placentia mutiny of Caesar's soldiers, Efrossini Spentzou demonstrates the working of the masculinity of domination, something that resonates with what I call a 'mythology of masculinity and domination'.[16] Efrossini Spentzou noted:

> The soldiers are overawed by the irresistible force of a sublime spirit that manipulates and dominates them. They are shattered by his abuse and yet lifted almost by force (certainly mental coercion) to a plane above norms and expectations, made to feel that they belong to something mighty, larger than (their) life, worth offering their own lives for . . . Passive to start with, immobilized by his might, they then, in a sudden great release of energy, offer their throats to be cut, providing themselves as victims of the exemplary punishment that he wants to exact.
>
> Spentzou 2018: 260

This resonates with something of a personality cult created by a leader to command fear and respect of his men. According to Eagleton in (Spentzou 2018: 267): 'The sublime is any power which is perilous, shattering, ravishing, traumatic, excessive, exhilarating, dwarfing, astonishing, uncontainable, overwhelming, boundless, obscure, terrifying, enthralling, and uplifting'. According to Efrossini Spentzou (2018) (my italics): 'Caesar's unlimited force, his sublime and at the same time abjecting violence, hints at a possible world made devoid of boundaries by his own limitlessness, a world where the allure and the *cult* of the individual have free, unfettered, anarchic reign.' In the words of the same author: 'The unfathomable might of Caesar pushed his soldiers to their own limits – and beyond, in such a way that, transported by their leader's incomprehensibility, the troops were caught up in the unfettered energy represented by Caesar, and his mighty destiny (and his imagination) became their mighty destiny (and imagination), though they barely understood it' (Spentzou 2018: 261). This illustrates how dominating masculinity in a leader may influence the behaviour of his followers in a desired direction.

Sometimes veterans transferred their allegiances from a general whose fortunes had declined to a more powerful general. Thus, to some extent, there was a relationship based on the notion of exchange (give-and-take), a relationship that was nominally based on constraining personal possibility but which also allowed for a great range of play and individual potential. There were various statuses that were inhabited by veterans. Scipio was also faced with the dilemma of how to address the soldiers, because of their insolence and insubordination which affected the state and hence the citizen status of the soldiers (Walsh 1961: 99). This in most cases signalled the dissolution of a homosocial order.

Although homosociality entailed a strong ideology of belonging to the guild, things could change, as criminal or rebellious elements could be eliminated from the guild through execution or dismissal. 'Belonging' refers to a spectrum of individual and collective statuses. Julius Caesar's soldiers at Placentia simulated old age and bodily weakness – a strategy to feign powerlessness and a wish to be discharged, as a way to manipulate Caesar into giving them more rewards (Dio Cass. 41.35.2, see Cary 1914, 61–3). In his response, Caesar gave them what they wanted, liberty to take leave – a counter-argument which showed the insignificance of the troops (Neely 2016: 63). As Neely (2016: 63) noted, Caesar, by reducing his men's power, was able to manipulate and control them: 'Caesar turns their claim into the mark of a shameful weakness that makes them unfit for war; *Fortuna* will provide him with *viros*, as if his current soldiers are not themselves men.'[17]

Sometimes through threats of dismissal or execution, a general could 'put aside the turbulent spirits' among his soldiers (Dio Cass. 42.55). Caesar executed those who had mutinied at Placentia. This was an example of a general exercising a brutal form of masculinity over their forces when their behaviour had become mutinous (Dio Cass. 42.53.6). Dio's account of a speech by Caesar has him saying: 'For no society of men whatever can preserve its unity and continue to exist, if the criminal element is not punished, since, if the diseased member does not receive proper treatment, it causes all the rest, even as in our physical bodies, to share in its affliction.' (Dio Cass. 42.29.1, Cary 1914: 51).

As Neely (2016) argued, Caesar's alternation between forms of address shows his ability to navigate the changing relationship between himself and his troops in which each situation required a different characterization of the army in order to be rhetorically effective. He would sometimes speak thus: 'Do not think, now, that, because you are soldiers, that makes you better than the citizens at home; for you and they alike are Romans, and they, as well as you, both have been and will be soldiers.' (Dio Cass. 41.31.1, Cary 1914: 55). To Caesar, his soldiers were sometimes equal soldiers with him,[18] and at other times fellow citizens/Romans (Dio Cass. 41.31.1, Cary 1914: 55), or comrades, or soldiers (Dio Cass. 41.27.1, Cary 1914: 47, and 41.31.1, Cary 1914: 55), or simply men (Dio Cass. 41.33.2, Cary 1914: 59). At Placentia, while trying to resolve a mutiny, Caesar found no name for his men: 'Give up your service, therefore, you – O what can I call you?'

(Dio Cass. 41.35.4, Cary 1914: 63). As Neely (2016: 76) noted, the soldiers have gone from *socii* to *Quirites* to *domitor (es)* – well suited to Caesar's pre-battle speech, as it reminded the soldiers of their past successes, suggesting that they would win the current conflict.

The various ways in which Caesar addressed, or is recorded by Lucan and Dio as addressing, his soldiers, in the patriarchal society of the time, would have had masculine connotations; yet by their plurality these different identifications of his soldiers demonstrate a variety of ways of conceiving masculinity.

A further examination of relations between the general and his veterans is possible. It is instructive that soldiers' violent impulses needed to be restrained. How did client-army generals deal with the violence of their men? This takes me to another form of masculinity which served to contain, tame and control the violence of their fighters – an oratorical or controlled masculinity.

## Violent, oratorical and reasoned masculinities in struggles for rewards

Oratorical/controlled masculinity was an elite type, which must have been adopted and adapted in military contexts outside of its traditional/courtly domain, such as in the senate or courts of law.[19] Its application outside this domain by client-army generals (for example in speeches they made to their soldiers) can thus be seen to register, though obliquely, the process of adaptation of oratorical masculinity from its traditional aristocratic/courtly domain to more complex situations, for example, in Roman generals' dealings with their troops. Thus, in contrast to a general's disposition to an unbending authoritative masculinity, there were times that called for the careful posturing and control of body, gestures and voice, in order, for example, to win over their men's violent impulses during crisis situations of apprehension, mutiny or rebellion over land demands or other rewards. Craig Williams (2010: 139) calls this disposition 'self-mastery', and it had deep roots in traditional Roman concepts of masculine identity. Cicero's treatise on the ideal orator's physical appearance demonstrates how masculinity became visible, enabling the speaker to gesticulate with confidence and authority (Connolly 2007: 86):

> idemque motu sic utetur, nihil ut supersit. in gestu status erectus et celsus; rarus incessus nec ita longus; excursio moderata eaque rara; nulla mollitia cervicum, nullae argutiae digitorum, non ad numerum articulus cadens; trunco magis toto

se ipse moderans et virili laterum flexione, bracchii proiectione in contentionibus, contractione in remissis.

At the same time he will use motion in such a way that nothing is superfluous. In his bearing, his stature will be upright and tall; his walking will be infrequent and not that broad (in scope); there will be stepping forward with restraint, and that will be infrequent; there will be no slackness in the neck, no quick motion in the fingers, no finger snapping according to the rhythm of the speech. Rather he will be restraining himself in his whole body and in the manly turn of his sides, in the projection of his arm in arguments, and in its withdrawal in relaxed moments.[20]

A lack of oratorical authority over one's forces would result in failure to deal with their demands or to control them. As Neely (2016: 12ff) convincingly argued, Caesar's troops showed dissatisfaction with his *cohortatio* (exhortation) at Ariminum, in which at first, one receives an impression of Caesar's weakness, as he was unable to rouse his soldiers, despite delivering an impassioned speech (Luc. 1.299-351). The troops' uncertain reaction in (Luc. 1.352) and their indiscriminate murmuring indicate that the speech had not achieved its goal (Neely 2016: 4). Nevertheless, the Placentia mutiny (where his Ninth legion demanded to be discharged and to be given their rewards of war (Luc. 5. 280), complaining of old age and battle weariness (Luc. 5.273) shows the importance of this type of masculinity. The following passage from Lucan demonstrates this point.[21]

. . . tremuit saeva sub voce minantis
volgus iners, unumque caput tam magna iuventus
privatum factura timet, velut ensibus ipsis
imperet invito moturus milite ferrum.
ipse pavet, ne tela sibi dextraeque negentur
ad scelus hoc, Caesar: vicit patientia saevi
spem ducis, et iugulos non tantum praestitit enses.

The passive crowd trembled before the ferocity of his threatening voice, and so great an army is cowed by a single man – a man they sought to depose – as if he could command their very swords and wield the steel against the soldiers' wishes. Caesar himself is afraid that weapons and strong right hands may be denied him for this crime: but the troops' compliance surpassed the expectation of their fierce leader and they offered up not just their swords but their necks.

This point is also demonstrated by Domitius' lack of oratorical firmness and skill to determine the course of action, in the face of Caesar's army which had surrounded Corfinium (a town he was defending). It was, for

Domitius, failure at a moment of typical masculine action. He failed to exhibit a masculinity expressible through words and comportment before this army (my italics):

> When the dispatch was read Domitius, concealing the facts, asserts in a public meeting that Pompeius would quickly come to their aid, and exhorts them not to lose heart, but to prepare whatever was required for the defense of the town. Privately he confers with a few of his friends and determines to adopt the plan of *flight. As his looks belied his words, and all his actions were marked by more haste and timidity* than he had usually shown on the previous days, while, contrary to his custom, he conversed much in secret with his own friends by way of taking counsel, *and shunned general deliberations and gatherings, concealment and dissimulation were no longer possible.*
>
> Caes. *BC*. 1.19, Peskett 1914: 29

Thus deportment and voice functioned as signs in the symbolic language of masculine identity (Gleason 1995: 103). The correct use of the voice was the physical instrument through which the generals found expression. Speaking with a voice suited to female screaming, argued Gleason (1995: 104), would not physically feminize the speaker, but masculinity in ancient Rome is a state that was also achieved through words. Thus in the context of a general addressing his veterans, the merest hint of the presence of cowardice or a lack of *animus* (*animus* implying a behaviour that combined anger, enthusiasm and confidence), would impair the virility of self-presentation in the eyes of the veterans being addressed.[22] Caesar's descriptions of battle suggest that it was highly unstable and quick to turn from victory to defeat 'and to turn its combatants from confidence to despair' in a single moment, hence the need for a well-composed general to instil confidence in his men.[23] Cicero himself commended Crassus for '... much flinging the body about and for speaking with no vocal swerves and without pacing up and down' (Cic. *Brut.* 43.158). This was a masculinity expressible through comportment/bodily movement/gait.

As Elaine Fantham (1985: 123) argued, the picture of a seditious crowd or mutinous force quelled by a man of strong personality and eloquence is a favourite theme of both epic and historical writing in the Roman tradition. Generals employed various means to tame violent impulses of their men. After his victory over Sextus Pompey in 36 BC, Octavian initially had tried to apply *disciplina militaris* to his rebellious troops. He had to back down and opted instead to offer them honours: in particular, centurions would be city councillors in their home towns and the military tribunes given special decorations

(Saddington 2012: 59). This is when Ofillius objected with the enthusiastic backing of his fellow soldiers. The troops were only cowed into submission the next morning when it was found that Ofillius had unaccountably disappeared (ibid.).

The mutiny at Sucro was caused primarily by the delay in payment of Scipio's soldiers. The stern expression on Scipio's face stopped the soldiers, and Scipio condemned the ringleaders to death (Liv. 28.26.5-14; see also Liv. 37.32.12–13). Julius Caesar killed the ringleaders of a mutiny in the army as happened after Pharsalus in 48 BC (Dio Cass. 41.35.5). Sometimes, Julius Caesar showed his strength, his strong and tough facade when dealing with his mutinous forces. With this kind of masculinized comportment, Caesar was a person who got what he wanted, a get-out-of-my-way general. Caesar had the ability to face his veterans with a penetrating and pacifying gaze – a masculinity that manifested itself facially. A good example is that of Caesar on a mound facing down the mutiny in Luc. 5:316-318: 'He stood on a mound of well-supported turf, fearless in expression. And he was not afraid but deserved to be feared, and spoke these words, as his anger dictated' (Luc. 5.316-318, Duff 1928: 262–3). In the words of Spentzou (2018: 267): Towering over his soldiers, Caesar crushed them with his assertiveness, keeping them trapped in an emotional rollercoaster that sustained in them insatiable hunger for war, while depriving them of any offsetting everyday reality. Whenever the situation demanded sternness, his countenance took on the unmistakable expressions of an indomitable general – an attribute of masculinity which other generals would not quite demonstrate effectively.[24]

Oratorical masculinity was yet another dimension of the working of masculinity, insofar as generals of client-armies handled their veterans' madness and violent land claims. It is in this process that the generals displayed a masculine superiority of speech in dealing with their forces. They exercised control over violent impulses and emotions of their veterans by use of 'masculinized reasoning'. Not only a strong character and a powerful will were a source of strength and authority over their men, but reason aligned with masculinity and *imperium* (the authority or dominion that generals exercised over their forces) (Williams 2010: 146). At Placentia, Caesar's soldiers mutinied but he was able to contain them by exhibiting a firm comportment,[25] and a 'reasoned masculinity'. His speech demonstrated his ability to face his forces and to resolve the crisis intelligently and authoritatively. Caesar was able to fathom the minds of his soldiers with greater penetration than most generals in the history of the late Roman Republic.

Cicero in his *Tusculan Disputations* masculinized reason in an imagery of *imperium* to describe the domination that reason ought to have over emotions (Williams 2010: 146). According to Cicero in *Tusc.* 2.47-8:

> est enim animus in partis tributus duas, quarum altera rationis est particeps, alter expers. Cum igitur praecipitur, ut nobismet ipsis imperemus, hoc praecipitur, ut ratio coerceat temeritatem. Est in animis omnium fere natura mole quiddam, demissum, humile, enervatum quodam modo et languidum. Si nihil esset aliud, nihil esset homine deformius. Sed praesto est domina omnium et regina ratio, quae conixa per se et progressa longius fit perfecta virtus. Haec ut imperet illi parti animi, quae oboedire debet, id videndum est viro. 'quonqm modo?' inquires, vell ut dominus servo vel ut imperator militi vel ut parens filio. Si turpissime se illa pars animi geret, quam dixi esse mollem, si se lamentis muliebriter lacrimisque dedet, vinciatur et constringatur amicorum propinquorumque custodiis; saepe enim videmus fractos pudore, qui ratione nulla vincerentur.
>
> For the soul is divided into two parts, of which one has a share in reason and the other does not. When therefore instruction is given that we should command ourselves, this instruction is given, that reason should compel rashness. For there is by nature in the souls of virtually everyone something soft, weak, humble, in some way enervated and languid. If there was nothing else, nothing would be more unsightly in man. But here reason is mistress and queen of all, which striving by itself and progressing further becomes perfect virtue (or valour). A man must see to it that she commands that part of the soul which ought to obey. 'How?' you will ask. As a master commands his slave, or a general his soldier or a parent their son. If that part of the soul, which I have said is soft, behaves most shamefully, as it surrenders itself to laments and tears in a womanly fashion, let it be bound and constrained by the guardianship of friends and neighbours; for we often see people broken by shame who would not be conquered by any reason.[26]

Because some generals had the 'masculine reason' allowing them to control their forces, they sometimes gained an upper hand in subduing their forces through reasoned speech. Julius Caesar tried to restrain his forces from plundering Italy. The Placentia incident was captured thus by Dio Cassius:

> 'Who would not be indignant at hearing that while we have the name of Romans we do the deeds of Germans? Who would not lament the sight of Italy ravaged like Britain? Is it not outrageous that we are no longer harrying the possessions of the Gauls whom we have subdued, but are devastating the lands south of the Alps, as if we were hordes of Epirots or Carthaginians or Cimbri? Is it not

> disgraceful for us to give ourselves airs and say that we were the first of the Romans to cross the Rhine and to sail the ocean, and then plunder our native land, which is safe from harm at the hands of our foes, and to receive blame instead of praise, dishonor in place of honor, loss instead of gain, punishment instead of prizes?'
>
> Dio Cass. 41.30.2-3, Cary 1914: 53–5. cf. 41.31.3

There were however cases where attempts to use the power of reason to control soldiers failed. Rubarth demonstrated how masculinity was constructed through Stoic reasoning in ancient Greece (Rubarth 2014). Musonius Rufus (a distinguished writer on Stoicism) tried to use Stoic reasoning, but failed to restrain the legions supporting Vespasian's attempt to become emperor who had besieged the city of Rome. Rufus mingled with the ordinary soldiers, the *manipuli* and discoursed on the values of peace (Tac. *Hist.* 3.81). According to Saddington (2009: 54), Musonius Rufus may have realized that decision-making had descended from the commander to the ranks, and that he thought the soldiers were amenable to logical argument (ibid.). His Stoicism proved completely inapposite in an army camp.

A further instance of failure to restrain soldiers may be added. After Philippi, Octavian failed to restrain his veterans, who plundered Italy as though it were enemy territory (App. *BC.* 5.12-15). This, together with the example of Musonius Rufus, goes to show that oratorical masculinity did not always prevail in ancient times.

## Conclusion

This chapter has examined how war veterans and their generals created a homosocial order, which was also fraught with challenges that threatened its existence and continuation, in spite of its unity of purpose. Transactions of power between veterans and their generals, it has been argued, were based on material considerations. The relationship between veterans and their generals can also be understood in terms of vertical and lateral masculinities.

The following chapter examines the body politics of war veterans in ancient Rome through the lens of African contexts, exploring the importance of the relation of cultural expressions of physicality – particularly the body of the war veteran – and the relation of masculinity concepts and land occupation to observable features of the physical body.

6

# The Deployment of the Veteran's Body: Masculinity, Disorder and Violent Expropriation

*But the body is also directly involved in a political field: power relations have an immediate hold upon it, force it to carry tasks . . . to emit signs. The political investment of the body is bound up, in accordance with complex reciprocal relations, with its economic use . . . the body becomes a useful force only if it is both a productive body and a subjected body*

Michel Foucault (Alan Sheridan [Trans])[1]

## Introduction

In Chapter Five, I argued that there is a degree to which the activities of Roman client-army soldiers, including land expropriation, through which they sustained their group goals in Rome's socio-political life, can be better understood as a function of homosociality and hegemonic masculinities – descriptors of how they organized themselves. Through a transcultural comparison with modern contexts of military veterans, I illustrated how homosociality and hegemonic masculinities could serve as descriptors of relations between client-army veterans and their generals – relations which were materialized by give-and-take transactions involving land allotments, booty, money and other rewards. Such relations, I have argued, though sometimes hierarchical, given the generals' prerogatives to wield and exercise power and control, also gave scope for the operation of vertical and lateral masculinities, where veterans exercised their agency and their power over their leaders. Ultimately, such relations established or created interdependence among veterans and their leaders, enabling them to achieve group goals.

In this chapter, I examine the politics of the physical bodies of client-army veterans as presented in the narratives of ancient Roman historians. Drawing on conceptualizations of the body and power in Bourdieu, Foucault and Butler, I frame the environment of expropriations and violence within which I may locate Roman veterans in order to make visible some of the scripts of masculinities, militarism, violence and disorder[2] that materialized in the processes of expropriation as represented in the Roman texts.

I also explore the complexities of the dynamics and politics of war, on one hand, and the emergence and stabilization of post-war regimes, on the other, with emphasis on the role of land and the political economy of masculinity in first-century BC Roman Republic. These two scenarios – war and post-war government – were characterized by challenges occasioned by the politics and social contingencies of redistribution, in which land became the main resource at the centre of redistribution challenges, ultimately representing concrete power and status. I view the expropriations from the perspective of 'the political economy of the body' (Foucault 1979), treating the body as 'a deeply political medium' (Wilcox 2015: 3) that functioned as a site for the 'redirection, profusion and transvaluation' (Butler 2004: 185) of power. The Zimbabwean veteran's body serves as a medium through which I consider notions of habitus involving bodily movements, training and emotions, to bring to life and better understand the Roman texts. The nexus between concepts of 'masculinity' and the 'body' of a veteran allows for the examination of the practical and symbolic value of veterans in a broader political framework. This necessitates investigating the positioning of veterans as part of the content and methods of politics in first-century BC Rome. Methodologically, I frame the veteran's combat motion, appropriation of space and exertion of force in land expropriation through the 'four categories schema' to analyse veteran masculinities in the two societies.

## The veteran's body and the practice of masculinity

My focus on physical bodies of war veterans goes beyond an isolated interpretation of masculinity via a focus on practice theory: Understanding masculinities foremost as habitualized and embodied ways of practising masculinity. Practice theorists conceive practices as embodied, materially mediated arrays of human activity centrally organized around shared practical understandings (Schatzki 2006: 11). Bodies and activities are constituted within practices (ibid.). That is, although there may be a prior conceptual understanding of masculinity among veterans, masculinities are actualized and lived out through specific practices. Masculinity comes alive through practices and performances. Here, the concept of practices must be understood as broad and inclusive. As Rouse has argued, meaning, discourses, vocabulary, constructions etc. also constitute practices (Rouse 2007). Social practices also derive from customs, beliefs, symbols etc. (Schatzki 2006: 12). But that practices are always embodied does not rule out the symbolic meaning and power they evoke and by which they are in turn shaped, hence I also include a constructivist perspective in the Geertzian sense. Clifford Geertz (1973) has shown that culture is a matter of publicly observable symbols and rituals and the organization of discourses and practices.

## The making of a veteran's body

Narratives in ancient Roman texts, involving men who fought in wars tell of severe and bloody war scenes in which the fighter's body took part. The quotation below is Livy's speech (Liv. 5.6.4-5) attributed to Appius Claudius which illustrates the exaltation of valorous bodies of Roman soldiers. It goes as follows (my italics):

> adeone effeminata corpora militum nostrorum esse putamus, adeo molles animos, ut hiemem unam durare in castris, abesse ab domo non possint? ut, tamquam navale bellum tempestatibus captandis et observando tempore anni gerant, non aestus, non frigora pati possint? erubescant profecto, si quis eis haec obiciat, contendantque et animis et corporibus suis virilem patientiam inesse, et se iuxta hieme atque aestate bella gerere posse, nec se patrocinium mollitiae inertiaeque mandasse tribunis, et meminisse hanc ipsam potestatem non in umbra nec in tectis maiores suos creasse.

> Do we think that the *bodies* of our soldiers are so effeminate, their minds so soft that they cannot last one winter in camp away from home? That they should wage war as if at sea watching the weather and observing the time of the year? That they cannot suffer *heat or cold*? They would indeed blush if anyone should lay these things to their charge and would contend that in both their minds and *bodies* there was a *manly* capacity for suffering and they could wage war in winter and summer alike and they had not entrusted to the tribunes the defense of softness and laziness and they remembered that their forebears had not created this very power while in the shade nor under roofs.[3]

It is necessary to examine the centrality of body-parts, scars, wounds etc. earned in battles, and of blood lost and/or shed during war in discourses of heroized masculinity in the world of military men of the two societies. Wounds, scars, blood and sweat became important substances in constructions of bodies of military men in discourses that set apart their bodies from those of ordinary civilians. The discourses created a view of strong and indefatigable bodies, worthy of honour and reward. Roman veterans tended to construct heroized masculinities from acts of valour in which they shed enemy blood.[4] As Milne (2009) has argued, the Roman soldier was by no means considered to be a disposable commodity (Sall. *Cat.* 58).

Because the body of a veteran (as it was represented) returned from war scarred, wounded or dismembered (this is in respect of those who suffered injuries or those who lost a limb/s), it became a special and an important 'marked' body in staking claims for political office or in laying claim to a heroic status in politics and society. As Milne (2009: 30)[5] argued, we gain a better understanding of why the scar was so important through a comment of the younger Seneca (*Prov.* 4.4), who explains the relationship between suffering and glory:

> Virtus is eager for danger and thinks rather of its goal than of what it may have to suffer, since even what it will have to suffer is a part of its glory. Warriors glory in their wounds and rejoice to display the blood spilled with luckier fortune. Those who return from the battle unhurt may have fought as well, but the man who returns with a wound wins the greater regard.

As Milne (2009: 30–1) noted:

> The idea of suffering augments the value attached to the practice of fighting, for the wound confirms that the task which the soldier achieved was not easy, but rather both difficult and dangerous. The unhurt soldier and the wounded soldier may, as Seneca says, have accomplished the same task. In fact, we might suspect the unhurt soldier was the more skilled. But the deed attracts more glory if it is difficult and dangerous, and the wound proves both; the opponent was no cowardly weakling to be dispatched before he had thrown a blow. The scar symbolizes the behavior of the soldier in battle, who put himself in danger, and perhaps more importantly, successfully mastered that danger. In this way, the scar is evidence of a situation which is in the past, and derives its meaning from suffering and pain, but also from the fact that it proves success and overcoming of significant difficulties. This success is integral to the model of the bloodless victory. Roman soldiers are not supposed to die gloriously, and nor are they supposed to shirk danger. They are supposed to throw themselves into danger and win.

The impact of war on the bodies of soldiers as variously recorded in ancient texts suffices to demonstrate how veterans bore the brunt of Roman wars (Scullard 1960: 63). Lucan 1.299-302, 340-345, Duff 1928: 25,29) put words in Caesar's mouth regarding the issue of injured veterans and the respect they deserved. The speech goes thus (my italics):

> Men who have fought and faced with me the peril of battle a thousand times, for ten years past you have been victorious. Is this your reward for *blood shed* on the fields of the North, for *wounds and death*, and for winters passed beside the Alps?. . .But, if I am robbed of the reward for my labours, let my soldiers at least, without their leader, receive the recompense of their long service; and let them triumph, be their leader who he may. What harbour of peace will they find for their feeble old age, what dwelling place for their retirement? *What lands will my veterans receive to till*, what walls to shelter their war-worn frames?

Suetonius (*Life of Julius Caesar* 68.4, Thayer 2013) described the importance of wounds and of losing a limb in the construction of heroism and triumphalism of individual soldiers thus:

> And no wonder, when one thinks of the deeds of individual soldiers, either of Cassius Scaeva the centurion, or of Gaius Acilius of the rank and file, not to mention others. Scaeva, with one eye gone, his thigh and shoulder wounded, and his shield bored through in a hundred and twenty places, continued to guard the gate of a fortress put in his charge. Acilius in the sea-fight at Massilia grasped the stern of one of the enemy's ships, and when his right hand was lopped off, rivalling the famous exploit of the Greek hero Cynegirus, boarded the ship and drove the enemy before him with the boss of his shield.

Sallust (*The Jugurthine War* 85.29-30, Perseus Digital Library n.d.d) mentioned what Marius qualified as his trophies of innumerable efforts and perils in battle. The list includes scars, in reference to his heroism. In this case again, we see General Marius' triumphalism. The passage goes thus:

> I cannot, to raise your confidence in me, boast of the statues, or triumphs, or consulships of my ancestors; but, if it be thought necessary, I can show you spears, a banner, caparisons for horses, and other military rewards; besides the scars of wounds on my breast. These are my statues; this is my nobility; honors, not left, like theirs, by inheritance, but acquired amid innumerable toils and dangers.
>
> Sallust, *The Jugurthine War* 85. 29-30, Perseus Digital Library n.d.d

The speech of Marius as given by Sallust in the following passage also makes reference to elegance as a female bodily characteristic, contrasted with military qualities. Latin for elegance is *munditias*, from *munditia* which means cleanliness [or orderliness] (Simpson 1959: 383). If we contrast the element of cleanliness with the sweat of the battlefield in the passage below, the body of a soldier is presented with distinctive masculinity qualities. In this passage there is also a reference to the body-parts of the senators put to shameful uses, as contrasted with the honourable deeds towards which soldiers deploy their body-parts. This is implicitly contrasted with Marius' own use of his body in his speech continued below (Sallust, *The Jugurthine War* 85. 39-41, Perseus Digital Library n.d.e):

> They reproach me as being mean, and of unpolished manners, because, forsooth, I have but little skill in arranging an entertainment, and keep no actor, nor give my cook higher wages than my steward; all which charges I must, indeed, acknowledge to be just; for I learned from my father, and other venerable characters, that vain indulgences belong to women, and labor to men; that glory, rather than wealth, should be the object of the virtuous; and that arms and armor, not household furniture, are marks of honor. But let the nobility, if they please, pursue what is delightful and dear to them; let them devote themselves to licentiousness and luxury; let them pass their age as they have passed their youth, in revelry and feasting, the slaves of gluttony and debauchery; but let them leave the toil and dust of the field, and other such matters, to us, to whom they are more grateful than banquets.

Marius' speech above clearly shows that he had fallen in love with toil and hardships of war. Such hardships, he considered sweeter than feasts. The common trend in Roman fighters' perception of their suffering in war was that of a triumphant masculinity.

In Zimbabwe, the masculinities of guerrilla veterans lay emphasis on the wounds and scars incurred during the war. Death is also mentioned in the rhetoric of dying for the country's independence hence the adage, 'We died for this country'. This statement puts spilt blood at the forefront of their discourses of claims for land allotments. In South Africa, armed Umkhonto weSizwe military veterans camped at former president Jacob Zuma's homestead in combat fatigues, in support of their leader in July 2021 (Ndou 2021). They reminded his 'detractors' of their sacrifices during the struggle and how blood was shed for victory against apartheid to be achieved. This is similar to Roman veterans' use of the notion of blood in their claims for land allotments. Lucan mentions a soldier, Scaeva, as *sanguine multo promotus,* 'promoted on account of much blood (shed)' (Luc. 6.145-146: Duff 1928: 314). The Zimbabwean context also emphasizes the blood lost by fighters during the war. We may refer to Mugabe's (2001: 141) speech on the commemoration of Heroes' Day on 11 August 2001, in which the centrality of lost blood is emphasized.

> Our notion of heroism thus comes directly from the bloody resistance to British imperial expansionism and the challenges, which come with foreign domination. These heroes we have here at the National Shrine and elsewhere in and outside the country come from the tradition of resistance and tell through their lives, the story of our struggle in its various constitutive facets; trade unionism, urban protests, nationalist politics . . . and of course liberation soldiery.[6]

A veteran of Zimbabwe's liberation war, interviewed by the author,[7] vowed to defend, by his blood, a farm he had expropriated. His motive for expropriating the farm he now owned was for him to experience some form of restorative justice.

It is instructive to mention how the war veteran constructed his current physical comportment. Because of a dislocated hip, he now questioned his masculinity. This kind of thinking resonates with two incidents in which Cicero was criticized by Calvus for being 'limp and enervated' and by Brutus as 'emasculated and loose in the loins' (*fractus atque elumbis*) (Gleason 1995: 107, 107 n.16). There is partly a degree to which a culture of masculinity in the two societies acknowledged no exceptions to its rules and would not accommodate any signs of human frailty in the guild of the masculine. Signs of loss were also badges of pride. The disabled Zimbabwean veteran in the above interview perceived himself as having lost his manliness by dislocating his hip during the war, but paradoxically, he got the farm posturing as a manly man, in spite of his dislocated hip and he got the farm perhaps because of it, too. The loss of a limb, life and blood during the war, injuries and scars incurred became central to their claims for compensation.

But a man's appearance does not matter if he is overly endowed with substitute phallic powers (Lehman 2007). Despite having appeared a coward after fleeing the battle without his shield, Horace even disparaged his shield as something replaceable. 'What is that shield to me? Stuff it! I'll get another just as good' (Bowie 1986: 109–10). In the case of Zimbabwe, the phallic powers which accrued to disabled veterans are the guns and the historical narrative of prowess associated with the body of a soldier which they obviously cherish as veterans of the liberation struggle who toppled the oppressive colonial regime. The symbolic importance attributed to some veterans, whose old bodies do not themselves announce anymore, are visually indicated somewhere and somehow. Things work in such a way that power is displaced from the old faces and old bodies themselves to various martial paraphernalia – guns, knobkerries, machetes, axes or clothes whose colour or form attract the eye to the site of martial power and potency.

Of course from Lacan's (1975) psychoanalytic perspective, a male's development through the mirror stage establishes a powerful mechanism for investment to prioritize in the male body. Lacan derives wants from the mirror stage of a young child's development (Cetina 2006). Wanting or desire is born in envy of the perfection of the image in the mirror (ibid.). In the case of the handicapped veteran, it is fathomable that he still thought of himself as a soldier regardless of his present disability. Indeed, once a soldier, always a soldier.

To further demonstrate the challenges of the impact of war on war veterans in politics, I refer here to Zimbabwean politics and the involvement of its ex-fighters. They strip their bodies in public places to show their scars and injuries (Sadomba 2011). Such an attitude towards one's scars is a part of constructing masculinity by Zimbabwean veterans. Peter Lehman argued that the scarred person gets mileage from his scars in that: 'He is not easily defeated or killed. He may not be perfect, but he perseveres. If he has done so in the past, he can do so again. Instead of (or, in the case of villains and enemies, in addition to) being ugly, he is more powerful for having been scarred' (Lehman 2007: 70). Such emotions which came as a result of the harm that the body of a veteran suffered during the war, at times caused violence.

## The 'body' as a focal point of analysis

My approach to the body takes into account Foucault's idea of the body and power. Foucault says that power acts on a body and power also forms a body. The distinction between the two is vexing, since it seems that to the extent that power acts on a body, the body is anterior to power; and to the extent that power forms a body, the body is in some ways, or to some extent, made by power (Butler 2004: 13). So how can both alternatives be true? There are two aspects of power in relation to the body to be taken into account. I articulate practical and symbolic meanings associated with bodies of war veterans, and in this context, I consider the notion of power as working on and through the bodies of war veterans. To explore the relation of concepts of masculinity and the body politics of war veterans, my approach emphasizes the moment when the relation of power to the body emerges, in which Foucault abandons the subject of power in his 'body and power' analysis. This abandonment forms for him the necessary background for an understanding of what power is (Butler 2004). In this context, the body emerges as a way of taking over the theory of agency previously ascribed to the subject (ibid.). While I do not neglect the role of the subject, nevertheless, like Foucault, I do not restrict my conception of the body to the human subject in isolation from its relations to other things. I focus on materialities (of which the body is an example), and observe how body-types and bodily substances (sweat, blood, wounds, scars etc.) come into play in a wider context of how masculinities were constructed and performed. I argue that the very materiality of the environments of war and of expropriations acted on the body of a veteran.

This power, said to be acting on a body, is not something belonging to one person exclusively but is part of the system of political relations in which the body exists (cf. Foucault 1979). Taking Foucault's insights into account, I conceptualize agency as extending beyond the theory of the isolated subject and including a strategy, which in my case consists of the action of the materiality of the environment of expropriations on and through, and in tension with, the materiality of the body. I rely on Judith Butler's conception of power, and for me the nexus of the body of a veteran and the environment of expropriations provides the condition for power to become redirected, proliferated, altered, transvaluated (Butler 2004). As Butler argues however, the introduction of the nexus is not simply, or exclusively, a way of thinking about power, but is also a way of redefining the body (ibid.). The body is not an inert or inherently docile object, nor is it merely a set of internal drives which qualify it as the locus of agency. So if the 'nexus' is related to power in the presence of a strategy involving activity and dispersion and transvaluation, this implies a new understanding of the body, as that which is a kind of undergoing, the condition for a redirection, active, tense, embattled (ibid.). Thus my analysis, to some extent, centres on the body of client-army veterans, to nuance more ways to understand the body-masculinity-land nexus of client-armies of first-century BC Rome.

As Judith Butler argued, power acts upon the body in the very formulation of powerful bodily emotion in its self-persistence and knowability (ibid.). I explore how power acted historically in each case (Roman and Zimbabwean) upon the body of a veteran in the formulation of compelling, powerful and violent emotion, as a mode by which veterans affectively seized upon a fundamental sense of identity and entitlement to land and other rewards. In this sense, the bodies of veterans developed these powerful and compelling emotions as a result of norms by which they felt obliged to recognize themselves as bearing the brunt of the wars in which they fought. Thus, veterans were, as it were, worked upon by many forces, and through being worked upon they became disposed to act with their trained bodies in ways which invites our attention to their bodies. I thus reflect on the context of the veterans of Rome and Zimbabwe from the viewpoint of power and land. In the first place, they claimed the land because they fought for their country (in the course of which veterans were maimed, handicapped etc. and even killed); and because of that, veterans believed that they deserved land. Secondly, they claimed the land because they could take it by force (and because they had the 'attitude' which came from having fought in their countries' wars). These two dimensions are discernible in veterans' responses in other African contexts, particularly in relation to reminding audiences of the sacrifices they made in the liberation struggles.

This brings me to the notion of habitus.

In Bourdieu's conception, mastery of the body is essentially the successful incorporation (literally, the taking into the body) of particular social meanings, inculcated through various bodily disciplines oriented to such mundane practices as 'standing, sitting, looking, speaking, walking etc.' (Brownell 1995: 15). Drawing on Bourdieu's (1977) concept of habitus, I explain how war veterans' culture of masculinity, martial aggression and heroism and their common history of war shaped social actions involving expropriations regardless of cultural differences. When dealing with Bourdieu's concept of habitus, I am cognizant of the problem of reflexivity. For Bourdieu (cited in Cowan 1990), reflexivity is not possible as the human body's sociality is masked in the reproduction of habitus, and therefore one cannot become aware of the social construction of their body. The embodied techniques, according to Bourdieu (in Cowan 1990) are placed 'beyond the grasp of consciousness and hence . . . cannot even be made explicit'. I do not think that Bourdieu's argument applies to my two case studies. The veterans of the two societies were reflexively conscious of their bodies. I will show in this chapter – if I may here borrow some convenient expressions from Cowan (1990: 24), which seem apt for my study - their "exaggerated postures of power" as "evidence of this kind of reflexivity." This allows for an illuminating investigation of notions of masculinity even between human beings of different cultures.

War veterans were aware of facts about their bodies but were not explicitly aware of social construction in the same way a sociologist or scholar would be aware. War veterans were aware of their own strength, their own sufferings, their manliness and gender and their own violence. These might be viewed as aspects of their bodily existence that can receive social interpretation. The veteran (in both societies) was aware that he had a body, and that he was a body. It has been argued that activity depends on shared skills or understandings, which are typically viewed as embodied (Geertz, cited in Swidler 2006: 85) – something which war veterans in the two societies mirror in their respective contexts.

In my analysis, the physical body of a veteran and his person are closely related. My descriptive endeavour, on the one hand, draws attention to the body to underscore the functionality, deployment, usability of the body of a veteran,[8] while on the other hand, to accentuate agency, rationality or initiative, I emphasize the person of a veteran. The involvement of the body, insofar as it relates to acts of expropriation by war veterans, may theoretically take various forms. The four categories below provide a framework upon which I draw in the interpretation of the Roman texts. This framework allows me to locate the Roman veterans and Zimbabwean veterans in an environment where their actions and the agency of their bodies can be analysed. It also allows me to perceive indications in the Roman texts of expropriation and proscriptions as productive of not only military violence, but also images of masculinity. The categories are as follows:

1. Appeal to weapons and physical achievement or the results of physical achievement (e.g. wounds or scars[9] in battle) to justify demands for land or office. This category allows visualization of the Roman veteran's body in deployment, masculinity and its communicative environment.
2. Physical invasion of land and exertion of force on owners of land to punish and drive them out or injure them. This category enables me to visualize the environment of expropriations. It also allows visualization of the Roman veteran and his victim in motion.
3. Combat with occupiers of land, or anyone resisting. This category allows visualization of the Roman veteran in combat motion.
4. Use of verbal communication and physical performance to intimidate or threaten the use of force to assert ownership of land. This category allows visualization of the Roman veteran in the practice and performance of violence and masculinity.

I illustrate below how the four categories assist in visualizing emotional effects involved with veterans and images of war, masculinity, violence and valour in the Roman texts. I juxtapose the Roman texts with the Zimbabwean cases of expropriation to enable consideration of emotions and to viewing the cultural and political logics of war, masculinity, violence and land expropriation.

## Appeal to a soldier's experiences and sufferings

In this section I consider more directly the corporeity of the soldier. Veterans of first-century BC Rome attached importance to their physicality – particularly their bodies and weapons as fighters. Dio Cassius (48.9, Cary 1917: 237–9) recorded episodes of violence, murder and arson to houses as Octavian's soldiers fought against civilians who were resisting the expropriations (my italics):

> They repeatedly came to blows and there was continual fighting between them, so that many were wounded and killed on both sides alike. The one party was superior by reason of the *arms with which it was equipped and of its experience in the wars*, and the other by its largest numbers and by their tactics in hurling missiles upon their opponents from the roofs.

This view of appeal to the veterans' physicality is represented by Lucan. Lucan portrays Caesar's soldiers' quest for land for expropriation, while boasting about their physical strength. Having asked, '*Quae noster veteranus aret?*' (What lands is our veteran to plough?) (Duff 1943: 29, see Luc.1.345) – raising the question of what land is to be given to war veterans – Caesar (347-348)[10] adds:

> Viribus utendum est quas fecimus. Arma tenenti
> Omnia dat qui iusta negat. Neque numina derunt . . .

This may be translated as follows: 'We must use the strength we have made. He who denies what is just to one who bears arms, grants him everything . . .' (Duff 1943: 28). Lucan's account reflects the violent disposition of client-armies of the first-century BC when, like Caesar's veterans to be,[11] they did not receive justice, they felt entitled, with the arms at their disposal, to collect what was due to them of their own accord. The merit of war determined what a veteran could get and influenced the behaviour for veterans.[12] Julius Caesar in his speech to his fighters showed that their past suffering made them undeserving of dishonour from Rome (Luc. 1.299-302). As a result, male honour was understood to be a result of attitudes towards gender.

Dio Cass. 42.53 also tells us that Caesar's Campanian legions '. . . had much to say about the toils and dangers they had undergone and much about what they had hoped for and what they declared they deserved to obtain.'

In his Annals, Tacitus reveals how a veteran's life, body and land were intertwined. Referring to the mutiny instigated by Percennius in the legions of Pannonia during the reign of Tiberius, Tacitus recorded how appeal was made to the threadbare garments and naked limbs of soldiers by Roman war veterans participating in this mutiny, who wished to show how much they had suffered (Tac. *Ann.* 1.18). Percennius, instigator of the mutiny (*Ann.* 1.16), objected that 'ten ases[13] a day is the value set on life and limb', suggesting that the bodies of the soldiers had been undervalued and should, given the risk undergone, be valued more highly (Tac. *Ann.* 1.17). In the same speech, reference is made to veterans getting 'soaking swamps or mountainous wastes' instead of good land (Tac. *Ann.* 1.18). This raises the question of a veteran-masculinity constructed through narratives of suffering and sacrifice, in which the body of the veteran's worth is deemed to deserve more value than it is given.

## Physical invasion of land, violence and disorder

Theorizing territorial invasion in a modern context, Connolly (1996: 144) argued that: 'To occupy a territory is to receive sustenance and to exercise violence.'[14] The expropriation of Italy by the *tresviri* perfectly suits Connolly's theory. The expropriations were premeditated and well planned to sustain the power of the *tresviri* through parcelling out land to their soldiers.[15] Appian recorded that (my italics):

> To encourage the army with expectation of booty they promised them, beside other gifts, eighteen cities of Italy as colonies – cities which excelled in wealth, in the splendour of their estates and houses, and which were to be divided among them (land, buildings, and all), just as though they had been captured from an enemy in war. The most renowned among these were Capua, Rhegium, Venusia, Beneventum, Nuceria, Ariminum, and Vibo. Thus were the most beautiful parts of Italy *marked out for the soldiers. But they decided to destroy their personal enemies beforehand, so that the latter should not interfere with their arrangements* while they were carrying on war abroad.
>
> App. *BC*. 4.3, White 1913: 145

Appian further demonstrates the violence committed by the triumviral soldiers after Philippi as follows (my italics): 'The soldiers *encroached* upon their neighbours in an *insolent manner, seizing* more than had been given to them and choosing the best lands.' (App. *BC*. 5.13, White 1913: 397). The Greek for 'encroached' is ἐπέβαινε[16] – which can also mean 'attacked' (Liddell and Scott 1876: 248). This suggests that soldiers may have been attacking civilians in the process of driving them away from their farms. This is supported by the phrase σὺν ὕβρει (in an insolent manner), lit. 'with hubris', a term which can refer to wanton violence (Liddell and Scott 1876: 723). This, according to Appian, characterized the expropriations. Such actions by the armies of the *tresviri* are consistent with masculinity. There is a masculinity which is territorial and expansionist, domineering and imposing, brooks no resistance and deploys violence to vanquish all in its path, to dominate and possess, to acquire more property for themselves (περισπώμενοι lit. 'draw off') (Liddell and Scott 1876: 553). Dio was emphatic about the *tresviri* client-army phenomenon of violent accumulation when he noted: 'Only those, indeed, who bore arms gained great wealth.' (Dio Cass. 47.17, Cary 1917: 151).

The physical invasion of land by veterans in first-century BC Italy played out images of masculinity, militarism and violence, in which client-army veterans and their generals claimed, embodied and wielded authority on the basis of their warrior image in their demands for land and political dominance. For example, after the battle of Philippi, Rome saw land confiscations by Octavian's and Antony's veterans, and this land was mostly taken from losers, supporters of Brutus and Cassius (cf. Polo 2019). The fact that the transfer of land to the veterans was mostly a transfer of property from the losers to the winners made the land confiscation in some ways a continuation of the war itself, wherein the losing party was humiliated, not only on the battlefield, but by losing their territory and their former mastery over that territory. Veterans also feature as forces of disorder.

Through an examination of Vergil's *Eclogues*, I explore the performance of a violent masculinity as a way to envision violent expropriations and disorder by triumvirate veterans. In the Ninth Eclogue (*Ecl.* 9:2-4)[17] there is a reference to the seizure of land by a war veteran, where we may view the episode as portrayed in performative utterance. This episode provides a window to explore performative violence during expropriations as depicted by Vergil. Vergil's *Eclogues* are for me a means not only of staging the argument or experiences of the dispossessed or the defeated faction in a civil conflict, but also of enunciating the modalities of violence of the political and social upheaval in a civil war. In addition, the element of warfare is accented by the fact that one of the persons in the poem, Moeris actually nearly got killed by the war veteran (Lee 1984: 95: see *Ecl.* 9.11-16). This war veteran's behaviour was a spillover of the combat masculine warrior disposition in the process of land confiscation.

Vergil's allusions to national conflict can be juxtaposed with scenes from Zimbabwe's national conflict involving confiscations of white-owned farms by Blacks. The two conflicts are productive of violent and barbaric veteran-masculinities, depicted also as harmful even to the orderliness of the farms. Both veterans in a way degraded national territory into chaotic space, reduced farmers to displaced persons. When relating their story and memories, both Vergil and former white farmers in Zimbabwe passionately comment on the beauty and idealism of their farms both in setting and lifestyle. Vergil (*Ecl.* 1.70-71), by referring to the neatness of the farm, calls to mind the kind of harmony that existed on the farm: 'An impious soldier shall possess these fallow lands so neat, a barbarian will possess these cornfields . . .' (*Ecl.* 1.70, Lee 1984: 29). The orderly setting is no longer possible when the violent and uncivilized veteran takes over Moeris' *neat* farm. Vergil thus portrays veteran-masculinities as barbaric and harmful even to the orderly and civilized environment of the farm. This is quite consistent with how Roman historians depict client-army veterans.[18] Sallust (*Cat.* 16.4, 28.4) describes Sullan veterans who joined Catiline in the 60s BC as spendthrift upstarts who had squandered their ill-gotten properties and hoped for new civil wars and confiscations, to escape their debts. Cicero (Cic. *Phil.* 8.9, 10.22, Yonge n.d.) had a cynical view on Antony's veterans whom he described as follows (my italics):

> While, then, the motives for war are so different, a most miserable circumstance is what that fellow promises to his band of *robbers*. In the first place *our houses; for he declares that he will divide the city among them; and after that he will lead them out at whatever gate and settle them on whatever lands they please.* All the Caphons, all the Saxas, and the other plagues which attend Antonius, are marking out for themselves in their own minds most beautiful houses, and gardens, and villas, at Tusculum and Alba; and those clownish men—*if indeed they are men, and not rather brute beasts . . .*

Dio Cass. 75.2.6. describes veterans from the frontier at the end of the Antonine period as 'most ferocious to look at, terrifying to listen to, and uncouth to talk with.'

On the other hand Zimbabwe's former white farmers depict the presence and work of a guerrilla veteran on the white men's once prosperous farm as harmful to nature on the farm – wild animals on the farm were killed, trees were cut, and buildings burnt to the ground, causing the once thriving forests to become like deserts. The image in Figure 5 shows destruction to a former white farmer's house in Zimbabwe.

The former white farmers had a friendly connection and attachment to nature (cf. Wiles 2005; Barker 2007; Buckle 2001). The 'ugly culture' of the veteran in the practice of agriculture is contrasted with a romanticized vision of the farm setting and of life before the farms were taken by veterans, in both the case of Tityrus in Vergil's poem (standing for Vergil of ancient Rome), and Catherine Buckle in Zimbabwe.[19] Buckle's view is characterized by a similar attitude to nature and romanticism as that of Vergil.

The veteran's rough masculinity is also evident in both cases. There is expression of feelings of dispossession and nostalgia with the farms (both in ancient Rome and in Zimbabwe) once under their control and ownership. This

**Figure 5** Dup Muller, a commercial farmer in Headlands had his farm house burnt by war veterans on 21 August 2002. Aaron Ufumeli/AFP via Getty Images.

reveals the veteran's rough masculinity and violence against nature, which Vergil (*Ecl.* 1.67-72) records below (my italics):

> En umquam patrios longo post tempore finis,
> pauperis et tuguri congestum caespite culmen,
> post aliquot, mea regna, videns mirabor aristas?
> *Impius* haec *tam culta novalia miles* habebit,
> *barbarus* has segetes: en quo discordia civis
> produxit miseros: his nos consevimus agros!

These lines are translated by Lee (1984) as follows:

> 'Look, shall I ever wonder, to see my native country a long time afterwards, and the roof of my poor cottage, packed with thatch; to see, afterwards, some ears of corn, my kingdom? An *impious soldier* shall possess these fallow lands so *neat*, a *barbarian* will possess these cornfields; look where civil discord has led us forth, wretches that we are; we have sown our fields for these people!'

Catherine Buckle (2001: 86–7) reminisces about the beautiful trees on her former farm:

> Trees I had planted with my own hands, pruned and nurtured, now stood high above my head and their leaves quietly rustled and whispered overhead. If I was

> really lucky I sometimes saw the barn owls flying low through the trees as they prepared for their nightly patrols ... I stopped when I got to Richard's tree (her son). As the trees had grown up, Richard had carved his name into the bark of one of the gums. I ran my fingers over his name, the bark smooth and cool under my fingers and for a moment lost myself in the memories of a decade.

Lee (1984: 35) translates line 70 of *Eclogues* 1.68-72 as, 'Some godless veteran will own this fallow tilth.' Referring to the veterans who invaded Tityrus' farm as uncultured. That the seizure of land is an act of war is indicated by the fact that the land seized is referred to as '*mea regna*' or 'my kingdom', indicating that the new veteran owner has in effect taken over a kingdom and dethroned the former ruler of the 'land' – an act of exercising *imperium* (dominion) over his new possession. Overtones linked with masculinity can also be traced here. First, the word *regna* comes from *rex*, a king. The ancient kings of Rome were males, and the owner of the kingdom is therefore male, a *paterfamilias*. We may recall at this point Aristotle's comparison of the father to a monarch (Rackham 1934: 493). By taking over land one takes over this masculine position and becomes the new *paterfamilias*. Appian (*BC*. 5.12) corroborates the above view with a graphic description of the Italians who came to Rome complaining in the forum and temples uttering lamentations that (my italics): 'they had done no wrong for which they, Italians, should be driven from their fields and their hearthstones, like people *conquered in war* ...' (App. *BC*. 5.12, White 1913: 395–7). Conquered people become emasculated and powerless.

Buckle also mentions how bands of guerrilla veterans who invaded her farm perceived the expropriation as war. She recounts how the war veterans who had broken into her farm yard were whistling and shouting: 'HONDO HONDO HONDO!' (War war war!) (Buckle 2001: 6). The armed guerrilla veterans invaded farms of unarmed white farmers in an ostentatious display of violence, ordering them to leave their farms. According to Carl Schmitt (2003), the specific political distinction to which political actions and motives can be reduced is that between friend and enemy, and the friend and enemy concepts receive their real meaning precisely because they refer to the threat and sometimes real possibility of physical killing.

Performance of a dominant violent behaviour is indicated when Moeris claims (*Ecl.* 9:2-4):

> 'O Lycida, vivi pervenimus, advena nostri
> (quod numquam veriti sumus) ut possessor agelli
> diceret: 'haec mea sunt; veteres migrate coloni.'

> 'O Lycidas, we have arrived alive, so that a stranger, as possessor of our small field might say – something we had never feared – "These things are mine. Go away, you old farmers."'
>
> Lee 1984: 95

This disorder and chaos of a Roman veteran-masculinity can be contrasted with a guerrilla veteran-masculinity on a white man's farm in Zimbabwe. One of the squatting veterans at Catherine Buckle's farm confronted the timid female commercial farmer demanding her shop! Below is the conversation between Catherine Buckle and her tormentor.

> 'I need this store,'... His needs had increased dramatically from a cup of milk to a store! 'It's not for sale.' 'But I need it,' he replied.
>
> Buckle 2001: 103

The utterances: '... Go away, you old farmers' and 'I need this store' are performances of dominant behaviour. A similar kind of authoritative and performative utterance demonstrated by a Roman centurion in a conversation with Jesus Christ of Nazareth: 'For I too am a man under authority, with soldiers under me. And I say to one, "Go," and he goes, and to another, "Come," and he comes, and to my servant, "Do this," and he does it.' (Matthew 8 verse 9). This testifies to a disposition to a dominant and violent authority by veterans in society.[20] It shows how military masculinity is built on the bedrock of instantaneous obedience. Moeris' description resonates with the case of a Zimbabwean white commercial farmer, Eric Harrison (2006: 11), who recounted how an elite war veteran in the company of two armed policemen ordered him out of his farm: 'We are the new owners of Maioio Farm... You have got 24 hours to get off ... now move it!' The two scenes reveal the impunity, injustice and lawlessness of veterans' acts of dispossessing farm owners in the two societies. Figure 6 shows guerrilla veterans' violent disposition through invasion of farms while armed.

*Ecl.* 9:2-4 also resonates with an account of a guerrilla veteran loyal to his wartime commander, General Solomon Mujuru, who simply invited his commander to Guy Watson-Smith's farm to see if he liked the farm. The farm was seized in 2001 by Solomon Mujuru, who simply ordered Watson-Smith to leave the farm, taking only his and his family's personal belongings (Tendi 2020: 254). Although Watson-Smith won a High Court order to recoup his movable assets, the former general resorted to violence as he unleashed a group of war veterans on Watson-Smith's farm to throw him out of his farm

**Figure 6** Independence war veterans led by Islam Burira (on the left) invaded the farm of commercial farmer Keith Kirkman (on the right) in Donnington, Zimbabwe, on 15 March 2000. Paul Cadenhead/AFP via Getty Images.

without his belongings.[21] The guerrilla veteran who invited general Solomon Mujuru said:

> I am the one who identified the general's farm in Beatrice. I used to see it and said, 'General, you do not have a farm from the land redistribution. I have seen a good tobacco farm in Beatrice for you. Come have a look.' He came with me to the farm and liked it and he decided to take it over.[22]

Catherine Buckle describes how guerrilla veterans invaded her farm. Her description offers insight into feelings and experiences of dispossession. Her books cover the most traumatic period experienced by the farming community in Zimbabwe, and reveal the kinds of intimidation they had to face (cf. Pilossof 2009). She referred in her writing to the war veterans who would later invade their farm as '. . . a bunch of crazed men . . . to come . . . and force you out of your house and off your land.' (Buckle 2001: 3). Buckle's narrative centres on the experiences of her family during the year 2000. Her farm was not designated by the government for redistribution, as the Buckle family had bought the farm through government approval in 1990. Buckle and her employees were continuously harassed and threatened, even at gun point on one occasion, until they shut down operations and left the farm (Pilossof 2009).

Thus, when Vergil's veteran ordered his victim to leave his farm, it must not be seen as a simple rhetorical expression of bravado that exists only in the world of poetic fiction. The performance part is asserted as an unquestionable higher gradation of machismo, consistent with the exercise of violence by military veterans as suffered in real life contexts by white farmers in modern Zimbabwe.

## Physical space and political order

I now pass on to the consideration of physical space and political order. To interpret the Roman texts in this section, I draw on one aspect of the views of a twentieth- and twenty-first-century critical theorist, Carl Schmitt (2003) – the idea that spatial politics can convert space into a political 'force-field'. Carl Schmitt's particular view on the politics of space sheds some light on the meaning of social action by veterans. I analyse the process through which the actions of first-century BC Roman generals, in their quest to gain land allotments for their men and political territory, reconfigured and transformed physical space into politically meaningful sites of contestation for power. I also draw upon Ika Willis' argument and theorization of the politics of physical space and political order. Ika Willis (2011) did not however refer to military veterans of the Roman Republic. The physical space that became Rome was carved out by fighters. Their claims for land were based on the fact that they identified the lands they fought for with the historic process in which they took part. There existed some interconnections between the political order reinforced by veterans, and the physical space – the political force-fields they occupied and appropriated.

According to Elden (2005), space is political, and the politics of space occur because politics is spatial. Land expropriation by war veterans was a political strategy used to transform physical space into a general's strongholds. The act of distributing land to veterans was a process that turned every part of those settlements into the 'force-field' of the general's political order. A better comprehension of the veterans of the triumvirs can be enhanced by brooking comparison with guerrilla veterans' strategies and scheme of operation. The same can also be said of the latter. This comparison helps us to comprehend the mechanics of reconfiguring physical space and political order, a strategy adopted to claim power and territory. I begin with Zimbabwe.

In Zimbabwe, war veterans settled on occupied farms in military bases. This process was inscribed with notions of martial masculinities. Symbols of masculine ideals, as seen in Figure 7, show a painting of a flexed muscle on the

**Figure 7** Schoolchildren pass the entrance of occupied Devonia farm on their way home from school in a rural area some 40 kilometres east of Harare, Zimbabwe, on 21 June 2000. The farm, renamed 'Black power farm', became a headquarters for the war veterans in the area. Odd Andersen/AFP via Getty Images.

signpost. There is also on the smaller signpost standing next to the big one with the caption: BASE FOUR which indicates the direction of the military base of the invading war veterans. The big signpost has the caption BLACK POWER, which indicates that the land occupations were seen as an act of struggle of the Black race against the white race.

It must be noted that the land occupations took on a symbolic character in the political debate around the elections of 2000 (and subsequently in 2002, 2005 and 2008), with the backing of Robert Mugabe and the ZANU-PF party (Sachikonye and Zishiri 1999). Mugabe marshalled and deployed practical occupation tactics to subdue his political opponents – the community of white farmers and their loyal workers. In so doing, he was simultaneously transforming physical space into a strategic political resource. On the one hand, he was emptying the space of a perceived threat, while on the other hand he was instituting a network of patronage. The war veterans and rural people who would take over the land would be indebted to him and would defend him at all costs.

The occupations not only became a means through which Mugabe could create new social and political spaces supportive of his regime, by garrisoning territories whose inhabitants were perceived as supporters of opposition political parties, but also constituted a process of disturbing and dismantling the vestiges of the colonial order, to conform with his post-liberation political project (Mlambo and Chitando 2015). Veterans were thus given the duty to garrison such spaces. In an interview with a guerrilla veteran, he related: '*Patakatora minda takazvisima pakati pevanhu munzvimbo dzose dzatinoziva kuti dzigere vanhu vasingadi musangano. Kuvepo kwedu pakati pevanhu vakadaro kunotonhodza vanotipikisa*' / (When we took the lands we planted ourselves in the midst of the people in all the places we knew there were people present who did not like the party [ZANU-PF]. Our being there in the midst of the people like that cools down those who are fired up against us). Thus, through manifesting physical presence, the image of the veteran served to avert and ward off the forces which threatened Mugabe's power and the spaces in which he exercised control. The occupations of white-owned farms by his veterans physically inscribed martial, heroic and violent masculinities in the process of defining spheres of political control. This was similar to what happened in neighbouring Mozambique. From the mid-1980s until 1992, residents across large areas of Mozambique were terrorized out of their villages by the South African-backed Mozambican rebel organization named RENAMO (Resistência Nacional Moçambicana). It was through the communal villages that Frelimo (byname of the Mozambique Liberation Front) had constituted space as state territory and individuals as state subjects (Lunstrum 2009). Such terror tells much about the relation between terror and territory and the ways in which terror is deployed to unmake and remake space (ibid.) across space and time.

The purpose of Mugabe's veteran settlement demonstrates how political strategies used in ancient times have endured over centuries. At Corsica in 82 BC the Roman leader Sulla established a colony to offset the Colonia Mariana (Marius' colony meant for his veterans) (Salmon 1969: 129). This was after the defeat of Marius by Sulla. Land was therefore used to strengthen the Sullan regime and to completely remove Marius' vestiges of power as represented by his veterans who were settled in Corsica.

The use of military symbolism in land expropriation, as shown in Figure 7, help us from our modern standpoint to envision the veteran settlements of Sulla and Caesar who marched into their allocated farms or colonies in military units under their standards. Sallust, relating the speech of Philippus, implies that Sulla's colonies (communities in Italy whose lands were allocated to his veterans) constituted a reserve of military manpower which could be mobilized to support the regime (Thein 2010: 79).

After Philippi, Appian also points out that the resettled veterans created colonies in Italy which composed of hirelings settled there by the rulers to be in readiness for whatever purpose they might be wanted (App. *BC*. 5.14). The five years of the *tresviri* were coming to an end so veterans and their leaders needed the services of each other for mutual security.

Sulla's activities with his veterans are comparable to those of the former leader of the ZNLWVA, Chenjerai Hunzvi. The Hunzvi-led veterans had become increasingly powerful and dangerous. Their actions can be construed as having effectively transformed physical space into political zones to harness a state of dictatorship. During periods leading up to the Zimbabwean elections, any sector of the community perceived to be opposed to the ruling ZANU-PF party was in danger of being attacked by these veterans (Feltoe 2004). The veterans functioned not only as storm troopers in the farm invasions, but also as a sort of strike force against Mugabe's political opposition generally.

## The exertion of military force

Having looked at physical space, I now consider how client-army veterans unleashed violence against their victims. Soldiers not only fought for their generals in battle, but also inflicted violence outside of a battle context. After Philippi, the triumvirs deployed a cavalry force in Southern Italy to operationalize expropriations of land for their veterans. The exertion of military force on communities and owners of land and other properties, to punish, drive them out or injure them in first-century BC Italy served as retribution for political opponents.[23] A speech supposedly by Antony as recorded by Appian shows the element of driving people out of their homes (my italics):

> There are twenty-eight legions of infantry which, with the auxiliaries, amount to upwards of 170,000 men, besides cavalry and various other arms of the service. The vast sum that we need for such a vast number of men you can easily imagine. Octavian has gone to Italy to provide them with the land and the cities — *to expropriate Italy*,[24] if we must speak plainly.
>
> App. *BC*. 5.5, White 1913: 385

Generals of client-armies led their men to believe that the prize of victory was plunder. Thus, military violence reinforced by ideas of being manly was transferred to expropriations in Italy and at Rome. Comparing Mugabe's use of guerrilla veterans as storm troopers to punish his political enemies (the white farmers) through plunder, I show how the Roman scenario can be understood in terms of how a general is often able to command/persuade his veterans because he is one of them – a comrade in both arms and crime. The general is, a 'man of men' insofar as he is the highest expression and embodiment of masculinity. I thus view Sulla's masculinities as having been in a way cerebral, insofar as he possessed the persuasive charisma and power to cause his veterans to march on Rome to face 'Rome's enemies'.[25] Facing the threat of losing turf to Marius, Sulla came to redefine the roles of his veterans. Mugabe's method of persuading his guerrilla forces to wreak havoc against not only white commercial farmers,[26] but Zimbabweans who supported or were perceived to support the opposition MDC,[27] allows us to consider the role of Sulla and veterans' masculinities in a war of attrition against his political enemies. Mugabe was known by his veterans to take revenge on his political enemies.

Using the similar logic of use of attrition against political enemies, if Sulla was known to be a person who took violent revenge on his enemies,[28] upon hearing Sulla addressing them to be ready to obey his unspecified orders (App. *BC*. 1.57), his veterans may have guessed that he was plotting revenge on Marius and those who had made him commander instead of Sulla, and this might involve fighting against Rome.

Military masculinities in first-century BC Roman Republic involved collateral damage. Those who got hurt and trampled were simply accidents that happened in the divine journey to masculine satisfaction. Thus even the designation 'political enemies' might be a misnomer. These were simply people/objects who held what the main man thought he was rightly entitled to.[29] Acquisition in masculinity was, in fact, a mere acquisition or retention of what one was entitled to by dint of his masculine gender and historical accomplishments. Thus Sulla's war involved what in modern terms is called 'total war', (cf. Clausewitz et al. 1984: Paret et al. 1986) where almost everything of his enemies was destroyed, including life, houses and cities (cf. Strab. 5.4.11, Flor. 1.11.8).

Mugabe (2001: 110) enjoined his veterans to 'bring home to the white commercial farmers that they have declared war against the people of Zimbabwe . . .' The specific political distinctions to which political actions and motives are reduced, in the kind of context in which land is forcibly taken by guerrilla veterans, is that of self and other, victor and defeated (Mlambo and Gwekwerere 2019). These distinctions receive their functional meaning from the reality of the acts of politically-motivated murder and other forms of physical attrition that war veterans resorted to in the bid to entrench or challenge a particular dispensation. Indeed after the defeat of Marius, Sulla gave his veterans land expropriated from Marius' veterans.

The following passage (Plut. *Sull.* 31.4-6, Perseus Digital Library n.d.g.) shows exertion of physical violence through proscriptions both in Rome and in Italy by Sulla as depicted by Plutarch.

> And what seemed the greatest injustice of all, he took away all civil rights from the sons and grandsons of those who had been proscribed, and confiscated the property of all. Moreover, proscriptions were made not only in Rome, but also in every city of Italy, and neither temple of God, nor hearth of hospitality, nor paternal home was free from the stain of bloodshed, but husbands were butchered in the embraces of their wedded wives, and sons in the arms of their mothers. Those who fell victims to political resentment and private hatred were as nothing compared with those who were butchered for the sake of their property, nay, even the executioners were prompted to say that his great house killed this man, his garden that man, his warm baths another. Quintus Aurelius, a quiet and inoffensive man, who thought his only share in the general calamity was to condole with others in their misfortunes, came into the forum and read the list of the proscribed, and finding his own name there, said, 'Ah! woe is me! my Alban estate is prosecuting me.' And he had not gone far before he was dispatched by someone who had hunted him down.

Appian sheds more light on Sulla's proscriptions and seems to indicate that it was Sulla's veterans who carried out the violence, murder and proscription of property (App. *BC.* 1.96, 100):

> In order to provide the same kind of safeguard throughout Italy he distributed to the twenty-three legions that had served under him a great deal of land in the various communities, as I have already related, some of which was public property and some taken from the communities by way of fine
>
> App. *BC.* 1.100, White 1913: 187

> There was much massacre, banishment, and confiscation also among those Italians who had obeyed Carbo, or Marius, or Norbanus, or their lieutenants. Severe judgments of the courts were rendered against them throughout all Italy on various charges — for exercising military command, for serving in the army, for contributing money, for rendering other service, or even giving counsel against Sulla. Hospitality, private friendship, the borrowing or lending of money, were alike accounted crimes. Now and then one would be arrested for doing a kindness to a suspect, or merely for being his companion on a journey. These accusations abounded mostly against the rich. When charges against individuals failed Sulla took vengeance on whole communities. He punished some of them by demolishing their citadels, or destroying their walls, or by imposing fines and

> crushing them by heavy contributions. Among most of them he placed colonies of his troops in order to hold Italy under garrisons, *sequestrating their lands and houses and dividing them among his soldiers*, whom he thus made true to him even after his death. As they could not be secure in their own holdings unless all Sulla's system were on a firm foundation, they were his stoutest champions even after he died.
>
> App. *BC*. 1.96, White 1913: 177–9

It appears that Sulla used his own soldiers, as they had the weapons and the willingness to do violence, and most of them would be sufficiently fanatical and aggressive to do the actual work of killing people and taking their property. The logic of Sulla's proscription was to cement his power by proscribing men of wealth and status from the elites of Rome and Italy, and who were all guilty of civil war opposition to him, but many were added to the lists because they had incurred the private enmity or greed of Sulla's adherents (Thein 2018: 1). Sulla's action was in a way a symbolic demonstration of his absolute superiority in Italy – an act of conspicuous destructive violence and killings which served to display the power of the perpetrators and to restore or enhance their status. Appian relates a speech by Brutus which demonstrates the military violence meted by Sulla and Caesar against innocent Italians whose lands and houses were taken by their veterans, and captures the injury and the violence committed against fellow Romans and fellow Italians by Caesar's men (App. *BC*. 2.140-141, White 1913: 485–89). The act of settling the war veterans is described in the same speech as an act of colonization (App. *BC*. 2.141, White 1913: 487–89):[30]

> οἱ δὲ ὑμῖν τὰ τῶν ὑμετέρων ὁμοεθνῶν διένεμον, τῶν ἐπὶ Κελτοὺς ὑμᾶς αὐτῷ Καίσαρι στρατευ-σάντων καὶ προπεμψάντων καὶ εὐξαμένων πολλὰ κατὰ τῶν ὑμετέρων νικητηρίων. καὶ συνῴκιζον ὑμᾶς ἐς ταῦτα ἀθρόους ὑπὸ σημείοις καὶ συντάξει στρατιωτικῇ . . .
>
> '. . . They divided among you the property of your own people, the very men who sent you with Caesar to the Gallic war, and who offered up their prayers at your festival of victory. They colonized you in that way collectively, under your standards and in your military organization . . .'
>
> App. *BC*. 2.141, White 1913: 487

Sulla's precedent was revived by the generals of the Second Triumvirate (Mark Antony, Octavian and Marcus Aemilius Lepidus) in 43 BC (Thein 2018). Proscriptions, and the summary execution of opponents, were the order of the day as Octavian, Antony and Aemilius Lepidus consolidated the power of the

Caesarean faction by rewarding their veterans with expropriated lands. In App. *BC.* 5.14 there is a description of expropriations by triumvirate veterans and the quarrels between two of the leaders, on one hand, Antony's representatives and on the other, Octavian over the issue of the assumption of authority to divide the lands to the soldiers. Appian also refers to the appeals made by civilians over the loss of their lands and properties to marauding triumviral veterans (App. *BC.* 5.12 , White 1913: 395–7). Thein (2018: 1, also App. *BC.* 4.13)[31] observed that in theory, the targets were political enemies sympathetic to Caesar's assassins, but many were victims of personal enmities or greed, and in some cases the triumvirs even sacrificed family members or friends to ensure the addition of a sworn enemy to the list.

The victory over Brutus and Cassius was a continuation in the now firmly entrenched habit of military violence to achieve political goals. Octavian after this turned his attentions to deposing and disposing of his nominal partners. He had been appointed triumvir for ten years with the purpose of restoring the state torn by civil strife (*RG.* 7.1). He continued to wield this virtually untrammelled authority in the course of his war with Antony and Cleopatra, and in the mop-up operations that followed. He acknowledges the fact unabashedly in the Res Gestae: 'I had total power in all matters.' (*RG.* 34.1). There was no reason not to acknowledge it. That was a revolutionary era, dominated by civil war and the almost constant threat of upheaval. Institutions may have survived, but military might ruled (Gruen 2011: 34). Nonetheless, after the disorders, he remained with the absolute power. Needless to stress is the fact that Caesar's veterans played a big role in the power equations of the life span of the triumvirate. The party which Caesar's veterans supported, the Caesarean party, and that was led by Octavian, took the state.

Caesar neutralized Lepidus, taking his army from him and left him the ceremonial role of pontifex maximus as the only memento from his time in the Triumvirate. Antony, considered weak, and despised by the Roman citizens for falling under the spell of his Eastern consort, Cleopatra, committed suicide. Ironically this was the only honourable path left to the vanquished of Actium. As for Octavian, he became sole ruler of Rome, wielding his *potestas* over the entire Roman Empire, which had become like his household. Below I elucidate how Octavian (who became Augustus) and his army expropriated not just land for his army, but Rome's entire political fields.

To aid his usurpation of power and *auctoritas*, Augustus seduced the military with gifts that included land, and seduced the people with free corn and the *ludi* (games), which numbed the humanitas of Roman citizens, too often now used to strife (Tac. *Ann.* 1.2). He granted land to his own veterans, as well as Antony's, in 41–40 BC, and settled some others in 36 BC on lands he acquired from a great deal of widespread confiscations. Some veterans were settled in lands sequestered from conquered peoples *ager publicus* (public land). Thus, in 25 BC, praetorians received allotments at Aosta on lands confiscated from the Salassi (Dio Cass. 53.25.5).

Having killed off all meaningful resistance, and with virtually all of the army on his side, Augustus circumvented the Senatorial *potestas* when he ceased to be a triumvir, but ruled as a tribune of the people. He established the omnipotent title princeps, with all authority. It is interesting to note that portraits of Augustus throughout his entire life, on coins, made a strong contrast with the realistic busts of older men favoured in Late Republican art (Osgood 2006: 116). Not a *puer* as his critics charged, he was rather a *iuvenis*, a vigorous youth with heroic qualities (ibid.), which spoke a great deal of his all-conquering masculinities. The boundaries of manliness were distinctly clear in Roman politics (see McDonnell 2006: 160ff).

## Conclusion

In this chapter, I have argued that the two concepts of 'masculinity' and 'veteran' bear witness to an intense investment in the body of the veteran. Veterans featured in the two societies as a destructive force, while exhibiting rough masculinities that resulted in violent disorder on farms and in a political context generally. The following chapter investigates the place of veteran-masculinities in politics more generally, while laying emphasis on the centrality of spaces upon which physical bodies of veterans in ancient Rome and contemporary Zimbabwe functioned. This allows for an examination of the political logic of spatial masculinities in advancing agendas for veterans and generals in first-century BC Italy.

7

# Veterans and 'Spatial Masculinities'

*With the situations on and around the farms deteriorating, war veterans then began to move in closer to the cities and wield their new-found power whenever it suited them. Their reign of terror, previously limited to farmers, their workers and opposition activists, now expanded to include anyone who stood in their way.*

Catherine Buckle[1]

## Introduction

The previous chapter examined the communicative environment of masculinities in which veterans took part in expropriation, confiscations and proscriptions in first-century BC Roman Italy. To make their grievances known, and also as an act of carrying out their general's assignment, client-armies occupied public spaces in the city of Rome. The Zimbabwean case shows a context in which the invasion or occupation of public spaces by war veterans allowed them to enact narratives and performances of war exploits, including violent acts involving rioting and looting. This offers the potential for seeing the appropriation of public spaces by Roman client-armies as productive of meanings greatly in excess of the simple denotation expressed in the ancient texts. My analysis of the Roman context conceptualizes such spaces as places where a war-based masculinity and violence was transposed, and the locus where we can envision the imagery of spatial-masculinities in public spaces in Rome. I argue that there was something of a 'spectacle' in the collective gesture of the masculinity of the group, with the aim to discern collective strategies and aims behind such occupations of public spaces.

As Guy Debord (1970) has argued, the concept of the spectacle unifies and explains a great diversity of apparent phenomena. Debord's concept thus allows for the analysis of images of masculinity, militarism and violence. Although

Debord studied specifically the role of spectacle in modern industrial/urban society and the media, there are significant nuances to his concept of spectacle as a specialized activity, touching on its specialization of power which is applicable to my context, especially its 'communication' which is essentially unilateral. The spectacle I have in mind includes the sight of armed Roman soldiers massing or walking in public places in public display of their power or virility. When reading passages on war veterans marching or assembling in public spaces, invading the senate or political spaces such as voting assemblies in Rome, the following questions may be asked:

1. What audience was being targeted during such processes, and what kind of gaze was being sought after by the veterans and their leaders from their targeted audience? I view the bodies of client-army soldiers as 'the terrain of politics and political communication'.[2] For example, Clifford Ando (2019) argued that politics conducted in a singular space, to wit, in the forum in Rome, was experienced by all relevant parties simultaneously. In fact, as Ando has argued, Roman narratives located politics in particular places, and focalized war through the movements *in space* of particular individuals.
2. What was being psychologically introduced into the minds of onlookers by marching/massing veterans?
3. What forces were at work in the process?

I thus deploy the concept of spectacle in my analysis of passages where Roman veterans assembled together, or where they mobilized to occupy the streets of Rome, to show how such gestures emphasize the conjunction of the masculinity of the group and its power. Hordes of soldiers in the city of Rome conveyed a potent image of masculinity.

## Veterans and political space

The image of Roman veterans I try to re-imagine is informed by the image of Zimbabwe's guerrilla veterans' invasion of streets during demonstrations. The occupation of space by veterans was a political advantage that accrued to the general who sponsored a particular group of veterans.

First-century BC Roman generals used their armies to forward their own political schemes. As Smith argued, there was no *patria* to claim the love of many citizens (Smith 1955), and hordes of men invested their loyalty and love in a group under individual generals. Legions belonged to generals, not to the state

(Plut. *Cato Min.* 45.3). Pompey was able to regard Spain as his when the civil war with Julius Caesar began, not merely because he had his personal lieutenants in command (Dio Cass. 41.10.4, 41.15.1, 41.18.3), but because his influence there was great, and it was his personal relationship with his army that counted, even though at that moment Pompey stood for the government (Smith 1955: 128). Roman armies only knew a loyalty to their generals, and were always ready to march on Rome at the behest of their commanders (Plut. *Sull.* 37.5).

Pompey's armed soldiers were deployed in some key political spaces in the city of Rome by their general in his struggle against Milo. I treat these gestures as disruptive masculinities of war veterans in Rome. Lucan (1.319-323) dramatically captured this – giving a vivid picture of a masculinity wielded by weapons – as follows: '*quis castra timenti nescit mixta foro, gladii cum triste micantes iudicium insolita trepidum cinxere corona atque auso medias perrumpere milite leges Pompeiana reum clauserunt signa Milonem*?' (Who does not know of the camp mixed with the frightened forum, when the glittering swords surrounded the place of judgement with an unaccustomed circle, and with the courage to break through the midst of the laws with military force, the standards of Pompey hemmed in the guilty Milo?)[3]

Kline's translation is palpable: 'Who does not know how the barracks *invaded* the fearful courts, how soldiers with grim blades gleaming *surrounded and stunned the anxious jurors*? How *warriors broke into the sanctuary of justice*, Pompey's *standards laying siege to Milo in the dock*?' (Luc. 1.289, Kline 2014)(my italics). This was in reference to Pompey's deployment of soldiers into the Forum during the trial of Milo. Thus, Caesar accused Pompey of mixing judicial and military business in his speech to his men (Neely 2016: 19). There was no more respect of legal space. Private property was attacked in an indiscriminate manner and in total disregard of law, order and authority.

In 59 BC an attempt to settle veterans was made by Julius Caesar. Pompey in this case enjoyed the support of Caesar as consul, and of Crassus, who united with him in the First Triumvirate. The parading of arms and military standards in the city and the parading of veterans' physical bodies and their involvement in forcing the passing of agrarian bills in voting assemblies are cases where veterans occupied political space. For example, upon Pompey's return from the East, the Senate refused to ratify his request for land for his veterans and to authorize his Eastern acta. Caesar in support of Pompey, proposed a legislation to give land to Pompey's veterans. The Senate's opposition was in vain, as it had only epigrams with which to parry the strokes (Smith 1955: 106). Bibulus (Caesar's fellow consul) had to content himself with publishing epigrammatic edicts, as Caesar had the martial masculinity in the physical presence of bodies of Pompey's veterans (Cic. *Att.* 2.20.6, 21.4, see also Dio Cass. 38.6). The Edicts of Bibulus, though biting in terms of the language of invective through which they were pronounced/gazetted, were of no effect in comparison to the intimidating physical presence in the assembly of Pompey's sword-bearing veterans. As Phang (2008) observed, the constitution of an *intentus*, combat-ready, upright *habitus* of a soldier did not complete the *vir militaris*: he also had to be armed, donning armour and bearing weapons. Pompey's armed veterans would have appeared in public spaces, and the atmosphere would surely have been intimidating to onlookers and voters. Although Figure 8 represents soldiers of a later period, it may give some idea of the impression Pompey's soldiers might have made to onlookers.

**Figure 8** The Praetorians Relief is a Roman marble relief dated to *c.* 51–2 AD. Wikimedia/Christophe Jacquand.

I therefore interpret the presence of Pompey's armed veterans in public spheres as an act of wielding a martial masculinity. Being skilled in military matters was more superior to civil law. Cicero admitted that the general's *auctoritas* is greater than the orator's art (Cic. *De Or.* 1.2.7, 8.34, see also *Mur.* 22-3). The doer of deeds and holders of the *gladii* prevailed over those of fine speeches. The *gladii* symbolized the Roman soldier more than any other equipment. It connoted aggression, manliness and courage. The presence of sword-wielding soldiers in civilian spaces exhibited a military masculinity, and the sword stood at the core of a soldier's *virtus* (Ward 2016: 310).

Referring to Caesar, Pompey and Crassus, Lucan states that the triumvirs desired to transcend the fatherland in power (Luc. 1.174f.). Apart from their veterans, the intimidatory presence of Pompey on the agrarian commission was significant (as it had 'surveillance effects' which in the language of Foucault entail a power relation of observation and domination), and still more so was the intervention of his veterans at the voting (cf. Dio Cass. 38.1. 3). According to Gabba (1976: 44), at this stage in Roman politics, we are no longer talking of measures taken through constitutional channels. The extra-constitutional position of the Triumvirate in the political scene harnessed by the interventions of their veterans shows that the provisions of Caesar's agrarian bill in 59 BC was just a formality. During those days, according to Plutarch, senators failed to attend meetings as they were afraid of Pompey's armed veterans. The senate had become emasculated. Thus, the details of the public gesture of Pompey's veterans must generally be connected with the managing and shaping of public spaces in Rome. In this sense, analysing such gestures by war veterans in Rome enables analysis of the spatial organization of power and the role of gesture in subverting power and its formal structures. The gesture of invasion of the senate and courts by veterans was associated with disorder and excess. To me the movement/occupation/assembling of veterans was a mastery of the body-plus-space politics, which in the process displaced one's opposing forces. The assembling itself or occupation of the senate house was a gesticulation framed in an embodied language (gestural comportment of military men), which subverted established boundaries and challenged contours of place, thereby making the courts or the senate house spaces of agonistic confrontation or male-self display. This embodied group-expression as soldiers was an assertion of their collective power and in some cases caused rival senators to flee the senate house or to be cowed to submission. This has the implications of Foucault's insight that the practice of seeing and being seen entails a power relation, and in this case, the invading veterans who invaded the senate and took seats therein caused the senate house to become a dominated space to those who could not withstand their presence.

It was a result of this culture by veterans that led Octavian's ascendancy as first emperor of Rome. At the expiry of the second triumvirate, the two consuls Gaius Sosius and Gnaeus Domitius, both supporters of Antony, tried to manoeuvre things in favour of Antony against Octavian as they had become the supreme authority in Rome (Bringmann 2007). There already existed grievances between Antony and Octavian. Antony was unhappy that Octavian had taken Lepidus' territory and his soldiers, including those of the defeated Sextus. Octavian accused Antony of holding Egypt and other countries without drawing them by lot (Dio Cass. 50.4). To gain power in Rome ahead of Antony, Octavian depended on his veterans. Octavian appeared with a horde of armed veterans and occupied his triumviral seat in the senate although his term had lapsed (Bringmann 2007, see also Dio Cass. 50.2). Octavian's action was a display of a threatening gesture of military/political authority in which his veterans acted as protagonists of the opposing faction. As a result of the intimidating tactics of Octavian and his veteran allies, the consuls and a large number of senators fled to Antony. Veterans were a factor in Republican politics at its most decisive phase. In fact, they played a key role in strengthening Octavian's military and political standing in Rome. Octavian's units were composed of battle-hardened soldiers of Caesar that formed the core of the Republican army. Needless to stress is the fact that Caesar's veterans played a pivotal role in the power equations of the life span of the triumvirate. The party which Caesar's veterans supported, the Caesarean party, led by Octavian, took the state. One can, therefore, conclude that veterans had become a force that facilitated the private seizure of the state's military power by a private soldier, Octavian. This Roman example shows how veterans served as a dominant visual embodiment of intimidating masculinities that cowed the senate to submit to their demands (cf. Álcalde and Seixas 2018: 7).[4]

## Massing of veterans in the city

There is also a sense in which through their speeches, Roman commanders invested emotional and mental energy in their forces. Would it be too far-fetched to suggest that the massing of soldiers in the city of Rome, for example, functioned as a force materializing the power and personal agendas of their leaders as echoed in the speeches mentioned of generals to their forces? Such speeches, I argue, served to summon and/or coax combat-related masculinities, providing the war veterans with an opportunity for generating militant-masculinities, leading to expropriation and violence.

For example, there is a strong rhetoric of violence in the speech to the senate in the temple of Bellona (Plut. *Sull.* 30.2), and in Strabo's comments on Sulla's idea of just vengeance against the Samnites which is reflected in the actual violence (Strab. 5.4.11). Rhetoric gave the green light to veterans to give rein to their own violent agendas of greed and expropriation. As Stathis Kalyvas (2006) in his book *The Logic of Violence in Civil War* has shown, in volatile civil war contexts, there is strong emphasis on the legitimacy of violence meted against one's enemies. An example of such type of speech is cited below where Octavian incited Caesar's veterans by playing their fears and uncertainty regarding whether they will be able to keep the lands they had received from Julius Caesar if another faction were to take over power (App. *BC*. 3.87, White 1913: 117). The passage goes as follows (my italics):

> 'What confidence can you have of keeping the *lands* and money you have received from him, or what confidence can I have in my own safety, while the *relatives of the murderers thus dominate the Senate*? ... I see only one path of safety now for both of us: if I should obtain the consulship by your help. In that case all my father's gifts to you will be confirmed, *the lands that are still due* to you will be forthcoming, and all your *rewards* will be paid in full ...'

In the passage below (Dio 50.22.1-4: Cary 1917: 483, 485), Antony incited violence against Octavian thus (my italics):

> 'Just as I, therefore, and the Romans associated with me foresee the danger, in spite of our enjoying a kind of immunity so far as the decrees are concerned, and as we comprehend his plot, and yet neither abandon you nor look privately to our own advantage, in like manner you, too, whom even he himself does not deny that he regards as hostile, yes, most hostile, ought to bear in mind all these facts, and counting both our dangers and our hopes as common to us all, you should cooperate in every way in what we have to do and eagerly share in our zeal, balancing against each other what we shall suffer (as I have explained) if defeated, and what we shall gain if victorious. For while it is a great thing for us just to escape being the victims of insult and greed, if by any chance we are defeated, yet it is greatest of all to conquer and thus to be able to accomplish all we have prayed for. On the other hand, *it is most disgraceful for us, who are so many and so valiant, who have weapons, money, ships, and horses*, to choose the worse instead of the better course, and when it is in our power to confer liberty upon the other side as well as upon ourselves, to prefer to share their slavery with them. Our aims, you must know, are so opposed that, whereas he desires to reign as a sovereign over you, I wish to free them as well as you, and this indeed I have

> confirmed by oath. Therefore, as men who are to struggle for both sides alike and to win blessings in which all will share, let us earnestly strive, soldiers, to prevail at the present moment and to gain happiness for all time.'

In the Zimbabwean context, Mugabe's public speeches for example, emphasized the legitimacy of revolutionary violence, the annihilation of political enemies and how this influenced veterans. One of the speeches goes like this (Mugabe 2001: 110): 'Let us bring home to the Commercial Farmers of the CFU that they have declared war against the people of Zimbabwe who have every determination to win it.' A speech by a leader of the liberation war veterans group, Chenjerai Hunzvi has it that: 'We are fighting for our land and whosoever is killed, it is tough luck. In fact, it is now going to be very hard for white farmers.'[5] Such speeches, I argue, served to summon combat-related masculinities, providing the war veterans with an opportunity for generating militant-masculinity which resulted in expropriation of land and other violent engagements against the white farmers and oppositional political parties and individuals.[6]

## The spectacle

Gibbon (cited in Beard 2007: 54) has reflected on Roman constructions of military might and glory, and the correspondence between the spectacular display of soldiers and the onlookers. Broadly, I draw upon this to shed some light on how one can make sense, for example, of the episodes in which soldiers are recorded to have marched or gathered in the city of Rome bearing arms. I also draw upon Barry Barnes' examination of practice theory. According to Barnes (2006: 35), members of a group depend on the existing repertoire of practices in their society.[7] Members may have innumerable objectives and interests, and very many different beliefs, but whatever their objectives and whatever their beliefs about how to attain them, they will have to draw on that existing repertoire (Barnes 2006: 35). He argued (ibid.):

> Hence the system of practices will in effect reproduce itself by being drawn upon, and this can confidently be predicted without any knowledge of what prompts the specific actions wherein it is drawn upon. Its very existence will indeed account for its continuation: practice will account for practice.

Thus to put the above in the context of the late Roman Republic, one easily recognizes a certain pattern where generals caused their men to occupy space in the city while bearing arms. It is always necessary to ask what disposed them to enact such a practice – their aims, their lived experience in which their shared and inherited knowledge counted. In this sense, soldiers have a body culture which refers to daily practices of fitness, movement, gestures, postures, manners, ways of speaking etc., and it also involves the way these practices are trained into the body (Brownell 1995). I thus attempt to explain those and similar deployments as practices whose logics bordered on displaying latent and manifest forms of power consummated in the struggles for hegemony, territory and rewards. I particularly examine Roman generals' constructions of masculinity through, for example, the display of soldiers and arms in the city.

In Zimbabwe, veterans had a practice which when contrasted with Rome can amplify the rationale of spectacle.[8] One feature of the veterans' claims to land in Zimbabwe was how they, as a strident paramilitary unit associated with Mugabe's claim to territory, sought through staging of drills, parades and simulation of battle actions, to dramatize the decisive defeat of the white farmers. Sara Phang has suggested that mass formation and drill in the Roman army suggests that drill was not used as a form of social control, as the Romans regarded highly coordinated mass formations as a spectacular entertainment rather than a display of power. While this was true especially in the context of Roman triumphs (cf. Beard 2007), the logic of deploying war veterans in public spaces had other political objectives such as intimidating of senators. A similar occurrence of this nature is what happened around 25 AD when Tiberius exhibited the training of the Praetorians to the senate, in order to intimidate the senators with the soldiers' numbers and vigour (Dio Cass. 58.24.5).

To understand the logic of deploying soldiers and the violent behaviour of client-army veterans, I use the concept of ideology. I draw upon Giddens' (1979) theory of ideology to provide a critique of domination. I use the term *ideology* in a sense that involves habitus and hegemony[9] – a sense similar to that of Joseph Alter (1992: 21) which ascribes to ideology the everyday relations of subordination and domination embedded in culture – the kind of domination that can be reflected with considerable power in seemingly innocuous circumstances or where one may not normally think of domination. For a veteran, combat life and all it entails (e.g. disposition to violence) involves an ideology. At the locus of this ideology is the identity of the veteran – what it means, among other things, to be strong, heroic, masterful. This view is similar to Steven Barnett's detailed and flexible model for understanding how persons act in terms of their ideological stance (in Alter 1992: 21).

Hegemony here is not understood as Alter argued, to mean anything denoting a formal structure of consciousness and control. In the case of Roman soldiers occupying the city, I argue that there was domination embedded in the soldiers' military disposition. For Geertz (in Alter 1992), an ideology is a powerful cultural system, an immutable paradigm for interpreting meaning and guiding action. Alter (1992: 21) aptly qualifies the term thus:

> ... the concept denotes some features of what Bourdieu calls habitus, 'the source of these series of moves which are objectively organized as strategies without being the product of a genuine strategic intention ...' What makes habitus 'ideological' is not only its 'strategic' quality but the fact that it operates in a covert manner. Those who are engaged in the practice of habitus—the replication and reproduction of various forms of domination—are not fully aware of all of the ramifications of their actions ...

This can be illustrated by a closer analysis of a passage at Dio 41.16.3, Cary 1914: 31. In this passage, Dio describes Caesar's marching on Rome in 49 BC after Pompey had left the city. Caesar's display of military hardware in Rome reinforces the connotative connection of this spectacle with his triumphalism over Pompey, performatively enacted. Julius Caesar went to Rome in the company of his armed forces. Dio Cassius recorded that '... his (Julius Caesar's) armed forces were many and were everywhere in the city ...' Caesar's aim in deploying his armed forces everywhere in the city was to '... tame the senate ... until he should bring the war to an end' (Dio Cass. 41.15.3, Cary 1914: 31). This, I argue, explains Caesar's preoccupation with the occupation of physical space with armed soldiers as expressing his deep sense of anxiety with regard to power – an expression of what he hoped to achieve and conquer with the practice of occupation of space. The armed soldiers represented dominion, authority, rule and Caesar's power. Thus, Caesar's invasion of Rome with his army was effectively a spatial organization of power in which the maintenance or subversion of power and its formal structure was realized (cf. Ando: 2019). In Clifford Ando's conception of 'spatial politics', the invasion of Rome by Caesar's armed men enables a spacious/spatial view of politics, since politics conducted in a singular space, for example, is experienced by the observers almost at the same time (Ando 2019). Through the act of invading Rome, Caesar and his army were therefore simultaneously marshalling consent and exercising hegemony.

A further example may suffice to illustrate this point. At Sulla's funeral we are told by Appian that many were afraid of soldiers (App. *BC*. 12.106). Thus, paraded soldiers could sometimes inspire fear. Their deployment in the city of Rome was not always done for entertainment and spectacular amusement of the public, and even when they were paraded for such reasons, e.g. at Sulla's funeral, they still inspired fear among the people. What I am driving at can be illustrated in a context where latent and/or manifest martial masculinity can be unleashed by veterans occupying, marching or deployed in a public space in their numbers as if on parade or ready to make a charge. The habitus of a soldier is conditioned by a military disposition, which he consciously or unconsciously reproduces even outside of a battle context. Figure 9 below shows Marcus Aurelius' soldiers marching in a battle campaign. A disposition similar to theirs, I argue, played out among armed soldiers deployed in the Roman Republic to achieve specific goals for their leaders.

Tacitus' (*Hist.* 1.80, Hadas 1942: 468) description of Otho's Seventeenth Cohort's unexpected charge into the city of Rome is a good example of a violent military disposition (my italics):

> ... The soldiers murmured, and charged the tribunes and centurions with treachery, alleging that the households of the Senators were being armed to destroy Otho ... the worst among them were seeking an opportunity for plunder, the mass was as usual ready for any new movement, and the military obedience of the better disposed was neutralized by the darkness. The tribune, who sought to check the movement, and the strictest disciplinarians among the centurions, were cut down. *The soldiers seized their arms, bared their swords, and, mounted on their horses, made for the city and the palace.*

**Figure 9** Detail from the Column of Marcus Aurelius in Rome. The Column represents an episode on one of the emperor's campaigns. The soldiers are on a march carrying shields, spears and bows. Wikimedia/Barosaurus Lentus.

We must note that Otho had ordered the Seventeenth Cohort to be brought up to Rome from Ostia, while the task of arming it was entrusted to Varius Crispinus. As Tacitus recorded, the timing of the dispatch of the cohort provoked suspicion, and the motive challenged accusation (Tacit. *Hist.* 1.80, Hadas 1942: 467).

Barry Barnes' cavalry imagery below (2006: 28–9) best demonstrates my argument about military disposition:

> A cavalry charge is a fearful unleashing of powers. It may unfold as a practiced routine, a manifestation of a shared social practice, but the target of the charge and the signal that unleashes it are further features of equal sociological interest. Both these things are extrinsic to the 'shared practice' itself, and need to be understood by reference to 'members' knowledge' in a broader sense. The company of cavalry knows that it should charge on the signal of its commanders ... This indeed is a nice symbol of the necessity of references to knowledge and experience in making sense of social activities.

Barnes' observations in the quotation above make sense in the context of Roman soldiers deployed in the city of Rome. Deployed soldiers possessed latent power even when they did not appear to threaten or to beat up people. According to Giddens (1979: 5), action does not follow a tangent of its own making; its course is set by pervasive structural themes. Thus, this latent power was well understood by their generals and upon this power, the generals counted to achieve their goals. The deployment of soldiers in the city must be understood not as a mere enactment of a practice, but as its knowledgeable, informed and goal-directed enactment.[10] It may be said, for example, that soldiers in the late Roman Republic traditionally did enter the city at the instigation of their leaders as the practice of the collective. The problem of why they enacted the practice might thereby be glossed over. According to Giddens (1979: 79), those who are engaged in the replication and reproduction of different forms of domination are not fully mindful of all of the ramifications of their actions. In this sense, it is possible that soldiers marching in the city of Rome might not have been performing masculinities knowingly. It is therefore not unnecessary to consider what moved them to do certain actions. By citing different incidents during the late Roman Republic I attempt to explain the possible explanations and reasons for actions involving armed soldiers' actions or their deployment.

In late April 44 BC, when Antony went to Campania to superintend the settlement of Legion VII at Casilinum, he also visited other groups of veterans and advised them to keep up a regular arms drill (Keppie 1983: 58). The purpose of the drills was in keeping with the broader aims of the *tresviri* of confirming Caesar's acts (see. Keppie 1983: 52, Cic. *Phil.* 2.100, *Att.* 14.21.2). This re-mobilization of veterans demonstrates their role in the broader matrix of the politics of their settlements, and the political battles between the Republicans and the Caesarean party. Since Roman masculinity by nature often invoked the notion of *imperium* (dominion) – in this case the veterans were asserting their dominance and presence in those territories. Since Roman masculinity often also invoked the notion of *virtus,* which can be translated to mean 'valour' (Williams 2010: 139), the drills were also conducted as a way of practising martialism and control of territory. In this situation, masculinity was performed as a constant enactment of power in the Caesarean party's territorial dominion as they were getting ready to wrest more territory and power from Brutus' faction (see Tacit. *Ann.* 1.1).[11] So masculinity was not merely something the Caesarean veterans simply possessed, but also a way of being that they had to perform and assert in the very possibility of losing not only their land allotments received from Caesar, but the very possibility of losing control of territory to the Republican forces. Brutus and his Republican Party were pledging to take back the land from Caesar's veterans to their rightful owners, the Roman citizens (App. *BC.* 2.140-141). So the military drills superintended by Antony were, matter-of-factly, preparation for war.

The secret mobilization of veterans to Rome which Cicero records was motivated by the political goals of having a law passed about veterans' pensions, and of passing through the *comitia* a number of other bills, the most important of which was aimed at reallocating the provincial commands to Antony (Cic. *Fam.* 11.2, *Att.* 14.22).[12]

More so, after the defeat of Brutus and company if Appian's account is anything to go by, Appian (*BC.* 4.5) recorded that the rich were proscribed due to the splendour of their estates and houses which the triumvirs promised to divide among the soldiers. No doubt, such promises motivated the actions of the soldiers as can be noticed in their actions afterwards. Describing the actions of the veterans of the triumvirs, Appian (*BC.* 4.7) further recorded that:

> As they arrived, the city was speedily filled with arms and military standards, disposed in the most advantageous places . . . A public assembly was forthwith convened in the midst of these armed men, and a tribune Publius Titius, proposed a law providing for a new magistracy for setting the present disorders, to assist of three men to hold office for 5 years, namely Lepidus, Antony, and Octavian, with the same powers as consuls. Among the Greeks these would be

> called harmosts, which is the name the Lacedaemonians gave to those whom they appointed over their subject states.

The promises made by the triumvirs to their soldiers served to summon combat-related masculinities, and this provided the soldiers with an opportunity to deploy militant-masculinity as seen by their actions described by Appian.

## Military fatigues and paraphernalia

An intimidating paraphernalia in the form of military boots also seems evident in Octavian's veterans' massing in Rome (Dio Cass. 48.12). To make Dio Cassius' description more palpable, I juxtapose this passage with the idea of marching Zimbabwean war veterans in the streets of Harare – a common political feature in Zimbabwe.

My epistemological position informed by the Zimbabwean context is my theoretical entry point for analysing Roman texts which describes appearances of veterans in ways that suggest the spectacle of a military, violent and threatening masculinity. The assembling, marching and dancing of Zimbabwean war veterans (in respect of their boots and fatigues) clearly fused the masculine, the beefy, the aggressive, the husky and the athletic as they showed the grand leap, the stamping of the feet, and the vigorous movements of the veteran's body which all acquire martial and muscular connotations.[13]

This is quite reminiscent of what happened in French West Africa. The African veterans of France's twentieth-century wars are living examples of how their experiences and political engagements affected the evolution of an emerging French African political community (Mann 2006). Their group activities and demonstrations against their colonial master, France, greatly manifested discourses of martial-masculinities (cf. Mann 2006). Upon their demobilization soon after the First World War from France and the Maghreb to West Africa they strutted and postured their physical toughness and their habits of combat in military fatigues as observed by Gregory Mann (2006: 63):

> The First World War represented the first large-scale mobilization in colonial West Africa, as some 200 000 men from the region served in the French army during the war. In its aftermath, ex-tirailleurs dressed in soldiers' puttees, in bright red caps, or in military issue coats returned from France and the Maghreb to West Africa. There they jammed the roads and cities, roughed up villagers, and momentarily changed the already shaky colonial order.

The images of masculinities constructed through group activities such as marching and mass gatherings allow for our examination of marching and massing Roman veterans in search of meaning. The assembling of Roman war veterans is described by Dio Cassius (48.12, Cary 1917: 243) as follows (my italics):

> After this the veterans assembled in Rome *in great numbers*, giving out that they intended to make some communication to the people and the senate. But instead of troubling themselves about this errand, they *assembled on the Capitol*, and after commanding that the compact which Antony and Caesar had made should be read to them, they ratified these agreements and voted that they themselves should be made arbitrators of the differences between them. After recording this action on tablets and sealing them, they delivered them to the Vestal Virgins to keep; and they gave command to Caesar, who was present, and to the other party through an embassy, to present themselves for the trial at Gabii on a stated day. Caesar showed his readiness to submit to arbitration, and the others promised to be there but did not go, either because they were afraid or because they thought it beneath them; at any rate, they were wont to make fun of the veterans, calling them among other names *senatus caligatus, on account of the military boots they wore* . . .

This passage can be analysed functionally, to explore the possible meanings of war veterans' actions. In this case, the veterans were called 'senators wearing soldiers' boots' on account of the military boots they were wearing which gives a sense of subversion of established boundaries and of challenging contours of place, by assuming a civic role or duty meant for senators. Dio's description gives a sense of what the veterans looked like in their military boots, and portrays the veterans' act as a subversive gesture. What Dio describes are the politics of appearance and gesture practiced by the assembled veterans. To some extent, but not in every respect, the passage conveys a sense of a masculinity expressed through the exhibitionistic and audacious display of hordes of veterans gathering in the city of Rome on their way to the Capitol.

Further analysis of Dio's passage can reveal some masculine motifs. The gathering of the veterans produced a spectacle, which proceeded in the form of an uninterrupted conversation which the veterans maintained among themselves for their intended purposes, in the moment of their mediation and management of the conflict between Antony and Octavian. Their gathering in Rome and eventually at the Capitol was a portrayal of their power, not just in terms of the spectacle of their mass gathering, but also as a loaded social and political gesture, constituting an embodied practice in the political economy of power and its representation. The spectacle can be understood as an embodied social and political practice which derived from their gathering as a custom, and a ritual that evoked meaning and power.

Since culture in anthropological terms can be understood as a matter of publicly observable symbols and rituals, and the organization of discourses and practices, this passage allows for reflection, inter alia, on the connotations of the veterans' boots in the passage in question, and allows us to explore the meaning of the boots. Figure 10 shows a Roman soldier's boot.

The term *caliga* signifies a stout shoe, especially a soldier's boot (Simpson 1959: 85). *Caligae* were a fundamental aspect of the soldier's identity and essential to his well-being (cf. Plin. *NH.* 7.44). They (*caligae*) had connotations of toughness. *Senatus caligatus* means a senate wearing soldiers' boots. The Greek words in Appian are 'boulen kaligatan' meaning a 'council with *caligae*'. Cary (the translator of the passage) has tried to reconstruct the Latin phrase which would have been used. It would not be plausible that veterans wore battle shoes off the battlefield, but in the passage above, they were wearing their boots. Or was the term used simply because they customarily wore them on the battlefield, being soldiers?

**Figure 10** A bronze caliga from an over life-size statue of a Roman cavalryman. Wikimedia/Carole Raddato from Frankfurt, Germany.

It is also possible that the *caligae* on the battlefield would have been dirty or dusty and so the title '*senatus caligatus*' would be to represent the veterans as animalistic and unrefined people wearing dirty military shoes. It is also possible that the people in this text calling the veterans *senatus caligatus* were trying to mock the veterans. It is to be expected that some people viewed veterans negatively, in view of their rough manner of comportment. The dirty military shoes may also be viewed from the point of view of onlookers not as an index of masculinity, but of animality – cause for mockery rather than admiration. According to Gleason, an ideal Roman masculinity did not equal deliberate untidiness – a certain amount, a degree, of refinement was in order (in Olson 2014: 187). When it comes to war veterans' contexts, this view may complicate the dynamics of gendered power gesticulation. It was expected for the war veterans to be rough and untidy due to the nature of their job. Soldiers are accustomed with tough and rough conditions of the field of war, where a rough masculinity is developed as opposed to a refined one. It has been argued that Roman masculinity was associated with a certain level of uncultivated roughness (Williams 2010: 142). Williams (ibid.) mentions the example of Vespasian who revoked the appointment he had bestowed upon a young official because the young man had come to him smelling perfume, and that of Juvenal's imagination of a young man desirous of promotion within the army being advised to affect neglect of his appearance, leaving his hair uncombed and his nostrils and underarms untrimmed.

Thus, the veterans in Dio's passage might have consciously, because of their distinctive boots, exhibited an animalistic appearance, which gave a palpable form or impression of soldiers on parade. Military boots are a marker of military status – something denoting totalitarianism in line with ideological functions of the veteran as a soldier. Dio himself in the passage conjectured that fear was the reason why some people wouldn't attend the rally of the veterans in Rome. A senator's boot has a history of authoritarianism in Rome. Coulston (2005: 90) describes how troops in ancient Rome could be paraded, in order to intimidate even senators.

Plutarch in his disquisition on city governance, advised mayors and city councillors in the cities of Greece to keep their eyes on the platform from which justice was administered by a Roman governor, 'seeing the Kaltoi above your head'.[14] Being under Roman governors' authoritarianism implied being under their officials who in the Roman world would basically be military personnel (Saddington 2012). Likewise, the veterans as described by Dio displayed their unfettered strength and power when they massed at the Capitol and made resolutions regarding the dispute between Antony and Octavian.

I proceed to explore the impact on society of veteran-masculinities in the two worlds of veterans.

## War veterans and society: A refined/intellectual masculinity vs a violent masculinity

This section illustrates the impact of a veteran-masculinity in society, as performed by Zimbabwe's liberation war veterans and ancient Roman veterans in two separate sections. The purpose of this endeavour is to provide insights into societies and cultures of violence that emerge in post-war situations.

### a) The Zimbabwean context

At this stage, I give some reflections on how Zimbabwe's guerrilla fighters' rough masculinities operated in competition with post-independence intellectuals in the country. It is worth noting that guerrilla combatants looked down upon the intellectuals with whom they waged the war. Mugabe himself, who was an intellectual, was looked down upon among the guild of guerrillas (cf. Mhanda 2011 and Tendi 2020) – a disdain which later led to his defenestration from power through a military coup largely orchestrated by guerrilla veterans. Just to remark on the fact that the liberation war veterans' behaviour met with some opposition, and that, as in Rome, Zimbabwean politics was shaped along the lines of a masculinity vs effeminacy discourse. But unlike in Rome where intellectuals were regarded as weak and effeminate, as Cicero said in the *Pro Murena* (22), educated oppositional leaders in Zimbabwe (without any military history) confronted the liberation war veterans with what counts as an intellectual masculinity, to thwart and counter a violent masculinity of veterans and their leaders. This intellectual masculinity, which appeals to masses of opposition supporters in Zimbabwe, would not have counted in Roman politics.

In a debate which straddled along the lines of the status of youth versus masculinity, Nelson Chamisa, leader of the opposition MDC (at the time of writing), was in real life convinced that he was the 'techno-metro' man: modern, IT (Information Technology) compliant, young, educated, of a great legal mind as an advocate, articulate, and above all, Christian. Reacting against the challenge to his manliness in Zimbabwean politics – as he was regarded as a baby in diapers, Chamisa activated and enacted a new form of masculinity – an intellectual masculinity, which actually shook the ruling ZANU-PF party.

Chamisa, on his part, armed himself with his soft intellectual masculinity, and augmented his youthful stature; a status which the veterans and ZANU-PF politicians demeaned with much disdain as woefully inadequate for him to challenge their tried and tested leader Emmerson Mnangagwa, a 'veteran of the Liberation War'. Chamisa was still in his mother's womb in 1978, two years before Zimbabwe's independence. He did not fight colonialism. He was not part of the veterans' struggle for land against colonialism, but he promised to enact a smart distribution of land without shedding blood.

In antiquity greatness is a quality that usually came at the cost of both great deeds and equally great flaws – with ordinary people ready to confer or deny individuals of this acclaim (Powell 2013). Similarly, masculinity in Zimbabwe and its various forms of manifestation and representations was variously analysed by ordinary citizens who also played a part in the discourses of its construction. In various ways, they discussed and shared their views on the statue of the political actors through WhatsApp and Facebook cartoons, depicting the politicians in a manner that testified to the existence of the public's universe of ideas insofar as the construction of masculinity was concerned. In such public conversations, some people felt Emmerson Mnangagwa's (president of Zimbabwe at the time of writing) performance during the 2018 presidential campaign rallies was lacklustre and dispirited. Some stated that his campaign was hamstrung by his lack of 'testosterone'-induced charisma and flowery language usually associated with not only his younger competitor, Nelson Chamisa, but even his predecessor Mugabe's rhetorical prowess. This shows how a liberation war masculinity was suddenly in a crisis as those born after independence felt Mnangagwa's liberation war masculinity was inadequate without a flare of intellectualism and loquacity.

Even the political supporters of Nelson Chamisa would not be beaten to it. They fought back by coining a joke which circulated on WhatsApp media platform through a cartoon in which Chamisa was shown in baby diapers. This was in acknowledgement of their favourite politician's youthfulness, but they still insisted that Mnangagwa would still lose the election to a baby in diapers. *'Mnangagwa achadyiwa semucheche semaJigisi'*/ (Mnangagwa will be munched like Jiggies [a baby food]). We may note that Chamisa also attempted to ride on the ideal of virile masculinity as a political actor to counter the veterans' derogatory utterances. He put much effort in trying to portray himself as possessing adequate manhood in Zimbabwean politics. At one time he did some push-ups during a demonstration march in Harare in June 2018, in display of his youthful and energetic body. This was in stark contrast to his then 75-year-old rival Mnangagwa, who obviously looked old and frail.

The crisis of ageing by self-styled 'liberation' leaders in African politics is a real one. Yoweri Kaguta Museveni, president of Uganda (at the time of writing) publicized his rigorous exercises by undertaking a six-day long march (195 kilometres) in early 2020 to re-enact his 1986 exertions when he took over power in Uganda. Political pressure principally from younger politicians such as Bobi Wine (real name Robert Kyagulani), forced Museveni to recalibrate his older body and redeploy it as agile and fit for purpose (Chitando and Mlambo, forthcoming). At the time of writing, Museveni was 76 years old, while Bobi Wine was 38 years old. Such younger politicians were clearly threatening Museveni's status as a Head of State, military commander and figure of authority.

Museveni's struggle is not personal or unique. Young people constitute the majority of citizens in Africa, and they ask hard questions regarding their exclusion from power as over-65 year old male politicians have continued to dominate the politics of their countries (ibid.). These men justify their continued stay in power on the basis of having waged struggles for freedom against colonialists (mostly in parts of Southern Africa) or against dictatorships (mostly in East and West Africa). As Chitando and Mlambo (ibid.) argued, they also project themselves as permanent fighters for one cause or the other: anti-colonialism, Black economic empowerment, fighting corruption, social decay of all kinds, and other initiatives. They project themselves as steeped in the warrior tradition and as embodying the masculinity of war (see for example, Mazrui 1977).[15] The rise of Julius Malema as an opposition figure in South African politics must also be located within the generational conflict and internal contestation within masculinities in Africa (ibid.). Malema took on the older veterans of the apartheid war, Jacob Zuma and Cyril Ramaphosa, challenging them to hand over power to the younger generation (cf. Posel 2014).

## b) An embodied rhetoric of masculinity: The sons of Roman centurions and the sons of Zimbabwe's guerrilla veterans

Having explored how war veterans-masculinities impacted the Zimbabwean political landscape, this section illustrates the impact of veteran-masculinities in society through an examination of selected passages in the *Satires* and the *Odes* of Horace. I illustrate the working of an embodied rhetoric of masculinity in societies beyond combat as exhibited by the sons of centurions described in Horace, and the sons of guerrilla fighters in Zimbabwe.

In *Sat.* 1.6 there is a possible reference to a masculine military ideal associated with war veterans. Here Horace gives a real-life history narrative of how his young life was impacted upon by the veteran phenomenon. He indicates that his father chose not to send him to school in a place where people of a military background were educated (Bovie 1959: 65). He uses the phrase *magni quo pueri magnis e centurionibus orti* ('where big boys, descended from big centurions . . .') (*Sat.*1.6.72-3: Fraenkel 1970: 2–3). The term 'big' is ambiguous since it may refer to the physique of the boys and their fathers or their social status. Bovie (1959: 65) uses the phrase 'prominent sons of centurions'. Fraenkel (1970: 3) suggests that the centurions' children might have bullied and insulted Horace as a boy; even if he did not go to school with them, Fraenkel talks of youngsters strutting up to the schoolmaster's house, and of centurions' children possibly insulting Horace when they were playing together. Although Fraenkel seems to relate *magni* in *magni . . . pueri* (*Sat* 1.6.72-3) to haughtiness among the young people, physical bullying might be held to imply a stronger male physique among the centurions' children. If *magni* refers to the size of the male physique, then the big boys descended from big centurions are sons with a strong male physique descended from war veteran fathers with a strong male physique. I may suggest that this maleness might have been a source of pride for both sons and fathers. This reveals the promotion of martial virtue and demonstrates that soldiers were feared for their martial virtue. The soldier's physical might was therefore not just metaphorical. Horace lived in Venusia where the army veterans were conceivably settled at the expense of local landowners whose land was parceled to veterans as punishment for their role in the Social War 91–88 BC. Post-Philippi veterans were also allocated land in Venusia. This must have been the environment in which Horace was living as a schoolboy.

Thus, ideals of heroic maleness were connected with the traditional notions of manly virtue as demonstrated by *Sat.*1.6.71ff, and also in his narrative of the defeat of the Republican forces at Philippi where he later recorded it as a day of embarrassment for himself, when he fled without his shield (*Odes* 2.7.10).

Horace's father's estate in Venusia and the poet Vergil's were among many throughout Italy to be confiscated for the settlement of veterans. Under those circumstances, Horace later claimed that he was reduced to poverty and this led him to try his hand at poetry.

This bit from Horace shed some light on how the children of centurions performed their father's masculinities in post-Philippi Rome. Such an image has fully played out in Zimbabwe. Children of Zimbabwe's National Liberation War veterans have formed an association namely, The Children of Zimbabwe National Liberation War Veterans Association, which has since become a vehicle through which their muscular arrogance is felt by many civilians. It is in both practical and ideological terms an extension of intimidation and muscular arrogance of their fathers. This example gives us an approximate idea of a shared masculinity, in more or less the same sense as Roman centurions' sons described by Horace.

It is important to highlight that there is a sense also even among Roman veterans in which masculinity could be lost. I recounted in Chapter Six about a Zimbabwean veteran who conceived himself as having lost his manliness because of dislocating his hip during the war. In this section, I attempt to show how such feelings were represented in ancient Roman texts. In the *Odes*, in the third stanza of *Carm.* 2.7, Michie 1964: 103, we read:

> Tecum Philippos et celerem fugam
> sensi relicta non bene parmula
> cum fracta virtus et minaces
> turpe solum tetigere mento.

> 'I endured with you Philippi, and a swift flight, having in cowardly fashion (lit. not bravely/creditably) left my shield behind, when courage was broken, and threatening people touched the vile ground with their chins.'

The phrase *non bene* is adverbial, and Lewis and Short (1879: 229) list among the acceptable meanings of *bene* the following: 'honourably, bravely, creditably, gloriously'. I view it as describing the action of abandonment of the shield rather than qualifying the shield itself. The translation of Michie (1964: 103) talks of 'my poor shield' and this may be influenced by the fact that Horace's abandonment of his shield is held to be related to a fragment of Archilochus which talks of a shield abandoned on the battlefield, but then says, 'What is that shield to me? Stuff it! I'll get another just as good' (Bowie 1986: 109–10); see also a chapter on 'A Counter-Culture of Honor' by Berkovich (2017: 165–94). This fragment seems to present the shield as something which is no great loss, and therefore of low quality; so that reading Horace under the influence of that fragment might suggest that Horace is representing his shield as poor. But in fact the adverb here grammatically cannot qualify the noun, but rather refers to the verbally-derived participle. It is the act of abandonment that is not done 'well' or 'bravely'. So we are looking at an ideal of conduct in wartime which Horace has violated.

That this conduct is linked with masculinity is suggested by the reference to *virtus*, courage, which is derived from *vir*, meaning a man. It is not clear whether the *virtus* broken here is Horace's own specifically, or the *virtus* of people generally; the reference to the *minaces* (threatening people) biting the dust suggests that he is saying that lots of people lost their courage, so that he is not unique.

The reference to *minaces* suggests people who are frightening rather than frightened on the battlefield, those who live up to the martial ideal. Michie brings this out by translating *minaces* as 'the strong men who frowned fiercest' (Michie 1964: 103). Yet these were humiliated, making Horace's loss of nerve and face more excusable. The reference to *mento*, the chin, the place where beards are grown, the sign of maleness, reinforces how martial masculinity was humiliated on the battlefield. The masculine chins were brought to the ground.

The fact that Horace has taken trouble to minimize and palliate or excuse his loss of nerve suggests that we are dealing with a real or historical lack of courage shown at Philippi. Why would one invent an embarrassing story about oneself and then try to palliate it, when it would be a simple matter not to invent the story in the first place? Yet since Horace's reference to abandoning his shield echoes a reference to shield-abandonment by Archilochus, mentioned above, it may be asked whether Horace's abandonment of his shield can really be a historical event. Are we not here dealing with an imitation of previous lyric poetry, and therefore something that did not happen in real life?

A possible answer may be that although Horace did in cowardly fashion flee at Philippi, the reference to abandoning the shield may be a metaphorical image describing this. We may recall the story of the Spartan soldier who was encouraged by his mother to return from battle either carrying his shield or being carried on it – these being metaphors either for victory or for dying in battle. Perhaps Horace is using abandonment of the shield as a poetic or metaphorical way of describing flight from battle generally, and his use of this metaphor or image is influenced by Archilochus. It is true that '*parmula*' is an unusual word, so we are not talking of a popular metaphor or proverbial expression, but of a metaphor specifically invented by Horace himself to fit a real occasion. Horace may not have literally thrown away his shield, but he literally fled at Philippi, and the abandonment of the shield represents this.

It should be noted that it does not follow that an event is historically unreal simply because imagery imitating earlier Greek poetry is used to describe it. Catullus' Poem 51 is based on an original by Sappho, (Simpson 1965: 106) but it does not follow that Lesbia was not a real person (Warrington 1961: 132) – although of course Catullus' real 'Lesbia' did not in fact come from Lesbos (ibid.) and her name is therefore a metaphor. The use of imagery imitating Greek poetry can therefore clothe a real event of some sort in history.

## Non-veteran, land/corn struggles and the political fields

There was also another dimension to land expropriation in both societies. The episodes of expropriation of political space cannot make sense if understood only in the context of military veterans alone, as a myriad of other actors also thronged such spaces to make the politics more complex. The urban crowd was a force that thronged streets and forums in protest for corn, land and against high prices. Because the city was functional as the focal point for political control and mobilization of political support, the mobilization involved soliciting mass support of crowds. There is however an important difference. Zimbabwe's guerrilla veterans mobilized ordinary citizens to join them in expropriations while the Roman veteran was seen in collision with the ordinary citizen as the ordinary people fought to resist them (Dio Cass. 48.9, App. *BC.* 5.12). It is in this respect that I find the Roman military veteran-masculinity to be very coarse as it brooked no cooperation with the ordinary citizen. Perhaps with the exception of Caesar whose tact involved giving land, corn and money to the ordinary people, first-century BC Roman veterans operated in an environment that allowed for no room for cooperation or sympathy with ordinary communities.

In another sense city protests reflected class struggle between the political elite and the poorer classes. Urban unrest reflected the dynamics of gender, class and other social cleavages, and the subordinated power relations characteristic of the powerful dynasties that controlled the levers of power in Rome. Appian recorded that (my italics): 'They came to Rome in *crowds*, *young* and *old*, *women* and *children*, to the forum and temples, uttering lamentations, saying that they had done no wrong for which they, Italians, should be driven from their fields and their hearthstones . . .' (App. *BC.* 5.12, White 1913: 397) This gives agency (passive or active) to non-combatants, not necessarily as participating in the expropriations themselves but in resisting them. Although Appian's account does not zoom in on women and children protesters, the fact that he mentioned them shows they were not passive platforms for client-army expropriations and violence. They went to Rome to occupy the streets as part of protesting crowds. I will begin with the Zimbabwean context.

In Zimbabwe, as the veterans mobilized languages of freedom, rights and sovereignty, so too did they foster the active and militant participation of youths in land occupation. The youths were made to believe that they were also instrumental in the completion of the revolution against colonialism which was started during the liberation wars, but could only be completed if and only if land was taken back from the white farmers (Mlambo and Gwekwerere 2019). Non-combatants who joined land expropriation were in a sense viewed as having joined the guild of heroes – a process which qualified them as fighters and patriots.

A shared masculinity between veterans and ordinary peasants functioned to camouflage conflict. In order to obscure the broad range of differences and conflicts between rural masses and the class that enjoyed the lion's share of the fruits of the war of national liberation as the nation's new rulers, war veterans functioned as occupants of the middle ground on which rural masses and the nation's leaders could meet (Mlambo and Gwekwerere 2019). They achieved this with relative success, partly through their willingness to refer to rural masses also as 'heroes', just like themselves. One might well have been an impoverished peasant, farm worker, civil servant or a gardener protesting against colonialism, but they were all allied in fraternity with veterans in the struggle. This implied a specious equality symbolically ratified by 'shared' masculinity or bravery and reinforced by songs such as '*Zvinoda vakashinga moyo*!' (The situation requires those who are brave) which valorized the courage that was perceived as necessary in militarily challenging the colonial regime and its remaining edifice. The result was the creation of a bond that brought together rural masses and veterans at an ideological level. This became clearer when veterans mobilized the language of Black freedom and sovereignty to foster active and militant participation of youths who were made to believe that they were spearheading revolutionary action for the sake of posterity.

Zimbabwe's case of deploying virile youths to support the settlement of veterans and hence to become a pillar of support of Mugabe's regime can be contrasted with Sulla's Cornelii – young former slaves whom Sulla recruited and gave citizenship to support his settlement scheme. Appian (App. *BC*. 1.100, White 1913: 187) refers to the 10,000 Cornelii – later described as young and strong, i.e. masculine, as one of the three pillars of Sulla's power, the other two pillars being veterans and the senate (my italics):

> To the plebeians he added more than 10,000 slaves of proscribed persons, choosing the *youngest and strongest*, to whom he gave freedom and Roman citizenship, and he called them Cornelii after himself. In this way he made sure of having 10,000 men among the Plebeians always ready to obey his commands. In order to provide the same kind of safeguard throughout Italy he distributed to the 23 legions that had served under him a great deal of land in the various communities, as I have already related, some of which was public property and some taken from the communities by way of fines.

Perhaps more close to Sulla's example was Mugabe's deployment of hooligans. Such a practice was confirmed by songs sung during the height of the expropriations to mobilize emotional energies from ordinary people as a way of encouraging them to participate in the proscription of political enemies through land occupations. One such song goes: '*VaMugabe vanofamba nemamonya, kwavanoenda vanofamba nemaRasta. VaMugabe vanofamba nemamonya, kwavanoenda vanofamba nemaHwindi*/ (Wherever Mugabe goes, he is followed by hooligans!'). There was deliberate deployment of bouncers by Mugabe for the sake of proscribing and intimidating political enemies. In periods of political instability like the late Republic and later empire, slaves trained in combat were deployed as bodyguards or used to threaten and even assault rivals and enemies (Lenski 2016). The late Roman Republic in particular was notorious for figures like P. Clodius Pulcher and T. Annius Milo, both of whom played a key role in the civil warfare of the 50s BC and intimidated their respective opponents using bands of armed slaves, especially slave gladiators (Lenski 2016: 292).[16] Mugabe's government was notorious for recruiting social miscreants, criminals, illegal and violent gold miners known as *mashurugwi* to terrorize his political rivals. Such moments manifested a masculinity of a violent mob deployed in political fields to maintain the dictator's grip on power. It is therefore necessary to understand the phenomenon of violence in politics not only in the context of land expropriation, but also in the broader context of expropriation of political fields by city mobs.

## The *cura annonae* and the politics of violent mobs

The corn dole does have a significant history in the 100 years between the Gracchi and Augustus. It is assumed that it was cancelled by Sulla;[17] certainly it was part of Lepidus' programme in 78 BC, and it was revived or increased by Clodius in 58 BC. Corn distribution was a contested issue, on which both sides competed for ownership and claimed to provide for the people and their material welfare. On the one hand, a populist policy was presented by the *populares* and others; on the other hand the senate, to reinforce their own position, also presented themselves as champions of the welfare of the people, from a more paternalist perspective. The role played by land and corn distributions in converting the urban plebs into an alternative source of political support, contested by both the senatorial government and the demagogues, is worth noting.

This brings us to the question of the power of the city plebs. We should not forget the issue of power residing in the cities, and of urban discontent as having been more politically dangerous than its rural equivalent. In the city of Rome, according to Appian, multitudes always sung the praise of those who spent their fortunes on the welfare of the public to please it (App. *BC.* 1.11), with Caesar stepping in later to capitalize on the support of the city plebs by distributing land and corn to them. This tradition started during the tenure of the Gracchi in the second century BC. Appian tells us that Tiberius also depended on the city plebs in his political programme. Appian recorded that Tiberius, fearing that evil would befall him if he should not be re-elected, '... summoned the rural people to come to vote; but they were busy with the harvest, and so under pressure from the short time still remaining before the day fixed for the election he resorted to the city population' (App. *BC.* 1.14, see also Plut. *Ti. Gr.* 16.1-2).

## The senate vs populares

In the first-century BC, corn distributions had become a stage of contestation for power between the *populares* and the senate. In 100 BC, Lucius Appuleius Saturninus proposed a radical corn law which pegged the price of corn at a far cheaper rate than the price stipulated by the *Lex Sempronia Frumentaria.* This trend was continued by Lepidus' *Lex Aemilia* in 78 BC. The motive was that of becoming more popular with the urban population. Clodius' corn law of 58 BC demonstrated the height of the politics of the belly, characterized by an unrestrained recklessness. Reacting against Clodius' Corn Law, Cicero protested against the free distribution of corn as it robbed the treasury of revenue (Dio Cass. 38.13, Cic. *Sest.* 55). Clodius' populism through corn distributions attracted more people into the city.

Julius Caesar is reported by Plutarch to have pursued a similar policy as he openly challenged the *senatus consultum ultimum.* This is why Julius Caesar's political goals, by the mid-60s BC, clashed with those of the 'establishment', and his approach was confrontational (Raaflaub 2010: 162). Plutarch (*Caes.* 8.4) corroborates this view:

> Cato, fearing above all things a revolutionary movement set on foot by the poorer classes, who were setting the whole multitude on fire with the hopes which they fixed upon Caesar, persuaded the Senate to assign them a monthly allowance of grain, in consequence of which an annual outlay of 7,500,000 drachmas was added to the other expenditures of the state.

This demonstrates how the crisis of hunger was to some extent a process worsened by politicians, who, in order to invest in the Roman political fields occupied by the urban plebs, undertook populist measures which drained the treasury. It is true that population growth played a part in causing the urban crisis of food shortages, but the solutions applied to the problem worsened the situation.

Rome imported grain to alleviate the shortage. The senatorial appointment of Pompey to a five-year *cura annonae* (57–53 BC) demonstrates that the senate also wanted to pose as the legitimate bread-winner for the urban plebs, as a counter to Clodius' Corn Law. Cicero's recommendation of Avianius' two sons Gaius and Marcus, who belonged to a reputable family of corn merchants, to the proconsulship of Sicily, is a pointer to the fact that the senate wanted to prove to be efficient in dealing with corn shortage at Rome (Cic. *Fam*. 13.79). Cicero, standing for the senatorial government, was clearly reacting to Clodius' Corn Law, which had not only drained the treasury but also caused riots in Rome, as Clodius was inciting the urban plebs against the government. Pompey's *cura annonae* was also a double-edged sword. On the one hand it was a genuine state sponsored programme; but on the other, it reaped political mileage for Pompey as someone considered beneficent.

## Pompey vs Caesar

The use of corn supplies as a political weapon was escalated in Roman politics during the civil war between Pompey and Caesar. Both men demonstrated a clever awareness of the importance of corn supplies. Pompey, during the civil war with Caesar, when he retreated to Greece, cut corn supplies to Italy. Pompey's control of Egypt and the East meant that Rome would starve (App. *BC*. 2.54, see also Cic. *Ad Att*. 9.9, Dio Cass. 41.18, Caes. *BCiv*. 1.30).

When Caesar defeated Pompey, and when he virtually became the most powerful individual in Roman politics, he tackled the problem of feeding the ever-growing urban population, as many people hoped to benefit from corn doles. Suetonius tells us that the figure of those eligible for corn doles was reduced to 150,000, down from 320,000 (Suet. *Div. Iul*. 41.3). By this process, Caesar was solely in control of the city populace. He endeared himself to the city populace that filled the political field that was Rome and won their political support ahead of the senate and its candidates.

## Octavian vs Sextus Pompey

Control of the political sphere was critical for Octavian and Sextus Pompey. In the late 40s BC, during the power struggle between the two, Sextus Pompeius' control of Sicily and of Sardinia and Corsica meant that the merchants of the Orient feared to lose their corn ships to Pompey. Appian observes:

> Thus there was a great rise in the cost of provisions, and the people considered the cause of it to be the strife between the chiefs and cried out against them and urged them to make peace with Pompeius. As Octavian would not yield, Antony advised him to hasten the war on account of the scarcity. As there was no money for this purpose, an edict was published that . . . those who acquired property by legacies should contribute a share thereof. The people tore down the edict with fury. They were exasperated that, after exhausting the public treasury, stripping the provinces, burdening Italy with contributions, taxes, and confiscations, not for foreign war . . . but for private enmities and to add to their power, for which reason the proscriptions and murders and this terrible famine had come about, the triumvirs should. deprive them of the remainder of their property.
>
> App. *BC*. 5.67, White 1913: 491

What this demonstrates is that the pursuit of political survival was important to these politicians, and not the welfare of the Roman population, who could be starved or fed depending on what suited the one seeking dominance (Cic. *Cat.* 2).[18]

## The case of Africa and Zimbabwe

The Roman corn dole was intended to capture the vote of the restive urban plebs. Bates' (1981) seminal work: *Markets and States in Tropical Africa: The Political basis of Agricultural Policies*, can be referred to in order to find a reflection, in an African context, of the politics of the belly in the Roman Republic. Bates demonstrates, with statistical data, why states in sub-Saharan Africa tended to pursue agricultural policies that have involved, among other things, buying export crops from farmers at very low prices and setting controls on the prices at which farmers can sell food crops to urban populations (Bates 1981: 4). These 'populist' policies, Bates argues, have allowed states to appease restive urban constituencies on whose quiescence states have depended for their survival (Ibid.). However, the same policies have contributed to the devastation of agriculture sectors in many countries.

Within the context of the populist politics of distribution of land and food, Zimbabwe experienced similar policies through price controls and the Basic Commodity Supply Side Intervention scheme (BACCOSSI), instituted in June 2007 (The Zimbabwe Independent, April 23, 2009). Masses in the rural areas and in towns were given food handouts. It is within this context that Mugabe emerged as the 'real' and popular man. However, this policy backfired, as food disappeared from supermarket shelves, and it also crippled production, as the price control model only made political sense, as opposed to economic sense.

The land expropriations era is reminiscent of Clodius' riotous and economically ruinous approach to the food crisis at Rome. The year 2000 saw mobs rampaging farms, in the process destroying and looting crops and infrastructure. This displaced thousands of farm workers and negatively affected production. Food shortages became severe and the end result was a scenario where the method of expropriation (characterized by violence and grabbing), though intended to solve rural and urban poverty and hunger, actually worsened the crisis. In fact, the process triggered a rise in food handouts as opposed to food production (Logan 2006).

A method with a result comparable to this was criticized by Cicero (*Dom.* 10-11), as he reacted to the economically ruinous Corn Law of Clodius (58 BC). Cicero accused Clodius of inciting the city mob, that led to looting and violence. Cicero (*Dom.* 13, Perseus Digital Library n.d.h) lamented the invasion of public and political spaces by hired mobs and excited crowds by the *populares* (my italics):

> Who are the men who were openly named in the senate by Quintus Metellus,—your brother, O Metellus,—the consul, by whom he said that he had been attacked with stones and actually hit? He named Lucius Sergius and Marcus Lollius. Who is that Lollius? A man who is not even at this moment by your side without his sword; who, while you were tribune of the people, demanded (I will say nothing of his designs against myself) to have the murder of Cnaeus Pompeius entrusted to him. Who is Sergius? The armour-bearer of Catiline, your own body-guard, the standard-bearer of sedition, the exciter of the shopkeepers, a man who has been convicted of assault, an assassin, a stoner of men, a man *who has depopulated the forum, and blockaded the senate-house.* With these leaders and others like them, when you, at the time when provisions were dear, *under pretence of espousing the cause of the poor and ignorant, were preparing for sudden attacks on the consuls, on the senate, on the property and fortunes of the rich*; when it was impossible for you to find safety if affairs remained in a tranquil state; when, the leaders being all desperate men, you had your *bands of profligates regularly enrolled and distributed into decuries*,—did it

> not behoove the senate to take good care that that fatal firebrand did not fall upon these vast materials for sedition?

The above passage shows us that instead of alleviating hunger, the distribution of corn actually had totally chaotic results. In fact, it created another crisis of plunder and looting. Similarly, the expropriation movement in contemporary Zimbabwe resulted in plundering and robbery on the farms, which spelt ruin and misery for both those who looted and for the rest of the population. As a result the price of bread soared, as bakers had to import wheat from South Africa. As was the case in Cicero' time, the high prices of foodstuffs were also identified as the cause of the people's suffering, when in actual fact the crisis stemmed from a wrong political solution to a purely economic problem. Within the discourse of the politics of opposition, Morgan Tsvangirai is said to have dismissed Mugabe's solution to rural poverty which involved giving land to every indigenous Zimbabwean. Tsvangirai is quoted as saying that no one could ever distribute land to everyone, and that there was no country in the world that developed by putting all people on the land (Moore 2003: 265). There was also in Zimbabwe a severe scarcity of mealie-meal, as the farming of maize was seriously affected by the confiscations. Such was the tragedy of the politics of distribution. To make matters worse, the government embarked on price controls of food commodities, and this worsened the situation as many shops closed down operations.

The two situations of Rome and Zimbabwe are also comparable in the area of political recrimination in the wake of the respective disasters. As a result of the Roman situation, accusations and counter accusations among politicians followed and then civil strife. Clodius clearly wanted to blame Cicero (of the Senatorial party) for the scarcity of food which his law had helped to bring about. Cicero was blamed at Rome for the price of grain (Cic. *Dom.* 13).

In both of the situations above, the common people constituted an important sphere of political influence, and leaders mobilized the people towards violent action, and sought to gain political influence and popular support through policies aimed ostensibly at the welfare and feeding of the people.

## Conclusion

In this chapter I discussed the deployment of war veterans in political spaces by competing dynasties of power in first-century BC Rome. This deployment, I have argued, radiated different forms of veteran-masculinities mobilized into political spaces by their commanders. My conceptualization of land in both contexts included the broader category of territory, conceived as political space by competing dynasties of power. My scope of analysis zoomed in on the examination of smaller political spaces such as law courts, streets and other political spaces, where bodies of war veterans performed masculinity in pursuit of political goals of their leaders.

The following chapter is the overall conclusion to the present book. It highlights the book's main argument and outlines the book's main achievements.

# 8

# Concluding Remarks

How can we re-imagine the expropriations of land by military veterans more than 2,000 years ago in ancient Rome? How can we join together the scattered pieces of evidence in the ancient Roman sources? This book has opened a window on the process of going through and contrasting different pieces of historical evidence, so as to re-imagine land expropriations in first-century BC Roman Italy. Using African approaches to study land expropriations in ancient Rome, despite all the possible differences, I argued that the Roman and African veteran's means to reach his goal of attaining land were very similar, particularly an emphasis on hyper-masculinity. I examined the political and social functions of the concepts of 'veteran' and 'masculinity' in the context of practices and social processes of expropriation by military veterans – analysing these phenomena by comparing violence, the passion for warfare and expropriation in two seemingly disparate societies, with a view to ascertaining their cultural meaning.

The distinctive contribution of this book is its defamiliarization of masculinity within two contexts: that of intersectionality and that of an ancient and a contemporary society, in which military veterans feature as subject actors in a larger drama of culture and power and their involvement in war, violence and expropriation. Intersectionality has generally been utilized in terms of understanding how gender is related to other factors such as race, ethnicity and class (Ferree 2018, Crenshaw 1989) that are constructed in the present. I have expanded this concept to include history, cultural behaviours, politics and economics within its purview. Thus the book interrogated why an African veteran and a Roman client-army veteran embraced a specific type of masculinity at a specific historical moment, within a peculiar political economy. In this regard, the study supported the idea of concreteness and situatedness in masculinity studies, while elaborating on the political economy that can influence violence and expropriations in societies. Employing intersectionality to study veteran masculinities in disparate politico-historical contexts also allows a broader approach to narratives of war and cultures of violence as this book has demonstrated.

The book also brings in the theme of masculinity into new areas, in particular through the association of masculinities and war veterans, politics, power and violence pertaining to land acquisition and the status thereof. While I am cognizant of the cultural particularities of constructions and performances of violence and the different repertoires of cultural knowledge in the two societies, one major conclusion the book draws is that the veteran's perception of those whose land or property he expropriated was mediated by norms of heroic and martial combat. These norms of heroic and martial combat were productive of cultural discourses and images of gender and masculinity bound up in violent practices and processes. Fighters in both worlds often did not question violence and plunder. Even when they did, reason was overcome by tumultuous madness, and competition for hegemony, control and the possession of material resources. As a result, they did not call into question the logic and the power of their dominant ideologies. Political rivals always sought to proscribe, expropriate, vanquish and obliterate each other.

Violence was thus a central feature of the experience of veterans and their cultural discourses. I have interrogated how these discourses were shaped and how they functioned within the particular cultural constructs of the world of military veterans in the two societies. I considered expropriation of land and political fields by military veterans as root and branch a gendered phenomenon whose mechanics, at its most extreme, happened in a pattern that played out the hostility of the veteran as a potent embodiment of violence, with ruinous consequences to society.

The book additionally analysed the issues of expropriation within the context of the political economy of physical bodies of military veterans' representation of masculinity in both societies. I have noted that bodies of veterans are physical, and have that physicality in common with another culturally significant factor, namely land. The histories and cultures of the two societies allow for the generalization of the significance of the physical body of a military veteran and land, as one notes how both contribute to a military veterans' self-perception. Thus, the meaning of the human body generally, and that of military veterans in particular, is linked with both physical nature and culture, and the different relations a soldier's body bears with both of these will give rise to different meanings and concepts associated with the soldier's body that manifest in history and society. Of particular interest are the meanings associated with the gender of the body and the use of the body in violent activity.

Finally, my thesis in support of an African approach to Classics is concerned with meaning-making and the interpretation of the historical phenomena of land, masculinity and war as manifest in two different worlds and histories. When we attempt to answer the question, 'What is history?' our answer, consciously or unconsciously, reflects our own global positionality in time and space, and forms part of our answer to the broader question what view we take of the global society and history in which we live (cf. Carr 1961).

My approach to Roman history in this book sought to challenge the selectivity existing in our approach to history as manifest in the relative emphasis of African and Western material. It is to be hoped that this study has shown the reader the relevance of African history to the study of Classics, and its importance in its own right. The exploits of Zimbabwe's military veterans are as much part of history as those of the ancient Roman armies.

I may remark that *Land Expropriation in Ancient Rome and Contemporary Zimbabwe: Veterans, Masculinity and War* has examined that the specific iconography of masculinity in the language and action of expropriation supports the view that there was close association between 'masculinity' and 'veteran' in the late Roman Republic. Juxtaposing ancient Rome and Africa allows veteran masculinities to be explored in ways that deepen our understanding of societies from far-off times, and prevents an overly isolated and compartmentalized scholarly study of modern phenomena that ignores the historical past. Such comparison also allows us to see how such remote societies may speak to the realities of today, and help shed light on many present-day phenomena.

# Notes

## Prolegomenon

1 For example, if we compare the Roman Legion and the Zulu Impi, there is a similarity in the weaponry of the individual fighters, and the fact that both favoured the practice of pressing (not rushing) forward – not as individuals, but as an entire formation. Nevertheless one may still find a Western historian de-emphasizing the collective aspect, referring to individual Zulu fighters as 'braves' or 'warriors' (cf. Otterbein 1964 and Cope 1995), even though the term 'soldier' is more appropriate than 'brave' or 'warrior', as soldiers are defined by a collective ethos rather than an individual one. I am grateful to Ilya Berkovich for sharing with me some insights on Zulu warfare.

2 For a detailed exposition of African masculinities, see Mbah 2019.

3 McClymont explores the problems that arise in establishing what Classics is not. It may be understood to exclude oriental civilizations, a viewpoint contested by the interest in them manifest in Bagnall (cited in McClymont 2007). Guite (1965) queried the exclusion of Christian Greek texts from Classics as an object of study.

4 My view here resonates with Ferree's illustration of the concept of intersectionality, where she argued that gender is continuously shaped in relationship to other distinct factors (in her case: race/ethnicity, social class, sexuality, age, nation, religion) – which in turn continuously affect those same intersecting distinctions (Ferree 2018: 7).

5 As Brunt (1962) has argued, the agrarian bills of Saturninus, Sulla's veteran settlement scheme, the proposals of Plotius, Rullus and Flavius, the agitation of Catiline, and the land allotments of Caesar, the triumvirs and of Augustus himself demonstrate the land redistributionary challenges that confronted the late Roman Republic. In the earlier phase of land struggles in the Roman Republic, reformers sought remedies for social distress and later on sought to provide homes for veterans (Brunt 1962). According to Thein (2010: 81), for Appian, there is a link between Sulla and his successors rather than his predecessors, as he (Appian) uses the Greek word ἐπινέμειν to refer to the distribution of land to veterans in the period from Sulla to Augustus, but διανέμειν and διαιρεῖν in reference to the agrarian laws down to the time of the Gracchi.

## Chapter 1

1 Interview with war veteran X3, 26 July 2012.

2 Especially considering that some Roman historians' accounts were written at least a hundred years after the events they describe.
3 See, for example, Alexander and McGregor 2004, Chung 2006, Tendi 2020.
4 Cic. *Tusc.* 2.37, here Cicero referred to weapons as a soldier's limbs.
5 For a detailed argument and discussion of Caesar's army's loss of subjectivity and personal agency, caused by Caesar's 'demonic genius', see Spentzou (2018: 260–8); cf. Silverman 1992.
6 For example, in the case where scars fulfilled the unusual function of making soldiers appear weaker, and also the sense in which war as a place for men to prove and affirm their masculinity became a site of a great deal of anxiety precisely about losing that masculinity, see Lehman 2007: 26–7.
7 Dio Cass. 40.41, Cary 1914: 469, brings this image clearly through his mention of Vercingetorix's disposition: 'Now Vercingetorix might have escaped, for he had not been captured and was unwounded; but he hoped, since he had once been on friendly terms with Caesar, that he might obtain pardon from him. So he came to him without any announcement by herald, but appeared before him suddenly, as Caesar was seated on the tribunal, and threw some who were present into alarm; *for he was very tall* to begin with, and *in his armour he made an extremely imposing figure.*' (my italics).
8 The Shorter Oxford English Dictionary (1973: 1284).
9 At Luc. 5.249-254, Caesar acknowledged the importance of his fighters as a way to motivate them. He showed how they possessed the power to determine their own fate and Caesar's. Losing the war meant losing everything, including benefits such as land and other rewards which would be given to Pompey's pirates (Luc. 1.343-5).
10 Commenting on Keaveney's assertion, Thein cautions that the sources are too few for their silence to be given too much emphasis.
11 Thein cites Cic. *Agr.* 1.16, 2.74, on colonies as garrisons, and Cic. *Agr.* 1.22, 2.77, 2.82, 2.84 and 2.98 on the view that colonists served as bodyguards.
12 For a detailed discussion of conceptions of power in the Roman Republic and the terms employed, see Drogula, 2007.
13 Giving the example of the tribune Laelius' agrarian proposal for Scipio Aemilianus' Punic War veterans, Scullard hinted at the limitations of tribunician *auctoritas*, arguing that Laelius' agrarian proposal suffered serious opposition from the *optimates* because it lacked the support of General Scipio Aemilianus' military *auctoritas* (Scullard 1960: 63).
14 To demonstrate that both the tribunician and military *auctoritas* were limited, let us consider the rewards for Pompey's and Metellus' veterans who had returned from the war against Sertorius. The tribune Plotius in 70 or 69 BC proposed the bill for land allocation to veterans and he succeeded with ease to get the nod of the government. It was, according to Gabba, because of the presence of Metellus among the interested military leaders that the proposal sailed through (Gabba 1976: 43).

However, Plotius' law, in spite of Metellus' military *auctoritas,* did not take effect. Cicero, who was speaking for the Senate, condemned the Lex Plotia, and in 59 BC, it still had not been implemented (Cic. *Att.* 1.18.6.). The abortive land reform bills of Marius–Saturninus, which were never seriously implemented, or the tribune Rullus' agrarian bill, which never made it into law (cf. Brunt 1962), bear further testimony to the limitations of military/tribunician *auctoritas.*

15 Rhetorical prowess in ancient Rome was, according to Gleason (1995), a typical marker of masculinity. My appropriation of this type of masculinity as a category of analysis is to advance the argument that struggles for land and other rewards took place also at the level of verbal contestations as can be illustrated by the many incidents involving quarrels, arguments and strife between generals and their forces. It is at this particular level where an oratorical-masculinity was performed.

16 See Connolly 2007: 86.

17 On the power of oratory see Fantham 1985: 123. Cicero, Quintilian and the Younger Seneca regard the orator as a paradigm of masculine deportment (see *Orator* 18.59, *De Officiis* 1.128-29. Letters. 78.5, 15.8; See also Plut. *Mor.* 130.). Even Octavian was also practiced in oratory, not only in the Latin language, but in Greek as well (Dio Cass. 45.1.). For Caesar, see Cic. *Brut.* 252. cf. *Ouint.* 10.114, Cic. *Brut.* 253.

18 See App. *BC.* 4.5-4.7. See also Dio Cass. 42.52.

19 App. *BC.* 4.7.

20 See for example the story of Hortensia at App. *BC.* 4.33-34.

21 According to Solomon-Godeau (1997), these are masculinities associated with the purview of the feminine.

22 The narrative of Antony's and Octavian's harangue of each other reveals how it is possible to understand client-army masculinities in terms of these two polar types. Feminized masculinity refers to a weak masculinity.

23 Harmless dogs that anyone can take away for their desired purposes.

24 Horace recorded '*Dulce et decorum est pro patria mori*' ('It is sweet and honorable to die for one's country' *Carm.* 3.2.13.

25 As quoted in Finley 1986: 54.

26 I am grateful to Orietta Cordovana for translating De Sanctis' article from Italian to English.

## Chapter 2

1 Bloch, M. 1992. *The Historian's Craft.* P. Putman. Trans. Manchester: Manchester University Press, 53.

2 See Roselaar 2010 for a detailed account of the social and economic history of *ager publicus* (public land) in the Roman Republic.

3 The origins of the veteran phenomenon in Roman politics is discernible right from the time of Scipio Africanus and partly during the tribuneship of Tiberius Gracchus. Scullard discusses the citizen-militia and property qualifications for service, and suggested that 'ex-soldiers' were living as or had been reduced to *proletarii / capite censi*. Emphasis, however, is laid on the suffering of the Italian small farmers. By definition, as Roman citizens, they were also the class of people who had fought in the Roman wars of conquest. It must be noted that the Roman People by definition included ex-soldiers (though they also included those who had yet to serve). Military service is cited by Tiberius Gracchus as a moral reason for helping the poor, but his emphasis is on citizenship and poverty rather than the problem of 'veteran settlement' as it later emerges. They are not his veterans, in a situation comparable to the case of Marius, Sulla, Pompey, Caesar, Antony and Octavian, or, arguably, of Scipio earlier. In these cases the settlers were given land as veterans, and they were a problem as veterans (Scullard 1960: 59–74). For the Gracchi the problem was (allegedly) the more general, broader problem of rural poverty. That is perhaps the reason why Scullard may have been trying to be careful when he used the term 'ex-soldiers' (rather than 'veterans'). But there is one issue in common in all cases: the fear that patronage of settlers would lead to excessive prestige and influence.

4 A largely silent instrumental component of Caesar's triumph was the army he had gathered for the civil conflict. Through possessing a proven record of rewarding loyalty amongst his men, Caesar's promises for honorable discharge and promises of acreage were more credible than Pompey's, and as a result, the better general, and the hungrier troops were all on the winning side at the battle of Pharsalus.

5 Cicero assessed one of Pompey's speeches as being 'of no comfort to the poor or interest to the rascals; the rich were not pleased the honest man were not edified.' (Cic. *Att.* 1.14).

6 *praemia* here means war booty.

7 Lewis and Short 1879: 1423 cf. 1416. cf. (Plut. *Life of Romulus.* 16.7, Thayer 2018: 139) '. . . such spoils were called "opima," because as Varro says, "opes" is the Roman word for *richness*; but it would be more plausible to say that they were so called from the *deed of valour* involved, since "opus" is the Roman word for *deed* or *exploit.* And only to a general who with his own hand has performed the exploit of slaying an opposing general, has the privilege of dedicating the "spolia opima" been granted.'

8 This is not to say the veterans were a homogenous group in their thinking about land invasions: cf. Sadomba 2011: 16.

9 See Sall. *Cat.* 16.4, 28.4. See also Cic. *Cat.* 2 where Catiline re-mobilized Sulla's veterans for insurgency purposes.

10 Dio Cass. 45.12. From these men was constituted the corps of evocati, which one might translate the 'recalled', because after having ended their military service they were recalled to it again.

11 Caes. *BCiv*. 1.3.2-3. Of men who have fought in all Caesar's campaigns, see also Luc. 5.274-277.

12 This translation is mine.

13 Lucius' speech to some former soldiers of Octavian as recorded by Appian testifies to the poverty and hunger of this lot (App. *BC*. 5.39, White 1913: 443).

14 In its historical context, '*veni, vidi, vici*' was a phrase attributed to Julius Caesar's message in a letter to the Roman Senate after his victory in his brief war against Pharnaces II of Pontus. It later became an English joke.

15 The nature and function in colonial politics of colonists' recourse to ancient Rome help us to understand justifications and anxieties regarding British imperialism (Vasunia 2013). Debates of the Legislative Assembly of Southern Rhodesia revealed the comparison of Southern Rhodesia with the pre-Roman peoples of Britain (Hadfield 1927, cited in Jeater 2005: 6). In the debates the native was considered as a child insofar as their present state of civilization was concerned (Thompson 1927, cited in Jeater 2005: 2). This comparison was appropriated to allow for the possibility that Africans could eventually develop to modernity in similar ways that ancient Britons had harnessed Roman civilization, thereby inscribing the white people as paternalistically responsible for African education and employment (Jeater 2005: 2).

16 I explore this theme in detail in Chapter Six.

17 The British rule of Southern Rhodesia is not the only reflection of ancient imperial conditions in history. Vasunia (2013: 121) refers to comparisons between the Roman and the British empire made by writers in India and Britain, and, moreover, by Britons and Indians. Even though the colonialisms and imperialisms of history are not carbon copies of each other (cf. Lenin in Vasunia 2013:119) nevertheless the general recurrence of imperial domination is something observable through history, and resemblances between Rome and later imperialisms have been assumed to exist. Such a comparison of the British Empire and ancient Roman imperialism is not forced, as argued elsewhere by Brunt (1965:1).

18 cf. Strabo's *Geography* and Pliny's *Natural History.*

19 It may seem problematic to attribute to the ancient Romans the sort of racial prejudice against Africa that existed among British colonialists. It has been regarded too simplistic to assume the Romans had no skin-colour prejudice Haley (2009: 49). While this claim might be 'applicable', it is not knowable for sure that skin colour contributed to Roman construction of difference (cf. Sinclair 1962: 269; Haley 2009: 30; Isaac 2004: 503ff.; Gruen 2011: 197).

20 Gregory Mann explored the challenges faced by Black West African veterans who served in France's colonial military in the twentieth century, whose recognition remained a challenge after their demobilization compared to their fellow French soldiers (Mann 2006: 3).

21 In Mexico in particular, and Latin America in general, public debate has addressed the broad cultural definition of masculinity in a long-standing discussion of 'machismo' and its roots in colonialism (Kimmel, Hearn and Connell 2005: 1–12, 6, Connell 2005), Dwyer and Nettelbeck 2018 and St. John 2007.

22 The 'Free Jacob Zuma' marches that started in July 2021 as mass protests against former president Jacob Zuma's incarceration are reminiscent to the looting and the violence of the apartheid era by indigenous Blacks of everything that looked like white men's privilege. The #FreeZumaNow violence started in KwaZulu-Natal and spread to other cities in South Africa, and grew into a brief revolution against poverty (in spite of it having started as a protest against Zuma's incarceration) in which anything that resembled privilege was targeted. The rage was blind to race and colour.

23 The author visited the farm of Saviour Kasukuwere (a former government minister) and saw a known war veteran, who has taken over the farm, harvesting oranges with his family and workers. Upon Mugabe's dethronement from power through a military coup in November 2017, some prominent politicians who belonged to his party fled the country and went into exile. Some of his closest allies' farms were confiscated by guerrilla veterans aligned to a victorious faction of the new government led by the president of Zimbabwe – at the time of writing, Emmerson Dambudzo Mnangagwa.

24 Interview with a war veteran WN, August 2011.

25 At some of the ZANU-PF political village meetings in 2008, former University of Zimbabwe students would narrate the story of the Gracchi and land distribution programmes to the landless by Peisistratus of Athens – encouraging villagers in attendance to regard Mugabe as a hero because he, like the Gracchi brothers and Peisistratus, was championing the distribution of land to the poor Zimbabwean peasant farmers. This was done to convince villagers that in contrast to the idea of Zimbabwe's exceptionalism, land struggles are a feature of every society. Such discussions among men and women who studied Classics, to a considerable extent, helped tilt the opinion of some families in favour of land expropriations.

26 Credit is due to Achille Mbembe's (2001: 14) words and turn of phrase in my formulation of this idea.

27 Xaba explained how for instance in South Africa, the armed struggle carried on by the resistance fighters on behalf of the African National Congress produced a generation of young men accustomed to violence. See Xaba cited in Connell 2005: 74).

28 This was the battle in Mozambique, where guerrilla fighters were bombed mercilessly by the Rhodesian forces on 28 April 1966.

29 This does not mean to say there were no fearful persons in the Roman armies, who fled from battle. Far from it. Horace writes of having fled the battlefield without his shield.

30 According to Fontein (2010: 431), what bones do in Zimbabwe is not confined to questions about representation of the past, or their symbolic efficacy, but also about their 'emotive materiality' as human substances and their 'affective presence' as dead persons; spirit subjects which continue to make demands upon society. Veterans in Republican Rome appealed to scars and wounds, but not to bones of dead persons in claims for acreage and other rewards.

31 I however need to emphasize that funerals were often occasions for stirring up clan violence; that's why Solon legislated against large funerals in Athens.

32 Seibert 2003; Gewald 2003. Accusing the ruling Frelimo party of showing total disrespect for local religion and culture, an insurgent movement known as The Mozambican National Resistance (Renamo), which fought Frelimo in the Mozambican civil war (1976 to 1992), claimed to fight in an alliance with the ancestral spirits to return the country to its ancestral traditions (Seibert 2003: 273). On the battlefield Renamo commanders, like ZANLA guerrillas, resorted to local diviners and spirit mediums to protect them in combat or to guarantee the success of an attack.

33 Luc. 1.347-8, Duff 1928: 28. On page 29, Duff identifies the speaker as Caesar.

34 Appian recorded that sacrifices were offered after Philippi (App. *BC*. 5.3, White 1913: 381).

35 cf. *Ecl.* 1:67 *patrios finis*. The word *patrius* comes from *pater* meaning father. Lewis and Short (1879: 1316) give the meaning 'of or belonging to one's native country or home, native.' Lewis and Short (1879: 1316) also explain the words *di patrii* which can mean gods 'of one's forefathers,' and the word *patrius* can mean 'handed down from one's forefathers'. But the meaning of 'native' or 'belonging to one's country' fits the text from Vergil best and seems to be corroborated by Fairclough (1999: 25 line 1.3). Vergil used the word *patrios* in association with *finis*, most probably thinking of Meliboeus' native land. One might call this, in a sense, ancestral land, without implying a conscious association with African-style ancestral spirits.

36 Connell's structural theory of gender is explained in detail by Messerschmidt et al. 2018.

37 Butler (1990) underscores the importance of discourse and performativity in the constitution of gender identities and practices.

38 In the Aeneid there is mention of a female soldier Camilla who had the power to run through grain without trampling it, and on the sea without wetting her feet. She fought with other warrior-maidens against Aeneas (Grant and Hazel 1979: 78–9).

39 The ravished Sabine daughters played more or less a similar role to avert war between Rome and the Sabines.

40 On men's status in Athens regarding possession of physical property (land, money, possessions), mastery of animate property (women, children, slaves) and possession of the political capital of citizenship and the moral authority to exercise it see Omitowoju 2016: 117.

41 For a more focused consideration of some of the prevailing ways in which the sexes were differentiated in classical literature, particularly in relation to political power, see Konstan 2002. See also Val. *Max.* 3.8.6 where he says: '*quid feminae cum contione*' [What do women have to do with public meetings?']. The elder Cato condemns women speaking in public (Liv. 34.2-3).
42 The saying 'their voice is in their sword' is based on the character Macduff in Shakespeare's Macbeth, Act V, Scene 8: 'I have no words, – My voice is in my sword.'
43 This translation is mine.

## Chapter 3

1 Catherine Buckle. 2001. *African Tears: The Zimbabwean Land Invasions*, 37.
2 I use this concept as deployed by Solomon-Godeau (1997), and to some extent, I draw upon Hannah Arendt's idea of the polis as a kind of organized remembrance (Arendt 1998, see also Willis 2011). However, I have indicated that Rome was not a polis in the strict sense of the word, as one would understand the Greek polis. Apart from not being a power confined to one city, Rome diverged from the Greek idea of the polis in its attitude toward membership in the state, its eagerness to assimilate conquered populations, and its control and use of colonies (Ando 1999: 14). For a detailed discussion see Ando 1999; 2002.
3 Primary sources focus on colonies created for veterans (*coloniae*) as loci of creating new farmer-soldiers. For a detailed discussion, see Amanda Jo Coles' article: 'Roman Colonies in Republic and Empire'.
4 Solomon-Godeau (1997) argues that the masculinity of the polis in the Roman Republic was materialized through heroism, citing the example of Consul Lucius Junius Brutus. She also argues that the Aeneid thematizes the supremacy of masculine and patriarchal bonds – Anchises, Aeneas and his son, and Augustus who founded a new polis – the principate.
5 Plut. *Mar.* 27.4-5. Plutarch's life of Camillus also stated that Romulus and Furius Camillus were the first and second founders of Rome for their role in defeating the Gauls who had destroyed Rome in 390/386 BC.
6 This translation is mine.
7 App. *BC.* 5.128, White 1913: 589. See also Dio Cass. 42.37, Cary 1917: 173 and especially 42.42.4, Cary 1917: 183.
8 App. *BC.* 5.128, White 1913: 589, 590.
9 The Greek word is ἀριστίνδην which is an adverb meaning 'according to rank or merit.' It is from 'aristos' meaning best, noblest, bravest – superlative of 'agathos'. The English translation is somewhat dynamic. The Greek does not have the idea of booty or plunder that the English might suggest. It is however consistent with the

idea of the nobility of the fighters or bravery which earned them whatever they asked for.

10 I acknowledge Alexander Thein's kindness in sharing his notes on insults and masculinities in Roman politics.

11 Takacs (2009: 52) is the source of the reference to Horace's poem, *Carm.* 3.2. Takacs (Ibid., 52) attests that: 'Horace's boy was Augustus, who at the time of the poem's composition and publication (23 BC), was planning a campaign against the Parthians, though he never set out against Rome's most eastern foe.'

12 For example, Homeric poetry depicts village life as something that preceded the polis.

13 It must be noted that these veterans were forcing Antony and Octavian to honour their agreement to give them land after the defeat of the Republicans at Philippi. Thus, their efforts as arbiters was motivated by their desire to get land promised them before the war.

14 The white commercial farmer was not a passive victim of expropriation. Semi-autobiographical writings of Eric Harrison's *Jambanja* (2006) and Jim Barker's *Paradise Plundered: The Story of a Zimbabwean Farm* (2007) are quite revealing. Both Harrison and Barker fought in the Zimbabwean bush war on the side of Rhodesia, and both lost their farms during the guerrilla veterans' expropriations. In addition to providing insights into masculinities, violence, patriarchy, as performed by white veterans of the war of liberation, these books also provide useful insights into the terror tactics of Black war veterans as they led the campaign to expropriate land from whites and deliver it to Blacks. See also A. R. Beattie's *Tengwe Garden Club: My Story of Zimbabwe* (2008).

15 Personal interviews with liberation war veterans in 2020. One war veteran of the liberation struggle operates a business in Harare.

16 As Gleason (1995: 161) noted, Cicero's contemporaries criticized him for being *Asianus, in compositione fractus, and paene viro mollior*. Gleason also cites Quintilian *Inst.* 12.10.12.

17 See H. Melber. 2003: 305–27.

18 Mugabe 2001: 141, Mugabe's speech on the commemoration of Heroes' Day on 11 August 2001.

19 See App. *BC.* 1.95, White 1913: 175, where Sulla was addressing Roman people, vaunting his past war exploits.

20 For a general illustration of societies where such practices occurred, see Cornford 1914: 266.

21 The source of this reference to Bourdieu is Cowan 1990: 23.

22 As quoted in Cowan 1990: 23.

23 Letter sent by Pioneer veteran J. A. C. Kruger to the governor of Southern Rhodesia on 19 May 1947), File No 283/1939 National Archives of Zimbabwe. This is not of

course, to say that all pioneer veterans failed to get land as promised. A number of files at the National Archives of Zimbabwe contain land and claim grants to pioneer veterans, e.g. Files No L 2/1 /22, L2/1 /222, LB 2/19, L2 /1 /222.

## Chapter 4

1 The Congolese war started in 1996 when Rwanda, Uganda and Burundi waged war on Mobutu's Zaire for accommodating Hutu militias and the defeated Rwandan government forces, leading to the ousting of Joseph Mobutu from power in 1997. The second phase of the war happened under Laurent Kabila (1998–2003). Fighting has continued in the North Eastern Kivu to this day, which can be regarded as the third phase of the war (Stearns 2012).
2 The translation is mine.
3 Interview with Comrade Wevhu, 20 October 2012.
4 Interview with war veteran Mabhunumuchapera, 15 January 2012.
5 Interview with Comrade Gidi, 12 August 2011.
6 This information was extracted from a life history of Cde CC, now a tobacco farmer, 2012.
7 Oral testimony by an eye witness of the event, Mr XV, 13 February 2020.
8 Raftopoulos 2009; Muzondidya 2009.
9 For the phenomenon of military involvement in politics in other African countries, see Tripp 2010; Huntington 1957.
10 μειρακιώδης = boyish, puerile.
11 Pompey on Caesar.
12 Curio underscores Caesar's potential in this regard.
13 The words in brackets are David Konstan's (2021: 61).

## Chapter 5

1 In ancient Rome, orature was a means for the elites to reinforce their power in transactions of authority and loyalty. Oratorically constructed masculinity was symptomatic of 'cultural fantasy', and was not a reflection of reality (Connolly 2007). A contrary perspective emerges from Rosanna Omitowoju's discussion of oratory in relation to reality. She argues that oratory offers the real world, that is, a world that is not self-consciously fictive, mythic, or heroic (Omitowoju 2016). I argue that both views apply in the case of client-army veterans' relations with their generals.

2 If we judge by the account in Lucan's *Pharsalia,* Caesar's journey as a cultic hero figure is in some respects mythical. Rondholz (2009) mentions the motif of the connection of Caesar's crossing of the Rubicon with a supernatural element – an apparition with a reed pipe (Suet. *Div. Jul.* 32).

3 I am aware that some elements of the *Pharsalia* are myth or fiction not based on history. It is the mythic that creates a personality cult and an aura of power and invincibility around individuals. The basic concept of the hero's journey in Campbell (2004: 28) involves separation, initiation and return. There is a quotation which encapsulates this: 'A hero ventures forth from the world of common day into a region of supernatural wonder: fabulous forces are there encountered and a decisive victory is won: the hero comes back from this mysterious adventure with the power to bestow boons on his fellow man' (ibid.). The hero's journey concept corresponds to the lives of Caesar and Mugabe. For Caesar going to Gaul and Britain amounts to the 'separation', while the 'initiation' and victory involves the explorations there and the victories won, and the 'return' is when he crosses the Rubicon and becomes ruler of Rome, and can provide boons for his veterans (see Suet. *Div. Jul.* 33). For Mugabe, the 'separation' is when he goes out into the bush for the purpose of guerrilla warfare; then the forces of Ian Smith are encountered and defeated, and finally Mugabe comes back as ruler of independent Zimbabwe, with boons for his people/ veterans.

4 Vance (1989: 27–8) has argued that in an ideological and political context it is often to the advantage of all groups struggling for resources to stress not only group unity (in this case based on ideals of male dominance) and historical privilege, but also their status as essential groups to which members have no choice but to belong. I do not stress, as Vance does, the issue of choice in belonging to a group, since fighters in both societies of ancient Rome and Zimbabwe had some choice whether to belong or not.

5 Inscriptions record moments when Roman military units acted as such both during service and afterwards (see MacMullen 1984: 442–3 n.12 and n.13).

6 According to Gabba (1976: 39), it became a necessity to reward soldiers when military service became professional as opposed to a service of the Roman citizen militia which existed before Marius (107–100 BC), and especially when the social and economic conditions of many families started to deteriorate at alarming levels owing to the fact that many soldiers had been away from their homes for very long periods.

7 For an extended discussion see Tendi (2020).

8 This translation is mine.

9 This translation is mine.

10 The word *σύστημα* is the source of the English word 'system'. Liddell and Scott (1876: 783) give for this word the meanings of: whole compounded of parts, system,

composition, organized government, constitution, body of soldiers, corps. It can also be used to describe the Roman senate. It is derived from the verb συνίστημι, for which Liddell and Scott (1876: 777) give the following meanings: to set together, combine, associate, unite, band together. In the passive, the verb means 'to stand together.'

11 Roller (2009) argued that performance of manly acts in the battlefield was crucial in republican battles. The acts required an audience of one's fellow soldiers and supervisors for recognition and conferment of rewards (Roller also cites Caes. *Gal.* 1.52, Sal. *Cat.* 7.4-6, Liv. 26.48).

12 In 36.12.2 Dio Cassius was referring to Mithridates, whose soldiers defected to his rebellious son, Pharnaces.

13 In 60 BC, Pompey repented of having let his legions go so soon, as he found himself helpless to have all his acts approved, including, in particular, to have some land given to his soldiers (see Dio Cass. 37.50.6 and 37.44.3 and 41.17.3). Caesar, in a speech delivered to his mutinous Campanian legions in Rome in 47 BC, as recorded by Dio, stated that there were two things which created, protected, and increased dominions – soldiers and money (Dio Cass. 42.49.4 cf. 42.55.

14 Thein (2010: 94) cites Brunt and Schneider to note that both their estimates (80,000 for Brunt and 70,000 for Schneider) and Appian's figure of 120,000 are too high, given as he argued, that so few settlement sites can be identified with certainty or any reasonable degree of probability. However, knowing the exact number of Sulla's men does not change the fact that Sulla and his men acted to pursue common interests during and after the war.

15 For a statistical presentation of Caesar's use of words that are generally violent more than Pompey and Cato, see Helzle 1994: 125ff.

16 In a contemporary African setting of liberation war leaders, such qualities resonate with how Mugabe created an aura around himself as the mythical Brave Son of Africa and mastered the art of oratory as part of his arsenal to claim loyalty of his forces. Mugabe would 'shock and awe' his veterans and audiences using hyperbole and high-end oratorical skills (see Moyo 2014: 25).

17 The words *fortuna* and *viros* are from Luc. 5.327.

18 At Luc. 1.299-302, Caesar started his speech by addressing his troops as *bellorum o socii*, a gesture implying the soldiers were his equals.

19 According to Connolly (2007: 92), Roman elites exploited the 'natural' language of gender to describe and evaluate themselves, through which the visible and verbal signs of masculinity become both evidence and source of political stability and power.

20 This translation is mine.

21 Spentzou (2018: 265–7) is the source of the reference to Luc. 5.364-70 as well as the translation.

22 Gleason was here not writing about client-army veterans, but her argument holds for a military context of client- army generals.

23 The words are Ward's (2016: 307).
24 On various arguments concerning Julius Caesar's comportment as a military general see: Olson 2014: 182; Raaflaub 1974. cf. Corbeill 2002.
25 See also Plut. *Life of Pompey.* 14.5. When some of Pompey's troops in the run-up to his 61 BC triumph demanded more handouts for them to participate in the triumph. Pompey stood firm in the wake of his soldiers' insubordination without giving in to their demands.
26 This translation is mine.

# Chapter 6

1 M. Foucault, *Discipline and Punish: The Birth of the Prison*, Alan Sheridan (Trans.), (New York: Vintage, 1979), 25–6.
2 For example, Lucan's Caesar and his men caused havoc by erasing boundaries and unleashing the chaos of civil war. For a detailed discussion of chaos and havoc in Lucan, see Ika Willis 2011, Chapter 2: *Fulmen* (Lightning): Paul Virilio's Politics at the Speed of Light.
3 This translation is mine.
4 Tac. *Ann.* 2.18.1 recorded a battle where Germanicus won a bloodless battle against the German tribes.
5 Milne's work is also the source of the textual references to the younger Seneca cited here.
6 Ancient Roman wars were not for liberation but for conquest; that is one difference. But Tacitus in Agricola, for example, praised the so-called barbarians who died to preserve their freedom.
7 See interview quote on page 1.
8 For example, in Laelius' speech to Caesar, he refers to Caesar's troops as bodies in which flows warm blood (Luc. 1.359-366).
9 cf. Dio Cass 54.14, Cary 1914: 317 '. . . one Licinius Begulus, indignant because his name had been erased, whereas his son and several others to whom he thought himself superior had been selected by the lot, rent his clothing in the very senate, laid bare his body, enumerated his campaigns, and showed them his scars . . .'
10 Duff (1943: 29) identifies the speaker as Caesar.
11 In translating the phrase *quaeritur armis* ('is sought by arms') into idiomatic English, Duff (1943: 29) talks of Caesar's 'warfare', which seems in context to refer to the fight in which he and his men are to engage, after which they will be veterans of that warfare. Hence my use of the phrase 'war veterans to be'.
12 As for the Roman Republic see App. *BC.* 1.9, App. *BC.* 5.2. 12 and Plut. *Ti Gr.* 9.5.

13 An *as* is a unit of currency, at first equivalent to a tenth and later to an eighteenth of a denarius (see Lewis and Short 1879: 545). Lewis and Short value the denarius at sixteen American cents, writing in the nineteenth century. Rather than trying to work out how much the coin is in modern money, we may recall that in the famous biblical story the workers in the vineyard were paid a denarius for a day's work; so the mutineers were not paid at a higher rate than this. The mutineers say in *Ann.* 3.17 that the praetorian cohorts, by contrast with themselves, get 2 denarii per man.

14 It may be noted that invasion need not only be physical, but can take other forms e.g. economic or political displacement, or even cultural invasion, whereby one is culturally displaced or marginalized. This last-mentioned has been alluded to in the context of African colonization in Chapter Two.

15 Appian (5.13, White 1913: 397–9) captures this as follows: 'The chiefs depended on the soldiers for the continuance of their government, while, for the possession of what they had received, the soldiers depended on the permanence of the government of those who had given it. Believing that they could not keep a firm hold unless the givers had a strong government, they fought for them, from necessity, with good-will. Octavian made many other gifts to the indigent soldiers, borrowing from the temples for that purpose, for which reason the affections of the army were turned toward him, and the greater thanks were bestowed upon him both as the giver of the land, the cities, the money, and the houses . . .'

16 ἐπέβαινε means to get a foothold, step onwards, advance (Liddell and Scott 1876: 723). Getting a foothold means lodging one's foot in a place to support oneself securely while making further progress. This contrasts the weak and unarmed civilians with the soldiers of the *tresviri* who took advantage of the civilians to rob them of their possession.

17 I am studying Vergil more from a political than a literary standpoint (cf. Weeda 2015). Vergil's political opinions cannot be ignored. Of course, worth stressing, is that the *Eclogues* are not set in a straightforwardly realistic Roman Italy; rather, they are set in a stylized world out of Theocritus. However it is the intrusions of 'real' Roman history that makes them an ideal source for envisioning land expropriations in Roman Italy, as in the passages I analyse. Theocritean and Vergilian pastorals are also different in that the bucolic idylls have nothing approaching the moral passion of the *Eclogues* – no moral outrage at a degenerate present characterized by wanton land-confiscations of 42 BC. Envisioning land expropriations, for example, through Vergil gives depth to historical analyses, as history is not written from one kind of evidence. Evidence is situated and it lies in relation to other evidence.

18 Caesar's Bill of 59 BC involved the displacement of flourishing state tenants in favour of men who had no aptitude and little real taste in farming (see Robinson 1938: 358).

19 Catherine Buckle (2001, 2002) wrote two books which cover the story of their violent eviction from their family farm – Stow Farm – along with a coverage on what happened to other white farmers.

20 cf. D. B. Saddington 2012: 122–30.

21 This may be compared with Vergil, *Ecl.* 1. 68-72.

22 Account of an ex-guerrilla fighter, a friend of the late general of the Zimbabwe National Army Solomon Mujuru, in Tendi 2020: 254.

23 Thein (2010), in reference to Sulla, comprehensively discussed this point.

24 ἀναστήσων τὴν Ἰταλίαν (to expropriate Italy). The verb is from 'anistemi' meaning to make someone get up, in this case making them get up to leave their homes (Liddell and Scott 1876: 64).

25 At App. *BC.* 1.57, White 1913: 105–7 Appian says: 'When Sulla heard of this (the news that Marius had been made commander of the war against the Mithridates in place of Sulla) he resolved to decide the question by war, and called the army together to a conference. They were eager for the war against Mithridates because it promised much plunder, and they feared that Marius would enlist other soldiers instead of themselves. Sulla spoke of the indignity put upon him by Marius and Sulpicius, and while he did not openly allude to anything else (for he did not openly allude to anything else (for he did not dare as yet to mention this sort of war), *he urged them to be ready to obey his orders.* They understood what he meant, and as they feared lest they should miss the campaign they uttered boldly what Sulla had in mind, and told him to be of good courage, *and to lead them to Rome. Sulla was overjoyed and led six legions thither forthwith*; but all his superior officers, *except one quaestor, left and fled to the city, because they would not submit to the idea of leading an army against their country.*' (my emphasis).

26 The guerrilla veterans looted white men's homes and stole livestock, destroyed household goods and crops and set fire to houses and fields.

27 Veterans were persuaded that by participating in the land reclamation movement, they were defending Zimbabwe against hostile foreign countries. 'Zimbabwe Will Never Be a Colony Again' became the mantra.

28 Sulla's epitaph indicates that none of his enemies surpassed him in doing evil (Plut. *Sull.* 38.4).

29 White farmers' homes were taken by Mugabe's storm troopers, the guerrilla veterans and hired gangs. See Barker (2007) and Buckle (2001).

30 The Greek verb συνοικίζω may be translated as 'colonize'. One of the senses of the verb συνοικίζω is 'to join in peopling or colonizing a country' (Liddell and Scott 1889: 778). In the English translation used the sense of 'colonize' seems to be to settle someone as a colonist, rather than to invade as a colonist.

31 According to Thein, the mechanisms of the triumviral proscriptions followed Sulla's template: the property of the proscribed was confiscated and sold, and there

were penalties and rewards for accomplices, bounty hunters and informers. He cites Appian's estimate for the total number of victims: 300 senators and 2,000 knights.

## Chapter 7

1 Catherine Buckle 2001: 80
2 This is Clifford Ando's formulation (2019).
3 This translation is mine.
4 The Roman context also demonstrates the importance of war veterans and the war experience in the construction of new regimes of power in other contexts as played out in the Third World during the late- and post-Cold War period in which veterans' roles as ideological and political agents loom large. In the Islamic Republic of Iran and independent Zimbabwe, anti-Western movements in the shape of anti-colonial armed struggle (Zimbabwe) and an Islamic revolution (Iran) were symbolically embodied by veterans (Álcalde and Seixas 2018: 7–8).
5 Chenjerai Hunzvi, in his speech at the 2000 ZANU-PF Congress.
6 For an extended discussion of this see Mlambo (2018).
7 He was referring to a battle context involving the charging of the cavalry.
8 Military displays by various states in the contemporary period seek to achieve the same objective of intimidating opponents and competitors. This was conceptualized by Achille Mbembe through the notion of the postcolony. The notion of the postcolony allows for exploring how state power organizes for dramatizing its own magnificence and ideology in the actual materials used in the ceremonial displays through which it makes manifest its majesty, and the specific manner in which it offers these, as spectacles, for its 'subjects' to watch (Mbembe 2001: 104).
9 For more on Raymond Williams and Gramsci's use of the term, see Alter (1992).
10 The turn of phrase is that of Barnes (2006: 29) which he used in the context of a cavalry charge in a real battle setting.
11 Tacitus (1.2, Grant 1971: 32) recorded that 'The violent deaths of Brutus and Cassius left no Republican forces in the field.'
12 For the date see Bailey 1978: 595.
13 "…the Roman moral tradition may have disapproved of movement in time to music, regarding dancing (outside certain ritual contexts) as unseemly and effeminate in a respectable man or youth; soldiers' singing and dancing was usually regarded as a form of indiscipline."
14 As illustrated by D. Saddington, *Kaltoi* was (Sicilian) Greek for *calcei*, the distinctive shoes worn by Roman senators and hence proconsular governors (see Saddington 2012: 12).

15 Aged African leaders' option for the masculine spectacle as instantiated through dramatic performances provides insights into the role of gender and age in African politics. Mugabe (1980–2017) would not use a walking stick despite an embarrassing incident where he fell in public. Thus, politics by aged African leaders is approached as 'performance', as '. . . both a doing of gender and its representation in . . . public spectacle . . . (Walsh 2010: 2).

16 The words are Lenski's.

17 Sall. *Oratio Lepidi cos.* 11.

18 Catiline, during his time, also used the politics of feeding to attract the masses. According to Cicero, Catiline was motivated by the opportunity of gaining support from the remnants of Sulla's veterans and the poor countrymen by attracting them with food.

# Bibliography


Akyeampong, E. A., and P. Obeng. 2005. Spirituality, Gender, and Power in Asante History. In: O. Oyewumi. Ed. *African Gender Studies: A Reader*. New York: Palgrave Macmillan. 23–48.

Álcalde, A., and M. Núñez Xosé Seixas. 2018. Introduction. In: A. Alcade and Xosé M. Núñez Seixas. Eds. *War Veterans and the World after 1945, Cold War Politics, Decolonization, Memory*. New York: Routledge. 1–14.

Alexander J., and J. McGregor. 2004. War Stories: Guerrilla Narratives of Zimbabwe's Liberation War. *History Workshop Journal*. 57. 79–100.

Alter, J. S. 1992. *The Wrestler's Body: Identity and Ideology in North India*. Berkeley: University of California Press.

Amadiume, I. 1987. *Male Daughters, Female Husbands: Gender and Sex in an African Society*. London: Zed.

Ando, C. 1999. Was Rome a Polis? *Classical Antiquity*. 18(1). 5–34.

Ando, C. 2002. Vergil's Italy: Ethnography and Politics in first-century Rome. In: D. S. Levene and D. P. Nelis. Eds. *Cloi and the Poets: Augustan Poetry and the Traditions of Ancient Historiography.* Leiden: Brill. 123–42.

Ando, C. 2019. The Space and Time of Politics in Civil War. In: C. R. Lopez. Ed. *Communicating Public Opinion in the Roman Republic.* Historia Einzelschriften. Stuttgart: Franz Steiner. 175–88.

Aranita, A. 2009. A Plague of Madness: The Contagion of Mutiny in Livy 28.24-32. Mania - Madness in the Greco-Roman World. *ACTA Classica: Proceedings of the Classical Association of South Africa. Supplementum* 3. 36–51.

Arendt, H. 1998. *The Human Condition*. Second Edition. Chicago, IL: University of Chicago Press.

Asso, P. 2010. *Texte und Kommentare: A Commentary on Lucan, 'De bello civili' IV: Introduction, Edition, and Translation.* Berlin/Boston, DE: De Gruyter.

Auret, M. 2009. *From Liberator to Dictator: An Insider's Account of Robert Mugabe's Descent into Tyranny.* Claremont: David Philip Publishers.

Bailey, D. R. S. Trans. 1978. *Cicero's Letters to Atticus*. Harmondsworth: Penguin Books.

Barker, J. 2007. *Paradise Plundered: The Story of a Zimbabwean Farm.* Harare: Jim Barker.

Barnes, B. 2006. Practice as Collective Action. In: T. R. Schatzki, K. K. Cetina, and E. von Savigny. Eds. *The Practice Turn in Contemporary Theory*. London: Routledge. 25–36.

Barrow, R. J. 2018. *Gender, Identity and the Body in Greek and Roman Sculpture.* Cambridge: Cambridge University Press.

Barton, C. A. 2001. *Roman Honor: The Fire in the Bones.* Berkeley and London: University of California Press.

Bassett, T. J. and Crummey D. E. Eds. 1993. *Land in African Agrarian Systems.* Madison: Univ. Wisc. Press.

Bates, R. H. 1981. *Markets and States in Tropical Africa: The Political Basis of Agricultural Policies.* Berkeley: University of California Press.

Beard, M. 2007. *The Roman Triumph.* Massachusetts: Harvard University Press.

Beattie, A. R. 2008. *Tengwe Garden Club: My Story of Zimbabwe.* Wilmington, NC: Ann Beattie.

Bederman, G. 1995. *Manliness and Civilization: A Cultural History of Gender and Race in the United States, 1880–1917.* Chicago: University of Chicago Press.

Berg, L., and R. Longhurst. 2003. Placing Masculinities and Geography. *Gender Place and Culture.* 10 (4). 351–60.

Berkovich, I. 2017. *Motivation in War: The Experience of Common Soldiers in Old-Regime Europe.* Cambridge: Cambridge University Press.

Blakely, S. 2006. *Myth and Ritual and Metallurgy in Ancient Greece and Recent Africa.* New York: Cambridge University Press.

Bloch, M. 1992. *The Historian's Craft.* P. Putman. Trans. Manchester: Manchester University Press.

Bloch, M. 1928–1953. Pour une Histoire Comparée des Sociétés Européennes, «Revue de Synthèse Historique», 15–50; English translation, 'Toward a Comparative History of European Societies'. In: F. C. Lane and J. C. Riemersma. Eds. *Enterprise and Secular Change. Readings in Economic History.* London: Allen & Unwin. 494–521.

Boucher, L. 2004. Masculinity Gone Mad: Settler Colonialism, Medical Discourse and the White Body in Late Nineteenth-Century Victoria. *Lilith.* 13. 51–67.

Bourdieu, P. 1977. *Outline of a Theory of Practice.* Trans. Richard Nice. Cambridge: Cambridge University Press.

Bovie, S. P. 1959. *The Satires and Epistles of Horace.* Chicago: University of Chicago Press.

Bowie, E. 1986. Lyric and Elegiac Poetry. In: J. Boardman, J. Griffin and O. Murray. Eds. *Oxford History of Greece and the Hellenistic World.* Oxford: Oxford University Press. 107–25.

Breed, B., C. Damon, and A. Rossi. 2010. Introduction. In: B. Breed, C. Damon, and A. Rossi. Eds. *Citizens of Discord: Rome and Its Civil Wars.* Oxford: Oxford University Press.

Bringmann, K. 2007. *A History of the Roman Republic.* Cambridge: Polity Press.

Brownell, S. 1995. *Training the Body for China: Sports in the Moral Order of the People's Republic.* Chicago: The University of Chicago Press.

Brunt, P. A. 1962. The Army and the Land in the Roman Revolution. *The Journal of Roman Studies.* Vol. 52. Parts 1 and 2. 69–86.

Brunt, P. A. 1971. *Italian Manpower, 225 B.C.–A.D. 14.* Oxford: The Clarendon Press.

Brunt, P. A. 1988. *The Fall of the Roman Republic and Related Essays.* Oxford: Oxford University Press.

Brunt, P. A. and Moore, J. M. Trans. 1967. *Res Gestae Divi Augusti: The Achievements of the Divine Augustus.* Oxford: Oxford University Press.

Buckle, C. 2001. *African Tears: The Zimbabwe Land Invasions.* Catherine Buckle: Johannesburg and London: Covos Day.

Buckle, C. 2002. *Beyond Tears: Zimbabwe's Tragedy*. Johannesburg: Jonathan Ball.

Bullock, C. 1927. *The Mashona: The Indigenous Natives of S. Rhodesia*: Cape Town.

Burbridge, S. J. 1923. 'How to Become a Witch Doctor.' *NADA*.

Burbridge, S. J. 1924. 'In Spirit-Bound Rhodesia.' *NADA*.

Burbridge, S. J. 1925. 'The Witch Doctor's Power: A Study of Its Source and Scope.' *NADA*.

Butler, J. 1990. *Gender Trouble: Feminism and the Subversion of Identity*. London: Routledge.

Butler, J. 2004. Bodies and Power Revisited. In: D. Taylor and K. Vintges. Eds. *Feminisms and the Final Foucault.* Chicago: University of Illinois Press. 183–94.

Butler, J. 2011. *Bodies that Matter: On the Discursive Limits of Sex.* London & New York: Routledge.

Campbell, J. 2014. *The Hero with a Thousand Faces.* Princeton: Princeton University Press.

Cantarella, E. 2003. Fathers and Sons in Rome. *The Classical World.* Vol. 96. No. 3. 281–98.

Carr, E. H. 1961. *What Is History?* New York: Vintage.

Cary, E. Trans. 1914 [1917]. *Dio Cassius, Roman History. Vol. V.* London: William Heinemann.

Cetina, K. 2006. Objectual Practice. In: T. R. Schatzki, K. K. Cetina, and E. von Savigny. Eds. *The Practice Turn in Contemporary Theory*. London: Routledge. 184–97.

Chitando, E. and Mlambo. O. B. forthcoming. 'I Have Got Stamina!' Yoweri K. Museveni, Masculinity and the Physical Right to Rule in Uganda.

Chitando, E., and J. Tarusarira. 2017. The Deployment of a 'Sacred Song' in Violence in Zimbabwe: The Case of the Song 'Zimbabwe ndeye ropa rama- dzibaba' (Zimbabwe Was/Is Born of the Blood of the Fathers/Ancestors) in Zimbabwe Politics. *Journal of the Study of Religion* 30 (1). 5–25.

Chung, F. 2006. *Re-living the Second Chimurenga: Memories from Zimbabwe's Liberation Struggle.* Harare: Weaver Press.

Clausewitz, C., Howard, M., Paret, P., and Brodie, B. 1984. *On War*. Princeton, NJ: Princeton University Press.

Clausen, W. V. Ed. 1994. *A Commentary on Virgil: Eclogues*. Oxford: Oxford University Press.

Coles, A. J. 2020. Roman Colonies in Republic and Empire. *Ancient History*. 3(1). 1–119.

Connell, R. W. 1995. *Masculinities.* Cambridge: Polity Press.

Connell, R. W. 2001a. The Social Organisation of Masculinity. In: S. Whitehead and F. Barrett. Eds. *The Masculinities Reader.* Cambridge: Polity Press.

Connell, R. W. 2001b. *The Men and the Boys.* California: University of California Press.

Connell, R. W. 2005. Globalization, Imperialism, and Masculinities. In: M. S. Kimmel, J. Hearn and R. W. Connell. Eds. *Handbook of Studies on Men and Masculinities.* London: Sage Publications. 71–89.

Connolly, W. 1996. Tocqueville, Territory, and Violence. In: M. J. Shapiro and H. R. Alker. Eds. *Challenging Boundaries: Global Flows, Territorial Identities.* Minneapolis: University of Minnesota Press. 141–64.

Connolly, J. 2007. Virile Tongues: Rhetoric and Masculinity. In: W. Dominik and J. Hall. Eds. *A Companion to Roman Rhetoric.* Malden, MA: Wiley-Blackwell. 83–97.

Cooley, A. E. Trans. 2009. *Res Gestae Divi Augusti, Text, Translation, and Commentary.* Cambridge: Cambridge University Press.

Cope, R. L. 1995. The Origins of the Anglo-Zulu War. DPhil Thesis, Johannesburg: University of the Witwatersrand.

Corbeille, A. 2002. Political Movement: Walking and Ideology in Republican Rome. In: D. Friedrich. Ed. *The Roman Gaze: Vision, Power and the Body.* Baltimore, MD: Johns Hopkins University Press. 182–215.

Cornford, M. Trans. 1914. *The Republic of Plato.* Oxford: Clarendon Press.

Cornwall, A., and N. Lindisfarne. 1994. *Dislocating Masculinity: Comparative Ethnographies.* London: Routledge.

Coulston, J. C. 2005. Armed and Belted Men: The Soldiery in Imperial Rome. In: J. C. Coulston and H. Dodge. Eds. *Ancient Rome: The Archaeology of the Eternal City.* Oxford: Oxford University Press. 76–105.

Cowan, J. K. 1990. *Dance and the Body Politic in Northern Greece.* New Jersey: Princeton University Press.

Crenshaw, K. 1989. Demarginalizing the intersection of race and sex: A Black feminist critique of antidiscrimination doctrine, feminist theory, and antiracist politics. In: S. A. Mann and A. S. Patterson. Eds. *Reading feminist theory.* New York, NY: Oxford University Press. 264–73.

Debord, G. 1970. *Society of the Spectacle.* Detroit: Radical America.

De Sanctis, G. 1932. *Problemi di Storia Antica: Sallistio e la Guerra Di Giugurta.* Bari: Laterza. 187–214.

Diop, C. A. 1981. *Civilization or Barbarism: An Authentic Anthropology.* Paris: Lawrence Hill Books.

Drogula, F. 2007. Imperium, Potestas, and the Pomerium in the Roman Republic. *Historia.* 56(4). 419–52.

Duff, J. D. 1928. *Lucan: The Civil War Books 1-X.* London: Heinemann.

Dwyer, P., and A. Nettelbeck. 2018. Savage Wars of Peace: Violence, Colonialism and Empire in the Modern World. In: P. Dwyer and A. Nettelbeck. Eds. *Violence, Colonialism and Empire in the Modern World.* Cham: Palgrave Macmillan. 1–22.

Eder, W. 2005. Augustus and the Power of Tradition. In: K. Galinsky. Ed. *The Cambridge Companion to the Age of Augustus.* Cambridge: Cambridge University Press.

Elden, S. 2005. Missing the Point: Globalization, Deterritorialization and the Space of the World. *Transactions of the Institute of British Geography*. 30/1. 8–19.

Erskine, A. 2002. Life after Death: Alexandria and the Body of Alexander. *Greece and Rome*. 49(2). 163–79.

Eyben, E. 1993. *Restless Youth in Ancient Rome*. London: Routledge.

Fagan, G. G. 2011. Violence in Roman Social Relations. In: M. Peachin. Ed. *The Oxford Handbook of Social Relations in the Roman World*. Oxford: Oxford University Press. 467–98.

Fagin, B. M. 1985. *In the Beginning*. Boston: Little Brown and Co.

Fairclough, H. R. Trans. 1999. *Virgil: Eclogues: Georgics: Aeneid I-VI*. Cambridge, Massachusetts: Harvard University Press.

Falconer, W. A. 1930. Trans. *Cicero: De Senectute, De Amicitia, De Divinatione*. London: William Heinemann Ltd.

Fanon, F. 1965. *A Dying Nationalism*. H. Chevalier. Trans. New York: Grove Press.

Fantham, E. 1985. Caesar and the Mutiny: Lucan's Reshaping of the Historical Tradition in De bello civili 5. 237-373. *Classical Philology*. 80(2). 119–31.

Feldherr, A. 1998. *Spectacle and Society in Livy's History*. Berkeley: University of California Press.

Feltoe, G. 2004. The Onslaught against Democracy and Rule of Law in Zimbabwe in 2000. In: D. Harold-Barry. Ed. *Zimbabwe: The Past is the Future*. Harare: Weaver Press.

Ferree, M. M. 2018. 'Theories Don't Grow on Trees': Contextualizing Gender Knowledge. In: J. W. Messerschmidt, P. Y. Martin, M. A. Messner, and R. Connell. Ed. *Gender Reckonings: New Social Theory and Research*. New York: New York University Press. 13–34.

Finley, I. M. 1986. *Ancient History: Evidence and Models*. New York: Viking.

Fontein, J. 2010. Between Tortured Bodies and Resurfacing Bones: The Politics of the Dead in Zimbabwe. *Journal of Material Culture*. 15(4). 423–48.

Foster, B. O. Trans. 1949. *Livy*. Massachusetts: Harvard University Press.

Foucault, M. 1979. *Discipline and Punish: The Birth of the Prison*. A. M. Sheridan Smith. Trans. New York: Vintage.

Fraenkel, E. 1970. *Horace* (reprinted). Oxford: Oxford University Press.

Gabba, E. 1976. *Republican Rome: The Army and the Allies*. P. J. Cuff. Trans. Oxford: Basil Blackwell.

Gale, M. R. and Scourfield, J. H. D. 2018. Introduction: Reading Roman Violence. In: M. R. Gale and J. H. D. Scourfield. Eds. *Texts and Violence in the Roman World*. Cambridge: Cambridge University Press. 1–43.

Geertz, C. 1973. *The Interpretation of Cultures*. New York: Basic Books.

Gell, A. 1998. *Art and Agency: An Anthropological Theory*. Oxford: Clarendon Press.

Gewald, Jan-Bart. 2003. Herero Genocide in the Twentieth Century: Politics and Memory. In: J. Abbink, M. Bruijn and K. van Walraven. Eds. *Rethinking Resistance: Revolt and Violence in African History*. Leiden: Brill. 279–304.

Giddens, A. 1979. *Central Problems in Social Theory: Action, Structure and Contradiction in Social Analysis.* Berkeley and Los Angeles: University of California Press.

Gilmore, D. D. 1987. *Aggression and Community: Paradoxes of Andalusian Culture.* New Haven: Yale University Press.

Glaser, B., and A. Strauss. 1967. *The Discovery of Grounded Theory: Strategies for Qualitative Research.* Chicago: Aldine Publishing Company.

Gleason, M. W. 1995. *Making Men: Sophists and Self-Presentation in Ancient Rome.* Princeton: Princeton University Press.

Goheen, M. 1994. *Men Own The Fields, Women Own the Crops: Gender and Power in the Cameroon Highlands.* Madison: Univ. Wisc. Press.

Graves, R. Trans. 1956. *Lucan, Pharsalia: Dramatic Episodes of the Civil Wars.* Harmondsworth, Middlesex: The Penguin Classics.

Grant, M. Trans. 1971. *Tacitus, The Annals of Imperial Rome.* Michael Grant Publications.

Grant, M., and J. Hazel. 1979. *Who's Who in Classical Mythology.* London: Hodder and Stoughton.

Greenfield, P. N. 2011. Virgin Territory: The Vestals and the Transition from Republic to Principate. PhD Thesis: University of Sydney.

Gruen, E. S. 2011. *Rethinking the Other in Antiquity.* New Jersey: Princeton University Press.

Guite, H. F. 1965. *What Kind of Classics?* London: Oxford University Press.

Hadas, M. Ed. 1942. *Complete Works of Tacitus.* New York: Random House.

Haley, S. P. 2009. Be Not Afraid of the Dark: Critical Race Theory and Classical Studies. In: L. Nasrallah and E. S. Fiorenza. Eds. *Prejudice and Christian Beginnings: Investigating Race, Gender and Ethnicity in Early Christian Studies.* Minneapolis: Fortress Press. 27–49.

Handford, S. A. Trans. 1963. *Sallust: The Jugurthine War; The Conspiracy of Catiline.* Harmondsworth: Penguin Books.

Harrison, E. 2006. *Jambanja.* Maioio Publishers.

Harold, C., and K. Deluca. 2005. Behold the Corpse: Violent Images and the Case of Emmett Till. *Rhetoric and Public Affairs.* 8. 263–86.

Haskins, C. E. Ed. 1887. *M. Annaei Lucani Pharsalia.* Cambridge: Deighton, Bell and Co.

Hearn, J. 1987. *The Gender of Oppression.* Sussex: Wheatsheaf Books.

Helzle, M. 1994. Indocilis Privata Loqui: The Characterization of Lucan's Caesar. Symbolae Osloenses. *Norwegian Journal of Greek and Latin Studies.* 69(1). 121–36.

Hinojosa, R. 2010. Doing Hegemony: Military, Men, and Constructing a Hegemonic Masculinity. *The Journal of Men's Studies.* 19(2). 179–94.

Hove, C. 1988. *Bones.* Harare: Baobab.

Huntington, S. 1957. *The Soldier and the State: The Theory and Politics of Civil-Military Relations.* Cambridge: Belknap Press.

Isaac, B. 2004. *The Invention of Racism in Classical Antiquity.* New Jersey: Princeton University Press.

Jackson, S. N. G. 1905. *Native Law in Southern Rhodesia.* London: Hurst & Blackett.

Jeater, D. 2005. Imagining Africans: Scholarship, Fantasy, and Science in Colonial Administration, 1920s Southern Rhodesia. *The International Journal of African Historical Studies.* 38(1). 1–26.

Kalyvas, Stathis. N. 2006. *The Logic of Violence in Civil War.* Cambridge: Cambridge University Press.

Kalyvas, Stathis. N. 2012. Preface. In: Nathalie Duclos. Ed. *War Veterans in Postwar Situations: Chechnya, Serbia, Turkey, Peru, and Côte d'Ivoire.* New York: Palgrave MacMillan.

Keppie, L. 1983. *Colonisation and Veteran Settlement in Italy 47–14 B.C.* London: British School at Rome.

Kirstein, R. 2017. Violence in an Erotic Landscape: Catullus, Caesar, and the Borders of Empire and Existence (Carm. II). In: M. Champion and L. O' Sullivan. Eds. *Cultural Perceptions of Violence in the Hellenistic World.* Routledge: New York. 191–207.

Konstan, D. 2002. Women, Ethnicity and Power in the Roman Empire. *Ordia Prima* 1. 11–23.

Konstan, D. 2021. Motivations and Justifications of Genocide. In: T. Taylor. Ed. *A Cultural History of Genocide in the Ancient World (800 BC-800 AD).* London: Bloomsbury Academic Press. 51–71.

Kroeber, A. L., and C. Kluckhohn. 1963. *Culture: A Critical Review of Concepts and Definitions.* New York: Vintage.

Lacan, J. 1975. *The Language of the Self.* New York: Dell.

Lambert, M. 2011. *The Classics and South African Identities.* London: Duckworth.

Lan, D. 1985. *Guns and Rain: Guerrillas and Spirit Mediums in Zimbabwe.* California: University of California Press.

Latour, B. 1999. *Pandora's Hope: An Essay on the Reality of Science Studies.* Cambridge, MA: Harvard University Press.

Lee, G. Trans. 1984. *Vergil, The Eclogues.* Harmondsworth: Penguin Books.

Lehman, P. 2007. *Running Scared: Masculinity and the Representation of the Human Body.* Detroit: Wayne State University Press.

Lendon, J. E. 2005. *Soldiers and Ghosts: A History of Battle in Classical Antiquity.* Yale: New Haven, CT.

Lenski, N. 2016. Violence and the Roman Slave. In: W. Riess and G. G. Fagan. Eds. *The Topography of Violence in the Greco-Roman World.* Michigan: University of Michigan Press. 275–98.

Lesejane, D. 2006. Fatherhood from an African Cultural Perspective. In: L. Ritcher and R. Morrell. Eds. *Baba, Men and Fatherhood in South Africa.* Cape Town: HSRC Press.

Lewis, C. T., and C. Short. 1879. *A Latin Dictionary.* Oxford: Clarendon.

Liddell, H. G., and R. Scott. 1876. *A Lexicon Abridged from Liddell and Scott's Greek-English Lexicon.* Seventeenth Edition. Oxford: Clarendon.

Liddell, H. G., and R. Scott. 1889. *An Intermediate Greek-English Lexicon Founded upon the Seventh Edition of Liddell and Scott's Greek-English Lexicon.* Oxford: Clarendon.

Lintott, A. W. 1971. Lucan and the History of the Civil War. *The Classical Quarterly.* 21(2). 488–505.

Logan, I. 2006. Ideology and Urban Food Security: Zimbabwe's Third Chimurenga. *Journal of African Studies.* (2). 202–24.

Lunstrum, E. 2009. Terror, Territory, and Deterritorialization: Landscapes of Terror and the Unmaking of State Power in the Mozambican 'Civil' War. *Annals of the Association of American Geographers.* 99(5). 884–92.

Lwambo, D. 2011. *'Before the War I was a Man': Men and Masculinities in Eastern DR Congo.* Goma: Heal Africa.

Lyons, T. 1999. Guns and Guerrilla Girls: Women in the Zimbabwean National Liberation Struggle. PHD Thesis: Adelaide University.

MacMullen, R. 1984. The Legion as a Society. *Historia.* 33. 440–56.

Mann, G. 2006. *Native Sons: West African Veterans and France in the Twentieth Century.* Durham: Duke University Press.

Maquet, J. 1972. Africanity: *The Cultural Unity of Black Africa.* New York: Oxford University Press.

Maringira, G. 2017. Politics, Privileges, and Loyalty in the Zimbabwe National Army. *African Studies Review, 60*(2). 93–113.

Martin, R. H. 1987. *Römishe Tempelkultbilder: eine Archäologische Untersuchung zur späten Republik.* Rome.

Masiiwa, M., and L. Chipungu. 2004. Land Reform Programme in Zimbabwe: Disparity Between Policy Design and Implementation. In: M. Masiiwa. Ed. *Post-Independence Land Reform in Zimbabwe: Controversies and Impact on the Economy.* Harare: Friedrich Ebert Stiftung and Institute of Development Studies.

Mazrui, A. 1977. The Warrior Tradition and the Masculinity of War. *Journal of Asian and African Studies.* 12(1–4). 69–81.

Mbah, N. L. 2017. Female Masculinities, Dissident Sexuality, and the Material Politics of Gender in Early Twentieth-Century Igboland. *Journal of Women's History.* 29(4). 35–60.

Mbembe, A. 2001. *On the Postcolony.* Berkeley: University of California.

McClymont, J. D. 2007. The Presuppositions of Classics: Towards a Philosophical Framework for doing Classics. Unpublished MPhil Thesis. University of Zimbabwe.

McClymont, J. D. and Mlambo. O. B. 2016. African Values in a Modern City: Threats and Benefits. In: Magosvongwe, R., O. B. Mlambo, and E. Ndlovu. Eds. *Africa's Intangible Heritage and Land: Emerging Perspectives.* Harare: University of Zimbabwe Publications. 112–20.

McDonnell, M. 2006. *Roman Manliness.* Cambridge: Cambridge University Press.

McInerney, J. 2003. Plutarch's Manly Women. In: R. M. Rosen and I. Sluiter. Eds. *Andreia: Studies in Manliness and Courage in Classical Antiquity.* Mnemosyne suppl. 238. Leiden: Brill. 319–44.

Melber, H. 2003. 'Namibia, Land of the Brave': Selective Memories on War and Violence within Nation Building. In: J. Abbink, M. Bruijn and K. van Walraven. Eds. *Rethinking Resistance: Revolt and Violence in African History*. Leiden: Brill. 305–27.

Meredith, M. 2002. *Mugabe: Power, Plunder and the Struggle for Zimbabwe*. New York: Public Affairs.

Messerschmidt, J. W. 1993. *Masculinities and Crime: Critique and Reconceptualization of Theory*. Lanham, MD: Rowman and Littlefield Publishers.

Messerschmidt, J. W., Martin, P. Y., Messner, M. A., and Connell, R. Eds. 2018. *Gender Reckonings: New Social Theory and Research*. New York: New York University Press.

Mhanda, W. 2011. *Dzino: Memories of a Freedom Fighter*. Harare: Weaver Press.

Michie, J. 1964. *The Odes of Horace*. Harmondsworth: Penguin Books.

Miller, W. 1993. *Humiliation: And Other Essays on Honor, Social Discomfort, and Violence*. Ithaca: Cornell University Press.

Milne, K. H. 2009. The Republican Soldier: Historiographical Representations and Human Realities. PhD Dissertation: Pennsylvania University.

Mlambo, O. B. 2014. The Dialectics of Land Redistribution in the Late Roman Republic and Contemporary Zimbabwe 2000–2008. Unpublished PhD thesis.

Mlambo, O. B. 2018. Veterans, Decolonization and Land Expropriation in Post-Independence Zimbabwe (2000 to 2008). In: A. Álcalde and Xosé M. Núñez Seixas. Eds. War Veterans and the World after 1945: Cold War Politics, Decolonization, Memory. London: Routledge. 167–83.

Mlambo, O. B., and E. Chitando. 2015. Blair, keep your England, and let me keep my Zimbabwe: Examining the Relationship of Physical Space and Political Order in Zimbabwe's Land Redistribution Program (2000–2008). *Journal of Pan-African Studies*. 8(8). 8–26.

Mlambo, O. B., and T. C. Gwekwerere. 2019. Names, Labels, the Zimbabwean Liberation War veteran and the third Chimurenga: The language and politics of entitlement in post-2000 Zimbabwe. *African Identities* 17(2). 130–46.

Mlambo, O. B., J. D. McClymont and E. Zvoma. 2017. Land, Political Power, and Violence in Republican Rome and Contemporary Zimbabwe: A Comparative View. *Africology: The Journal of Pan African Studies*. 11(1). 153–78.

Mommsen, T. 1895. *A Well-Meaning Conservative Who Leads a Revolution: The History of Rome*. New York: Charles Scribner's Sons.

Montserrat, D. 2000. Reading Gender in the Roman World. In: J. Huskinson. Ed. *Experiencing Rome: Culture, Identity and Power in the Roman Empire*. Oxford: Routledge in Association with The Open University. 153–81.

Moore, J. 2003. *Zimbabwe's Fight to the Finish: The Catalyst of the Free Market*. New York: Kegan Paul.

Morrell, R. 2006. Fathers, fatherhood and masculinity in South Africa. In: L. Richter and R. Morrell. Eds. *Baba, Men and Fatherhood in South Africa*. Cape Town: HSRC Press.

Morey, W. C. 1903. *Outlines of Greek History.* New York: American Book Company.

Moyo, S. 2014. Regime survival strategies in Zimbabwe in the 21st century. *Journal of Sociology and Social Work.* 2(1). 21–49.

Moyo, S., and W. Chambati. Eds. 2013. *Land and Agrarian Reform in Zimbabwe. Beyond White Settler Capitalism.* Dakar: CODESRIA.

Muchemwa, M. 2011. Zimbabwe's War Veterans: From Demobilisation to Remobilisation. *Transformation: Critical Perspectives on Southern Africa 75.* 122–31.

Mugabe, R. G. 2001. *Inside the Third Chimurenga.* Harare: Department of Information and Publicity.

Murphy, A. Trans. 1908. *The Annals.* London: Everyman's Library.

Mutambara, A. 2014. *The Rebel in Me: A ZANLA Guerrilla Commander in the Rhodesian Bush War, 1975–1980.* Pinetown: West Midlands: Co-published by Hellion and Co Ltd and 30° South Publishers Pvt Ltd.

Muzondidya, J. 2009. From Buoyancy to Crisis, 1980–1997. In: B. Raftopoulos and A. Mlambo. Eds. *Becoming Zimbabwe, A History from Pre-Colonial Period to 2008.* Harare: Weaver Press. 167–200.

Nagel, J. 1998. Masculinity and Nationalism: Gender and Sexuality in the Making of Nations. *Ethnic and Racial Studies.* 21(2). 242–69.

Ndlela, N. 2005. The African Paradigm: The Coverage of the Zimbabwean Crisis in the Norwegian Media. Westminster Papers in Communication and Culture. Special Issue. 71–90.

Ndlovu-Gatsheni, Sabelo J. and Wendy Willems. 2009. Making sense of cultural nationalism and the politics of commemoration under the Third Chimurenga in Zimbabwe. *Journal of Southern African Studies* 35(4). 945–65.

Neely, E. T. 2016. *Lucan's Characterization of Caesar through Speech.* MA Thesis: University of Georgia.

Ocobock, P. 2017. *An Uncertain Age: The Politics of Manhood in Kenya.* Ohio: Ohio University Press.

Olson, K. 2014. Masculinity, Appearance, and Sexuality: Dandies in Roman Antiquity. *Journal of the History of Sexuality.* 23(2). 182–205.

Omitowoju, R. 2016. The Crime That Dare Not Speak Its Name: Violence against Women in the Athenian Courts. In: W. Riess and G. G. Fagan. Eds. *The Topography of Violence in the Greco-Roman World.* Michigan: University of Michigan Press. 113–15.

Osgood, J. 2006. *Caesar's Legacy: Civil War and the Emergence of the Roman Empire.* Cambridge: Cambridge University Press.

Otterbein, K. F. 1964. The Evolution of Zulu Warfare. *The Kansas Journal of Sociology.* 1(1). 27–35.

Parchami, A. 2009. *Hegemonic Peace and Empire: The Pax Romana, Britannica and Americana.* New York: Routledge.

Paret, P., Craig, G. A., and Gilbert, F. 1986. *Makers of Modern Strategy: From Machiavelli to the Nuclear Age.* Princeton. N.J: Princeton University Press.

Parker, G. 2012. *Mixed Capital: Classicism in Unexpected Places*. Princeton/ Stanford Working Papers in Classics. Version 1. 1–43.

Paxton, R. O. 2004. *The Anatomy of Fascism*. New York: Knopf.

Peskett, A. G. Trans. 1914. *Caesar, The Civil Wars*. Cambridge, MA: Harvard University Press.

Petrie, A. 1963. *An Introduction to Roman History, Literature and Antiquities*. Oxford: Oxford University Press.

Phang, Sara E. 2008. *Roman Military Service: Ideologies of Discipline in the Late Republic and Early Principate*. Cambridge: Cambridge University Press.

Pilossof, R. 2009. The Unbearable Whiteness of Being: Land, Race and Belonging in the Memoirs of White Zimbabweans. *South African Historical Journal*. 61(3). 621–38.

Pilossof, R. 2012. *The Unbearable Whiteness of Being: Farmers' Voices from Zimbabwe*. Harare: Weaver Press.

Pitt-Rivers, J. 1968. Honour. In: D. L. Sills and R. K. Merton. Eds. *International Encyclopaedia of the Social Sciences. Vol. 6*. New York: Macmillan. 503–11.

Polo, F. P. 2019. Losers in the Civil War Between Caesarians and Pompeians: Punishment and Survival. In: K. J. Hölkeskamp and H. Beck. Eds. *Verlierer und Aussteiger in der, Konkurrenz unter Anwesenden: Agonalität in der politischen Kultur des antiken Rom*. Stuttgart: Franz Steiner Verlag. 147–68.

Posel, D. 2014. Julius Malema and the Post-Apartheid Public Sphere. *Acta Academica*. 46(1). 31–52.

Powell, L. 2013. *Eager for Glory: The Untold Story of Drusus the Elder, Conqueror of Germanicus*. Pen & Sword Military.

Raaflaub, K. 1974. Dignitatis Contentio: Studien zur Motivation und Politischen Taktik in Bürgerkrieg zwischen Caesar und Pompeius. *Vestigia*. 20. 293–307.

Raaflaub, K. A. 2010. Creating a Grand Coalition of True Roman Citizens: On Caesar's Political Strategy in the Civil War. In: Brian Breed et al. Eds. *Citizens of Discord: Rome and Its Civil Wars*, Oxford, Oxford University Press. 159–68.

Rackham, H. Trans. 1934. *Aristotle: Nicomachean Ethics*. London: Harvard University Press.

Raftopoulos, B. 2009. The Crisis in Zimbabwe, 1998–2008. In: B. Raftopoulos and A. Mlambo. Eds. *Becoming Zimbabwe, A History from Pre-Colonial Period to 2008*. Harare: Weaver Press. 201–50.

Reinhold, M. and P. M. Swan. 1990. Cassius Dio's Assessment of Augustus. In: K. A. Raaflaub and M. Toher. Eds. *Between Republic and Empire: Interpretation of Augustus and his Principate*. Berkeley: University of California Press. 155–73.

Riphenburg, C. 1997.Women's Status and Cultural Expression: Changing Gender Relations and Structural Adjustment in Zimbabwe. *Africa Today*. 44(1). 33–50.

Robinson, G. E. 1938. *A History of the Roman Republic*. London: Methuen.

Roller, M. 2009. The Exemplary Past in Roman Historiography and Culture. In: A. Feldherr. Ed. *The Cambridge Companion to Roman Historians*. Cambridge: Cambridge University Press. 214–30.

Rondholz, A. 2009. Crossing the Rubicon. A Historiographical Study. Mnemosyne: *A Journal of Classical Studies*. 62. 432–50.

Rosen, M. and I. Sluiter. Eds. 2003. *Andreia: Studies in Manliness and Courage in Classical Antiquity*. (Mnemosyne suppl. 238. Leiden: Brill.

Rubarth, S. 2014. Competing Constructions of Masculinity in Ancient Greece. *Athens Journal of Humanities and Arts*. Vol. 1. No. 1. 21–32.

Sachikonye, L. 2011. *When a State Turns on Its Citizens: Institutionalized Violence and Political Culture*. Harare: Jacana.

Sachikonye, L. M. and O. J. Zishiri. 1999. *Tenure Security for farm Workers in Zimbabwe*. Harare: Friedrich Ebert Stiftung.

Saddington, D. B. 2009. Mens Exercituum: The Pathology of Roman Soldiers in Conflict. In: P. Bosman. Ed. *Mania: Madness in the Greco-Roman World. Acta Classica Supplementum III*. Pretoria: Classical Association of South Africa. 52–68.

Saddington, D. B. 2012. Under the Centurion's Boot: Corruption and its Containment in the Roman Army. In: P. Bosman. Ed. *Corruption and Integrity in Ancient Greece and Rome. Acta Classica Supplementum IV*. Classical Association of South Africa: Pretoria. 122–30.

Sadomba, Z. W. 2011. *War Veterans in Zimbabwe's Revolution; Challenging Neo-Colonialism and Settler and International Capital*. Harare: Weaver Press.

Salmon, E. T. 1969. *Roman Colonization Under the Republic*. London: Camelot Press.

Scarnecchia, T. 2006. The 'Fascist Cycle' in Zimbabwe, 2000–2005. *Journal of Southern African Studies*. 32(2). 221–37.

Schatzki, T. R. 2006. Introduction: Practice Theory. In: T. R. Schatzki, K. K. Cetina and E. von Savigny. Eds. *The Practice Turn in Contemporary Theory*. London: Routledge. 10–23.

Schmitt, C. 2003. *The Nomos of the Earth in the International Law of the Jus Publicum Europaeum*. Trans. G. L. Ulmen. New York: Telos Press. First Published in 1932 as *Der Nomos der Erde im Volkerrecht des Jus Pulicum Europeaum*. Berlin: Duncker and Humblot.

Scullard, H. H. 1960. Scipio Aemiliunus and Roman Politics. *The Journal of Roman Studies*. 50. 59–74.

Sedgwick, E. K. 2015. *Between Men: English Literature and Male Homosocial Desire*. Columbia University Press.

Seibert, G. 2003. The Vagaries of Violence and Power in Post colonial Mozambique. In: J. Abbink, M. Bruijn and K van Walraven. Eds. *Rethinking Resistance: Revolt and Violence in African History*. Leiden: Brill. 254–76.

Shakespeare, W. s.a. *The Complete Works of William Shakespeare*. London: Collins' Clear-Type press.

Sharwood Smith, J. E. 1977. *On Teaching Classics*. London: Routledge and Keagan Paul Ltd.

Shipton, P. 1994. Land and Culture in Tropical Africa: Soils, Symbols, and the Metaphysics of the Mundane. *Annu. Rev. Anthropol*. 23. 347–77.

Shoko, T. 2006. My bones shall rise again: War veterans, Spirits and Land Reform in Zimbabwe. Leiden: African Studies Centre. 1–17.

Silverman, K. 1992. *Male Subjectivity at the Margins.* New York: Routledge.

Simpson, D. P. Ed. 1959. *Cassell's New Latin-English English-Latin Dictionary.* London: Cassell & Company Ltd.

Simpson, F. P. 1965. *Select Poems of Catullus.* Second Edition. London: Macmillan and Co. Ltd.

Sinclair, T. A. Trans. 1962. *Aristotle: The Politics.* Harmondsworth: Penguin Books.

Sinha, M. 1995. *Colonial Masculinity: The 'Manly Englishman' and The 'Effeminate Bengali' in the Late Nineteenth Century.* Manchester: St. Martin's Press.

Smiley, C. J. and D. Fakunle. 2016. From 'Brute' to 'Thug': The Demonization and Criminalization of Unarmed Black Male Victims in America. *J. Hum. Behav. Soc. Environ.* 26(3–4). 350–66.

Smith, R. E. 1955. *The Failure of the Roman Republic.* Cambridge: Cambridge University Press.

Solomon-Godeau, A. 1997. *Male Trouble: A Crisis in Representation.* London: Thames and Hudson.

Spentzou, E. 2018. Violence and Alienation in Lucan's Pharsalia: The Case of Caesar. In: M. R. Gale and J. H. D. Scourfield. Eds. *Texts and Violence in the Roman World.* Cambridge: Cambridge University Press. 246–68.

Stearns, J. K. 2012. *Dancing in the Glory of Monsters: The Collapse of the Congo and the Great War of Africa.* New York: Public Affairs.

Stewart, M. E. 2014. Some Disputes Surrounding Masculinity as a Legitimate Category of Historical Inquiry in the Study of Late Antiquity. *Masculinities Journal.* 1. 77–91.

Stewart, M. E. 2016. The Soldier's Life: Early Byzantine Masculinity and the Manliness of War. *Byzantina Symmeikta.* 26. 11–44.

St. John, L. 2007. *Rainbow's End: A Memoir of Childhood, War and an African Farm.* New York: Scribner.

Strauss, A. and Corbin, J. 1990. *Basics of Qualitative Research: Techniques and Procedures for Developing Grounded Theory.* California: SAGE Publications Inc.

Summers, C. 2013. Boys, brats and education: Reproducing white maturity in colonial Zimbabwe, 1915–1935. *Settler Colonial Studies* 1(1). 132–53.

Swidler, A. 2006. What Anchors Cultural Practices. In: T. R. Schatzki, K. K. Cetina, and E. von Savigny. Eds. *The Practice Turn in Contemporary Theory.* London: Routledge. 83–101.

Takacs, S. T. 2009. *The Rhetoric of Empire: The Construction of Authority in Ancient Rome and Byzantium.* Cambridge: Cambridge University Press.

Taylor, C. 1994. Interpretation and the Sciences of Men. In: M. Martin and L. C. McIntyre. Eds. *Readings in the Philosophy of Social Science.* Cambridge: The MIT Press. 181–211.

Tendi, Blessing-Miles. 2020. *The Army and Politics in Zimbabwe: Mujuru, the Liberation Fighter and Kingmaker.* Cambridge: Cambridge University Press.

Thein, A. 2010. Sulla's Veteran Settlement Policy. In: F. Daubner. Ed. *Militärsiedlungen und Territorialherrschaft in der Antike*. (Topoi / Berlin Studies of the Ancient World 3). Berlin: Walter de Gruyter. 79–99.

Thein, A. 2016. Booty in the Sullan Civil War of 83–82 B.C. *Historia 65*. 2016/4. 450–72.

Thein, A. 2018. Proscriptions. In: Roger S. Bagnall, Kai Brodersen, Craige B. Champion, and Andrew Erskine. Eds. *The Encyclopedia of Ancient History*. John Wiley & Sons Ltd.

Togarasei, L. 2020. State as Patriarch and Biblical Discipline: Theorising State Sponsored Violence in Zimbabwe. *African Identities*. DOI: 10.1080/14725843.2020.1813549.

Trigg, R. 1982. *The Shaping of Man*. Oxford: Blackwell.

Tripp, A. M. 2010. *Museveni's Uganda: Paradoxes of Power in a Hybrid Regime: Challenge and Change in African Politics*. Boulder: Lynne Rienner Publishers.

Vance, C. S. 1989. Social Constructionist Theory: Problems in the History of Sexuality. In: D. Altman et al. Eds. *Homosexuality, Which Homosexuality? Essays from the International Scientific Conference on Lesbian and Gay Studies*. London: Gay Men's Press. 13–34.

Vasunia, P. 2013. *The Classics and Colonial India*. Oxford: Oxford University Press.

Walsh, F. 2010. *Male Trouble: Masculinity and the Performance of Crisis*. Basingstoke: Palgrave Macmillan.

Walsh, P. G. 1961. *Livy*. Cambridge: Cambridge University Press.

Ward, G. 2016. The Roman Battlefield: Individual Exploits in Warfare of the Roman Republic. In: Werner Riess and Garrett G. Fagan. Eds. *The Topography of Violence in the Greco-Roman World*. Michigan: University of Michigan Press. 299–324.

Warner, R. 1958. *Fall of the Roman Republic*. Harmondsworth: Penguin Books.

Warrington, J. 1961. *Everyman's Classical Dictionary*. London: J. M. Dent and Sons.

Weber, M. 1972. *Basic Concepts in Sociology*. H. P. Secher. Trans. Secaucus, New Jersey: Citadel Press.

Webster, G. 2003. *Roman Invasion of Britain*. London: Routledge.

Weeda, L. 2015. *Vergil's Political Commentary in the Eclogues, Georgics and Aeneid*. Berlin: De Gruyter Open Ltd.

West, H. 2000. Girls with Guns: Narrating the Experience of War of Frelimo's Female Detachment. *Anthropological Quarterly*. 73(4). 180–94.

Westall, R. 2014. Triumph and Closure: Between History and Literature. In: H. L. Carsten and F. L. Vervaet. Eds. *The Roman Republic Triumph Beyond the Spectacle*. Rome: Edizioni Quasar di Severino Tognonn srl.

White, H. Trans. 1913. *Appian: Roman History Vol. III*. Massachusetts: Harvard University Press.

White, L. 2000. *Speaking with Vampires: Rumor and History in Colonial Africa*. Berkeley: University of California Press.

Widlok, T. 2008. The Dilemmas of Walking: A Comparative View. In: T. Ingold, J. L. Vergunst Eds. *Ways of Walking. Ethnography and Practice on Foot*. Aldershot: Ashgate (Anthropological Studies of Creativity and Perception). 51–66.

Widlok, T. 2017. *Anthropology and the Economy of Sharing.* London: Routledge.

Wilcox, L. 2015. *Bodies of Violence: Theorizing Embodied Subjects in International Relations.* Oxford: Oxford University Press.

Wiles, R. F. 2005. *Foredoomed Is My Forest: The Diary of a Zimbabwe Farmer.* Victoria: Trafford.

Willems, W. 2004. Peaceful Demonstrators, Violent Invaders: Representations of Land in the Zimbabwean Press. *World Development.* 32(10). 1767–83.

Williams, C. 2010. *Roman Homosexuality.* Oxford: Oxford University Press.

Wills, G. 1966. *Roman Culture: Weapons and the Man.* Toronto: Ambassador Books.

Willis, I. 2011. *Now and Rome: Lucan and Vergil as Theorists of Politics and Space.* London: Continuum.

Witzke, Serena S. 2016. Violence against Women in Ancient Rome: Ideology versus Reality. In: W. Riess and G. G. Fagan. Eds. *The Topography of Violence in the Greco-Roman World.* Michigan: University of Michigan Press. 248–74.

Worby, A. 2001. Redivided Land? New Agrarian Conflicts and Questions in Zimbabwe. *Journal of Agrarian Change.* 1(4). 475–509.

Woodman, A. J. 2006. Mutiny and Madness: Tacitus Annals 1.16-49. *Arethusa. 39(2).* 303–29.

Zhou, Z. 2016. Post 2010 Evaluation of Zimbabwe as a Preferred Tourist Destination. *African Journal of Hospitality, Tourism and Leisure.* 5(1). 1–15.

## Online resources

Basore, J. W. Trans. n.d. [1928]. *Seneca: Moral Essays Vol I.* Internet Archive. <https://archive.org/stream/moralessayswithe01seneuoft/moralessayswithe01seneuoft_djvu.t> Accessed 1 September 2021.

Brunt, P. A. 1965. Reflections on British and Roman Imperialism. *Comparative Studies in Society and History,* 7(3). 267–88. http://www.jstor.org/stable/177793.

Evans, E. B. 2003. Iraq and the New American Colonialism. *Moebius.* (1)2. <https//digitalcommons.calpoly.edu/moebius/vol1/iss2/10>. Accessed 20 July 2021.

Fontein, J. 2009. The Politics of the Dead: Living Heritage, Bones and Commemoration in Zimbabwe. *ASAonline.* 1(2). 437–48.

Greene, R. A. 2020. Who is Cecil Rhodes and why are UK demonstrators protesting at his statue? *CNN,* 10 June 2020. <https://edition.cnn.com/2020/06/09/uk/cecil-rhodes-protest-oxford-intl/index.html> Accessed 25 November 2021.

Hammaren, N., and T. Johansson. 2014. *Homosociality: In Between Power and Intimacy.* SAGE Open. <https://doi.org/10.1177/2158244013518057>. Accessed 10 October, 2020.

Jones, H. L. Trans. 1917. Strabo: *Geography. In 8 Volumes.* Loeb Classical Library. London: William Heinemann. <https://archive.org/details/Strabo08Geography17AndIndex> Accessed 15 August 2021.

Kline, A. S. Trans. 2014. *Lucan: The Civil War (Pharsalia): Book I.* Poetry in Translation.<https://www.poetryintranslation.com/PITBR/Latin/PharsaliaImaster.php#anchor_Toc390000078> Accessed 10 October 2020.

Laband, J. 1998. Zulu Strategic and Tactical Options in the face of the British Invasion of January 1879. *Scientia Militaria. South African Journal of Military Studies.* 28(1). 1–14. <scientiamilitaria.journals.ac.za> Accessed 2 September 2021.

Mbah, N. L. 2019. African Masculinities. *Oxford Research Encyclopedia of African History*: Online. DOI: 10.1093/acrefore/9780190277734.013.270. 1–42. Accessed 1 January 2020.

Ndou, C. 2021. MKMVA Defies ANC Call to Disband. *The Witness,* 6 July 2021. <https://www.news24.com/witness/news/mkmva-defies-anc-call-to-disband-20210706> Accessed 24 July 2021.

Perrin, B. n.d. Trans. *Life of Antony*. Lexundria. <https://lexundria.com/plut_ant/35/prr> Accessed 31 August 2021.

Perseus Digital Library. n.d.a. *Polybius, Histories, Book 6, the Causes of Roman Superiority.* <http://data.perseus.org/citations/urn:cts:greekLit:tlg0543.tlg001.perseus-eng1:6.52> Accessed 1 November 2021.

Perseus Digital Library. n.d.b. *Aristotle, Economics, Book 1, Section 1343a.* <http://data.perseus.org/citations/urn:cts:greekLit:tlg0086.tlg029.perseus-eng1:1.1343a> Accessed 31 August 2021.

Perseus Digital Library. n.d.c. *Aristotle, Politics, Book 1, Section 1254b.* <http://data.perseus.org/citations/urn:cts:greekLit:tlg0086.tlg035.perseus-eng1:1.1254b> Accessed 31 August 2021.

Perseus Digital Library. n.d.d. *Sallust, The Jugurthine War, Chapter 85. 29-30.* <http://data.perseus.org/citations/urn:cts:latinLit:phi0631.phi002.perseus-eng1:85>. Accessed 15 October 2021.

Perseus Digital Library. n.d.e. *Sallust, The Jugurthine War, Chapter 85. 39-41.* <http://data.perseus.org/citations/urn:cts:latinLit:phi0631.phi002.perseus-eng1:85>. Accessed 15 October 2021.

Perseus Digital Library. n.d.f. *Pliny The Elder, The Natural History, Book VII.* <http://data.perseus.org/citations/urn:cts:latinLit:phi0978.phi001.perseus-eng1:7.29> Accessed 16 October 2021.

Perseus Digital Library. n.d.g. *Plutarch, Sulla Chapter 31.* http://data.perseus.org/citations/urn:cts:greekLit:tlg0007.tlg033.perseus-eng1:31 Accessed 31 August 2021.

Perseus Digital Library. n.d.h. *M. Tullius Cicero, On his House. 13.* http://www.perseus.tufts.edu/hopper/text?doc=Cic.+Dom.+13&fromdoc=Perseus%3Atext%3A1999.02.0020 Accessed 31 August 2021.

Roche, P. Ed. 1997. *Lucan, De Bello Civili, Book 1.* Oxford University Press. ProQuest Ebook Central. <http://ebookcentral.proquest.com/lib/nyulibrar ebooks/detail.action?docID=472360. Created from nyulibrary-ebooks> Accessed 7 December 2019.

Roselaar, S. 2009. *Assidui* or *Proletarii*? Property in Roman Citizen Colonies and the *Vacatio Militiae. Mnemosyne* 62: 609–23. https://doi.org/10.1163/156852509x384266.

Roselaar, S. 2010. *Public Land in the Roman Republic: A Social and Economic History of Ager Publicus in Italy, 396–89 BC*. Oxford: Oxford University Press. https://doi.org/10.1093/acprof:oso/9780199577231.001.0001.

Rouse, J. 2007. 'Practice Theory'. *Division I Faculty Publications*. 43. <https://wesscholar.wesleyan.edu/div1facpubs/43> Accessed 15 March 2020.

Stewart, A. 2021. [1900]. Trans. *Seneca, Of Consolation: To Helvia.* Wikisource. <https://en.wikisource.org/wiki/Of_Consolation:_To_Helvia> Accessed 31 August 2021.

Thayer, B. 2013. *Suetonius, The Lives of the Caesars: The Life of Julius Caesar.* Bill Thayer's Website. <http://penelope.uchicago.edu/Thayer/E/Roman/Texts/Suetonius/12Caesars/Julius*.html> Accessed 25 October 2021.

Thayer, B. 2018. *Plutarch, The Parallel Lives: The Life of Romulus.* Bill Thayer's Website. <https://penelope.uchicago.edu/Thayer/e/roman/texts/plutarch/lives/romulus*.html> Accessed 25 October 2021.

United Nations. 2007. *General Assembly Official Records, 62nd Session : 7th Plenary Meeting, Wednesday. 26 September 2007. New York.* <https://digitallibrary.un.org/record/607840?ln=en#record-files-collapse-header> Accessed 2 August 2021.

Yonge, C. D. Trans. n.d. [1852]. *The Orations of Marcus Tullius Cicero, Vol. 4.* London: H G Bohn. <https://lexundria.com/cic_phil/8/y> Accessed 4 November 2021.

Yonge, C. D. Trans. 2005. [1877]. *Cicero's Tusculan Disputations, Also, Treatises On The Nature Of The Gods, And On The Commonwealth.* Project Gutenberg. <https://www.gutenberg.org/files/14988/14988-h/14988-h.htm> Accessed 31 August 2021.

# Index of Greek and Roman Passages Discussed

# General Index